Three Men
On Third____

Three Men On Third___

And Other Wacky Events
from the World of Sports

Carl Sifakis

PRENTICE HALL GENERAL REFERENCE
New York   London   Toronto   Sydney   Tokyo   Singapore

For Stefan Kohlenberger

PRENTICE HALL GENERAL REFERENCE
15 Columbus Circle
New York, New York 10023

Library of Congress Cataloging-in-Publication data

Sifakis, Carl.
   Three men on third : and other wacky events from the world of
sports / Carl Sifakis.
      p.   cm.
   Includes index.
   ISBN 0-671-86502-1
     1. Sports—Anecdotes. 2. Sports—History. I. Title.
GV707.S54   1994
796'.0207—dc20   93-32140
                                           CIP

Designed by Irving Perkins Associates, Inc.

Manufactured in the United States of America

10 9 8 7 6 5 4 3 2 1

First Edition

ILLUSTRATION CREDITS

ARD, CNN via the AP, 264; George Brace, 33, 39, 49, 123, 127, 174; D&G Photos,
64, 88, 167, 231; Grambling, 246; University of Kentucky, 190; National Baseball
Library, Cooperstown, NY, 31, 44, 89, 93, 94, 97, 113, 171; New York Public Library
Picture Collection, 4, 8, 10, 13, 15, 19, 61, 67, 83, 86 (left), 115, 137, 141, 150, 157;
Wide World, 194, 238, 251; York Pictures, 147; Author's Collection, 29, 36, 86 (right,
upper & lower), 112, 155, 183, 216, 221, 240.

796.0207
SIF

6/94

Contents

Three Men On Third___

Introduction

In a short series good pitching will always beat good hitting—and vice versa.

It was Casey Stengel who came up with that gem of baseball wisdom. Admittedly a zany statement on the face of it, it does have an element of logic—both ways. That in large measure is the key to understanding zaniness in sports. In any sports contest, the emotional involvement is so intense that the zany moments that occur are understandable and even follow their own "logic," as warped as it may be.

Entire volumes have been compiled about the wit and wisdom of Yogi Berra, who deserved a place in the Baseball Hall of Fame as much for his bizarre observations as for his playing ability. We are forever indebted to Yogi for reminding us that it ain't over till it's over, but we have been blessed by his other keen baseball insights as well. Yogi was always a bad-ball hitter, and one afternoon he went after three wide pitches in succession and struck out. He returned to the dugout, a deep scowl on his face, and his teammates awaited his customary outburst of self-blame. Instead Berra offered his evaluation of the hurler who had just victimized him: "How does a pitcher like that stay in the league?"

Probably baseball is the font of more wacky tales than any other sport because the leisurely course of the contest allows for more introspection, more time to concoct misadventures and to permit the bizarre to flower.

Sometimes, especially in baserunning, zaniness can burst forth in instant mindlessness, as when that daffiest of all Dodgers, Babe Herman, triggered the madness of the infamous "Three Men on Third" caper in which he just raced around the bases like a loose cannon until three Dodgers found themselves all trying to occupy a bag made for one.

In the old days, when there was a single umpire, the legendary John J. McGraw was a star third baseman for the cheatingest team in baseball, the old Baltimore Orioles. He had a patented play whereby he grabbed a runner's belt as the man tagged up to run after a fly ball. Since the lone umpire had to watch the outfielder's catch, he seldom spotted McGraw's caper, and the runner would be unable to make a dash for the plate. Louisville's Pete Browning decided one day to avenge himself. When the batter unloaded a long ball, Browning unfastened his belt buckle and took off for home. It was a zany play on Browning's part even though he scored. As he streaked down the baseline, his pants slipped down around his lower hips, and he had to scamper home trying to keep his trousers up, much to the appreciation of the spectators. The only one not laughing was an embarrassed McGraw, who stood there with nothing but Browning's belt in hand.

The entries in this book are arranged chronologically by year and then alphabetically by sport, so that basketball entries follow baseball, etc. That is the orderly element of the book. The wackiness belongs to the players—two-legged or four-legged.

In the second category would be the legendary Lucky Maury, who put on an unforgettable performance at the Hollywood Greyhound Track in 1978. It would be hard to say if Lucky Maury was addle-brained or just plain brainy.

In dog racing, the greyhounds never catch the mechanical rabbits— at least not until Lucky Maury came along. After scores of frustrating races, Lucky Maury may have sat on his haunches and contemplated his sad record. However in one outing, Lucky Maury decided to head off that speedy bunny at the pass. As the race started, the dog blithely turned around, headed *up* the track, and nailed that bunny coming straight to him. He went for the kill, ripping into the bunny so the fur flew. When the rest of the field got there, they merrily joined in the melee. It was a mess for the track. All $47,000 wagered on the Lucky Maury race had to be refunded and a new bunny produced for the next race.

Babe Herman, meet Lucky Maury.

Wacky Events: 1846–1993

1846

BASEBALL

Paying the Penalty

The first official baseball game played in America between the "New York Nine" and the Knickerbockers saw a player named Davis guilty of swearing at the umpire. He drew a hefty fine for that grievous infraction—six cents.

1853

BOXING

Too Many Foes

In a heavyweight championship bout between Yankee Sullivan and John Morrissey, the volatile Sullivan exhibited some of his more aggressive traits that made him a villain in the ring. Before a fight Sullivan was notorious for going after the handlers of his opponents and, at least verbally, even the referee. The battle between Sullivan and Morrissey soon turned into a pier-six brawl, with Yankee subjected to vicious catcalls from Morrissey fans. Between the 36th and 37th round, Sullivan suddenly bolted from the ring into the seats and started to belt around a number of his tormentors. He punched one into dream land and sent a second crashing through three rows of seats, and then proceeded to give two others a horrendous lacing at the same time.

Unfortunately Sullivan neglected to get back into the ring in time for the start of the next round, and Morrissey was declared the winner.

Yankee Sullivan was a pier-six brawler who not only took on his opponents but also the rival handlers, referees, and even fans rooting against him.

It should be noted that Yankee Sullivan continued his penchant for mayhem both inside and outside the ring, and in 1856 he was arrested by San Francisco Vigilance Committee as an enforcer for corrupt politicians. Overhearing a vigilante saying that he would be hanged the next morning, Yankee Sullivan killed himself.

1865

BILLIARDS

Off, Off, Damned Fly!

Billiard champion Louis Fox was playing a $1,000 winner-take-all match with John Deery at Rochester, NY, and was holding a commanding lead when a fly landed on the cue ball and resisted all efforts to be shooed away. Fox became so unbent that he miscued, lost all concentration, and ended up blowing the match. He stomped angrily from the hall. A few days later his body was found floating in a nearby river, and it was generally believed the incident of the stubborn fly had driven him to suicide.

1871

BOXING

Boxing's No-Hitter

What if they staged a boxing match and nobody threw a solid punch? That was what happened in a one-rounder in Ontario, Canada, in a bare-knuckle contest between Joe Coburn and Jem Mace. Under the boxing rules of the era, a round lasted until one of the competitors was knocked down (but not out) or slipped to the canvas. So when the two "competitors" entered the ring, they marched to their own strategic drummers. Coburn was a master at using the ropes, while Mace was a center-of-the-ring slugger. It was a case of water and oil not mixing. Coburn went to the ropes and Mace took possession of the center of the ring, and neither would abandon his fight plan. According to one sportswriter's account, "At times the men stood contemplating one another for as much as five minutes without raising their arms."

The fans turned up the boos as the first round went on and on with nonaction. Occasionally one of the "combatants" ventured into the other's domain and almost threw a solid blow, but thought better of such madness and scurried back to his own territory. The spectators grew more raucous, and it may well have been that their jeering informed the authorities of the locale of the illegal contest. By the time the police mercifully crashed the fight and stopped the nonaction, the first round was in its 69th minute, with neither boxer landing a punch.

1873

FOOTBALL

Nonsensical Game

When a game was scheduled for the Cornell football team to journey to Cleveland to play the University of Michigan, Cornell President Andrew White vetoed the idea, declaring, "I will not permit thirty men to travel 400 miles merely to agitate a bag of wind."

HORSE RACING

Instant Replays

On a hot summer day at New York's Gravesend race track two horses, Mort Jordon and Bing Aman, finished in a dead heat after a grueling 1¾-mile race. Despite the hot temperatures it was decided that the two horses should rerun their race. They did so and, remarkably, finished in a dead heat a second time. They were sent around on a third running, and the evenly matched animals again finished with the same incredible result. So around they went a *fourth* time. This too seemed to have been a tie, but the judges ruled that Bing Aman had won by a nose. This was enough to get bettors who had wagered on Mort Jordon very hot under the collar, and in fact they rioted and destroyed much of the track.

1876

BASEBALL

Look, Ma, No Hands!

It was a day to live in baseball infamy. The Boston Reds topped the St. Louis Browns 17–6, but neither team had much to brag about, and fans showered boos down on both of them. Between them the clubs managed to set a major league record, which undoubtedly will never be surpassed, of committing a one-game total of 40 errors.

Faded Glory

Early in 1876 Boston pitcher Joe Borden was on the top of his game and in fact threw the first no-hitter in the National League. But after that accomplishment Borden's career went down a slippery slope. He lost his control, and when he did get the ball over the plate, the pitch was a fat one that batters murdered. Giving up on Borden's pitching, management tried to convert him into an outfielder, but Borden's slugging was not up to par. Still, Borden was around at season's end in Boston, but he was no longer a player; he was retained as the club's groundskeeper.

1879

FOOTBALL

Bloody Good Show

An outstanding athlete in a number of sports at Yale, 18-year-old Frederic Remington was most fond of football, which he played with total abandon. In an 1879 game against Princeton, Remington appeared especially ferocious, being covered with blood. As a result, when he snarled, the Princeton boys listened. Actually, before the game Remington had gone to a nearby slaughterhouse and coated his jersey with blood so that the contest would "look more businesslike." This was undoubtedly an early manifestation of the artistic creativity that would bring him worldwide fame for his realistic paintings and sculptures of the American West.

1880

BASEBALL

Defensive Ambush

When it came to roguish trickery in old-time baseball, no one could match Mike "King" Kelly of "Slide, Kelly, Slide!" fame. In the words of baseball historian Charles Alexander: "In keeping with the winning imperative of professionalism, he mastered the rules and took advantage of every possible loophole, as well as the inability of the sole umpire to watch everything at once."

One day when not in the game—most likely on account of nursing a hangover—Kelly was on the Chicago White Stockings bench when the batter slapped a pop fly in his direction. Realizing that catcher Frank "Silver" Flints could not possibly get to the ball in time, Kelly jumped to his feet and shouted, "Kelly in for Flint," and caught the ball. Under the prevailing rules of the game, Kelly's caper was perfectly legal and, notes Alexander, "The umpire had no choice but to call the batter out."

Kelly got away with this bit of diamond larceny a few times until finally the rules were changed so that substitution of players could be made only when time was out and the umpire so notified.

Frederic Remington immortalized football roughness with the same enthusiasm he later exhibited in his portrayal of violence of the Western frontier.

FOOTBALL

Hand-to-Hand Combat

Back in the early days of football, various rules were imposed and then dropped when they proved less than viable. The craziest rule of all was the so-called maul-in-goal rule, which was a carryover from rugby. Before a team could be credited with a touchdown, the ball carrier had to touch the ball to the ground beyond the goal, while any opposing players who had hands on him when he crossed the goal line could try to keep him from doing so. If the defense succeeded, the scoring play was disallowed.

In an exhibition game between the Yale varsity and Yale scrubs, 290-pound Alex Coxe rammed over the goal line, falling on his back. One small player named Tillinghast clutched at him and tried to keep him from turning over and downing the ball. Little Tillinghast held on gamely, not permitting Coxe to roll over. Coxe was handicapped since he could not use his full strength without letting the football loose—which would constitute a fumble and wipe out the possible score. The battle went on for a full 15 minutes, as the other players could only stand around and watch the struggle. Finally Coxe got winded and the feisty Tillinghast was able to wrestle the ball free. No touchdown!

1881

BOXING

No-Tipping Policy

In many respects the fight between John L. Sullivan and Professor John Donaldson was a grudge match even though it was "Boston Strong Boy" Sullivan's first regular bout. Sullivan was known to resent Donaldson's claim to the title "Professor"—he claimed it on the basis of teaching boxing in addition to fighting on his own—and the fact that Donaldson considered him an unintelligent fighter. The two met in Cincinnati, and Sullivan, the much stronger man, knocked out his foe in the 10th round. Sullivan took the heavyweight championship the following year and in a long reign never hid his disdain for Donaldson. Frequently after a fight Sullivan would feel sorry for opponents he beat and give them a tip of $15 or $25 for their absorption of so much punishment, but it undoubtedly rankled Donaldson when Sullivan was reported saying he would willingly tip all opponents except "professors."

During Sullivan's long reign, Donaldson taught boxing and finally latched on to a Californian, John J. Corbett, who he felt had the skills and brains to best Sullivan. Corbett did so in 1892. In a lavish tribute to Donaldson, Billy Edwards, former lightweight champion-turned-author, wrote: "Corbett's great success as a ring general is no doubt due to the fact that he has wisely availed himself of the tips given him by the Professor, who is a master of boxing tactics, and believes

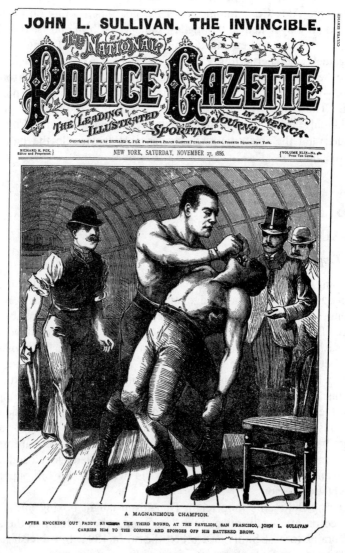

A MAGNANIMOUS CHAMPION.

AFTER KNOCKING OUT PADDY RYAN IN THE THIRD ROUND, AT THE PAVILION, SAN FRANCISCO, JOHN L. SULLIVAN
CARRIES HIM TO THE CORNER AND SPONGES OFF HIS BATTERED BROW.

While John L. Sullivan (shown here ministering to Paddy Ryan) was famous for showing compassion for most foes after kayoing them, even tipping them $15 or $25 for medical costs, his failure to do so with "Professor" John Donaldson made the latter his mortal enemy.

that brains, coupled with activity and muscle, will, at any time, be more than a match for mere brawn, unbacked by intelligence.'' The use of such phrases as ''mere brawn'' and ''unbacked by intelligence'' and most certainly the word *tips* were all a way of giving the needle to the fallen champion. The ''Professor'' finally had his revenge.

1885

BASEBALL

Hiding the Talent

In the 19th century baseball clubs were notorious for getting around all established rules when it came to fielding the best team they could get. In 1884 it was obvious that some of the teams in the American Association (then considered a big league) were going to fold. Charlie Hackett, manager of the Cleveland club, saw the handwriting and arranged to manage Brooklyn in 1885. Determined to corral the best talent, Hackett ignored the established rule that players from a defunct team had to wait 10 days before signing with another club, to give all teams a chance to join the bidding. Hackett simply moved to grab the top Cleveland players and got them to agree to come to Brooklyn. Then when the formal dissolution of the Cleveland franchise occurred, he hustled all the players from their homes into a Cleveland hotel incognito and baby-sat them the entire 10 days, so that other teams could not locate them. Just after midnight when the 10-day waiting period elapsed, Hackett got a pen and had all his ''prisoners'' sign their contracts. It was, according to the *New York Times,* ''the biggest sensation ever made in Brooklyn.''

1886

BASEBALL

Slide, Williamson, Slide!

While King Kelly was known as the premier base stealer of the 19th century, and was serenaded by his loving fans with the call, ''Slide, Kelly, Slide!'' perhaps his grandest caper was the one in which he helped a teammate execute a most remarkable theft. The King and teammate Ed Williamson had long plotted the running scam and had only to wait for an appropriate time. The situation presented itself in a game their Chicago White Stockings played against the Detroit Tigers. Kelly was on second and Williamson on first in the last of the ninth with the score knotted. As step one of their inventive caper, the pair pulled a double steal so that Kelly was on third and Williamson on second. King then gave Williamson the high sign, and phase two was set in motion on the next pitch. Kelly broke off third and Williamson went flying from second. Oddly, Kelly was not quite as fast as he usually was, and in fact, when he was still 20 feet or so from the plate, Williamson, who never broke stride, was steaming up behind him. Kelly barreled straight forward into catcher Charlie Bennett, who got the ball and slapped the tag on the King. But as the tag was made Kelly spread his legs apart, and Williamson slid through them for the game-ending run. Clearly Bennett had never even noticed Williamson, having concentrated on Kelly, and he was rejoicing at supposedly getting the best of the master of the base stealers.

1887

BASEBALL

Great Performance

Shortly after King Kelly was sold by the Chicago White Stockings to the Boston Beaneaters, that nefarious player demonstrated once again there were endless ways to win a game, honestly or otherwise. In the gathering gloom in the final inning of a game with New York, the bases full and two out for the Giants, Roger Connor hit a line drive—home run written all over it—toward the right-field fence. Kelly, eyeing the ball carefully, backed to the fence and, timing his leap perfectly, made an incredible catch just above the fence line. The Boston fans cheered wildly as Kelly held up his glove in triumph and raced off to the clubhouse with a show of exuberance. Kelly's teammates were likewise impressed with his magnificient game-saving catch, and howled in glee and pounded his back. One of the players asked to see the ball. Kelly put on a wicked grin and said, "Can't do that. It went way over the fence."

RING Nº1
FIGHTING IN THE RISING
TIDE WATER

RING Nº2
THE FINISH

N.Y. PUBLIC LIBRARY
PICTURE COLLECTION

The illegal middleweight championship bout between Jack Dempsey "the Nonpareil" and Johnny Reagan was fought first in a makeshift ring that was flooded by tidewater. Then the fighters and the crowd were hauled by tug to a new site where the fight continued amidst hail and snow until Reagan's handlers tossed in the towel after 45 rounds.

BOXING

Washout

One of the oddest of all boxing matches involved the defense of the middleweight title by the first Jack Dempsey "the Nonpareil" and Johnny Reagan. This was in the days of illegal bare-knuckle fisticuffs, and to avoid police interference it was slated outdoors in Huntington, Long Island, December 18, starting at 8 A.M. with a ring quickly pitched. However, flooding interfered with the match in the 5th round when a nearby river overflowed and the tide from the Atlantic started coming in. By the 8th round the two battlers were standing knee-deep in water. It was then decided to move the bout down the coast. The boxers, their handlers, and the referee and judges and as many fans as could fit aboard a ship were floated down to another site, where the match continued. In the 21st round it started to hail, and in the 30th it began to snow. After the 45th round, Reagan's handlers decided their boy could take no more combined blows from Dempsey and Mother Nature, and they threw in the towel.

1888 _____

BOXING

Suicide Lament

Perhaps the most "elitist" boxing bout ever held was an illegal one between John L. Sullivan and Charlie Mitchell on the training grounds of the estate of Baron Rothschild near Chantilly, France, with no more than 30 or 40 wealthy society men and "fight swells" in attendance. Among those present was Billy Porter, the socially accepted bank burglar, who was destined to die in the German salt mines. He was weighted down by a revolver in each overcoat pocket and informed Mitchell's corner that Sullivan was to have fair play. Generally Porter's message had its effect, although once Mitchell did tramp on Sullivan's instep with his spike shoes, which the fighters wore because the contest was staged during a heavy rain that made the footing precarious. While Sullivan remonstrated with Mitchell to "be a gentleman," the watchful Porter was satisfied the stomping had been accidental. The contestants fought with bare fists soaked in walnut juice, and each round ended when either man went down to one knee. There were no gate receipts, no purse, only enormous side bets placed by the viewers with each fighter bankrolled by supporters. After 39 rounds the seconds agreed to halt the bout and call it a draw.

Just as the bout ended, gendarmes arrived and clapped both battlers behind bars. The French jailer reported he had taken away their silk handkerchiefs "to prevent their hanging themselves." Both men were said to have wept in jail, having lost out on an enormous payday. The French authorities could think of no reason to charge Rothschild with the slightest offense.

Only 30 or 40 "sporting gentlemen and high rollers" were in attendance when John L. Sullivan (right) and Charlie Mitchell faced each other on the French estate of Baron Rothschild.

1889

BOXING

Stranding the Enemy

It was the last bare-knuckle championship fight that July day in Richburg, Mississippi, when John L. Sullivan met Jake Kilrain. Like many other matches of the era, the bout was subjected to harassment by authorities who tried to stop the illegal fight. A sporting event under such conditions presented special problems for the media covering it. Not only did they have to dodge the law, they had to find a way to beat the competition in reporting the results. This was even more complicated on this occasion since the nearest telegraph office was in New Orleans, 100 miles away. To rush the story of the contest, Addison Thomas of the Associated Press came up with a plan for chartering a railroad engine and two cars, which were kept waiting on a siding near the ring.

The struggle was a long one, lasting 75 rounds and consuming 2 hours, 16 minutes, and 3 seconds, before Sullivan emerged victorious. During the fight Thomas wrote his running story at ringside, but he knew he would face another headache. Since he was far in the rear of the ring, there was a good chance he would be caught up in the jam of humanity when the contest ended. So as soon as it was over, Thomas stuffed his finished story into some hollow wooden balls and threw them over the spectators' heads to some waiting assistants. The A.P. men rushed for the train without Thomas and set out for New Orleans. However, several competitor newsmen figured out the A.P. strategy and managed to smuggle themselves into the cars with their stories at the ready. Reporter Thomas had anticipated this, though, and had his men clamber forward to the engine of the speeding train, disconnect the two cars, and leave them behind, with the competition stranded on the tracks. The A.P. scored a beat of several hours before anyone else in the media could get a report out.

FOOTBALL

Steamrolling Through the South

It was in its way as devastating as Sherman's march through Georgia. In 1899 the football team of the University of the South, then known as Sewanee, took on five of the region's toughest teams and defeated them all. While a five-game winning streak might not appear to be so outstanding, there were some very marked distinctions in the Sewanee sweep. First of all, the games were all on the road. On November 8, Sewanee knocked off previously unbeaten Texas 12–0. On November 9, they destroyed Texas A&M 32–0. On November 10, Tulane fell to Sewanee 23–0. Then on November 12, they rolled over Louisiana State 34–0 and followed that up on November 13 by beating Mississippi State 12–0. Thus, Sewanee concluded their five-game sweep *in six days* (it never was explained why the school embarked on such a hectic schedule). Furthermore, many of the opponents were powerhouse teams, but Sewanee never gave up a single point to any of them! Even more amazing was the fact that Sewanee, apparently to cut down on costs, took only 12 players on the steamroller march through the South.

1890

BASEBALL

The Original Hidden-Ball Trick

Baseball's original hidden-ball trick did not involve anything so relatively antiseptic as concealing a ball in a glove and tagging out a base runner when he unsuspectingly stepped off the bag. Instead, it originated with the 1890 Baltimore Orioles, generally held to be the decade's most dishonest baseball club. Since the grass in most ball fields at the time tended to be cut irregularly and therefore often was quite long, it provided excellent camouflage for several extra baseballs secreted at strategic points on the field. When an opponent smashed a mighty blow over the outfielder's head, that worthy would fall back in pursuit, pick up not the correct ball but one that had been conveniently hidden for just such an emergency, and fire it back to the infield, holding the hitter often to a single on what he surely felt was a clout good for two or three bases.

Baltimore got by with this deception the better part of the season until, alas, tragedy struck. A ball went soaring into left-center with the left fielder bounding after it. He picked up a hidden ball and pegged it in, cutting off the extra-base hit. Unfortunately, a very diligent center fielder in the meantime ran down the right baseball, picked it up, and fired it in, not noticing that one ball had already been retrieved. The umpire duly noted the surplus of balls, nodded somberly, and declared the Orioles to have lost the game by forfeit. It was said this sad experience cured the Orioles of hidden-ball deception, but it was long suspected their outfielders did from time to time continue the practice, having devised a signal for warning their fellow players that they were putting a hidden ball into play.

Take Me Out to the Other Ball Game

In the 1880s there were two major leagues, the National League and the American Association, but in 1890 the Players League was formed, taking many of the top players from the other two leagues. The older leagues and the new organization fought pitched battles for supremacy, and the National League especially sought to undercut the new competition by scheduling games at the same time in the same city as the Players. The Players in turn sought out ways to intensify the struggle

for fan support, and in New York, the Players team found a way to
go head-to-head with its rival.

At the time the New York Giants played in what was called Manhattan Field, at Eighth Avenue and 155th Street. The Players leased
another piece of property between Eighth Avenue and the Harlem
River, and put up a ballpark under the rock cliff known as Coogan's
Bluff, right next to the Manhattan Field, and moved into this new
Brotherhood Park. Only a canvas fence separated the two parks, and
as a result fans in either park could watch the action in both fields by
scrambling into a strategic position. One time the New York Giants'
Mike Tiernan blasted a mighty drive that cleared the Manhattan Field
barrier and landed in Brotherhood's outfield. Fans in both fields
cheered him lustily. With that sort of competition, both teams lost
fortunes that year and, facing financial collapse because of competition
in their other cities, the two older leagues were forced to absorb most
of the Players teams into their setups.

1891

BASEBALL

Proud Buccaneers

In a distribution of players from the collapsed Players League, infielder
Louis Bierbauer was slated to be assigned to Philadelphia, but the
Pittsburgh Nationals ignored the agreement and signed him up. This
prompted angry talk around the league about the "pirates" in Pittsburgh. Pittsburgh was not taken aback by the perjorative term, and
soon adopted it as the team's official nickname.

1892

BASEBALL

Decoy

King Kelly was one of the most versatile players of the 19th century,
seeing effective duty at every position except pitcher during his 17-
year career. Some say he was best at catcher, especially since it permitted him to con the opposition with embarrassing regularity. Kelly was
behind the plate for the Boston Beaneaters in a game against Cleveland

Note the second ring surrounding the fighting area in the Fitzsimmons–Maher heavyweight bout. It was meant to keep unruly partisans of the combatants out of the battle. Fitzsimmons is at left.

when he pulled off one of his grandest catching hoaxes. Late in the game Cleveland's Jesse "The Crab" Burkett was on second with two men out, when the batter slashed a base hit to left field. As Burkett rounded third he saw Kelly stomp the ground disgustedly and then throw away his mask and catcher's mitt, apparently an indication that the ball had gone through the left fielder and that Burkett could romp home easily. Burkett slowed to a trot coming down the third-base line. Meanwhile, Boston's left fielder fired home to Kelly, who caught the ball in his bare hands and put the tag on the chagrined Burkett.

BOXING

Keeping the Fans Away

When heavyweight title contenders Bob Fitzsimmons and Peter Maher met at the Olympic Club in New Orleans, the latter was much concerned about the rowdiness of the fans and insisted a second ring be installed outside the main ring to prevent mob interference. Free of such distractions, Fitzsimmons went on to knock out his foe in a slashing 12-round battle.

1893 _____

BOXING

Fight to the Finish

It was to be the longest and one of the most damaging boxing matches ever fought. It took place on April 8 in New Orleans between Jack Burke and Andy Bowen to decide who would take over the lightweight crown following the retirement of champion Jack McAuliffe. By agreement of both fighters the purse of $2,500 would be a winner-take-all affair, and as it was for the championship it would go to the finish, until one or the other was no longer standing.

Both fighters came out slugging from the opening bell, causing each other damage but not enough for one or the other to go down for the count. The spectators cheered the brutal action, but as 3-minute round after round went by, the fans were wore down to stillness as they watched the two fighters continue to battle furiously, barely able to walk back to their stools between rounds. Ten rounds went by . . . 20 . . . 30 . . . 40 . . . 50 . . . 60, and still both scrappers went at each other without let-up. Finally, at 2 A.M., more than 7 hours after the start, the bell sounded for the 111th round. Burke tried to get to his feet but failed. Bowen then fought to a half-standing position and collapsed back on his stool. The fight-to-the-finish ended with both fighters finished, and the referee was forced to rule the match ''no contest.''

Neither man ever became lightweight champion. Burke's strength had been so sapped that he never fought again. He urged Bowen likewise to retire, but Bowen decided to continue. He died after being knocked out in 18 rounds in his next fight.

1894 _____

BOXING

Thomas Edison's Fixed Fight

Thomas Edison gets credit for first filming a sporting event, a boxing match between Jack Cushing and Mike Leonard. It was also the first fixed fight ever filmed. Edison set the bout up at his West Orange, NJ, laboratory and had the ring reduced in size to 12 feet square so that his stationary camera could take in all the action. Edison required the two ''contestants'' to go a sufficient number of rounds to make the film interesting for boxing fans and allow the film itself to become profitable. That being accomplished, Leonard, following the script, knocked out Cushing. The film turned up at a Kinetoscope parlor within 60 days with the admission set at 10 cents per round. What viewers were not told was that the action had all been prearranged.

1895

BASEBALL

Superbobble

Almost every baseball infielder has had one or more nightmare games or even innings in which he made several errors, but third baseman Mike Grady of the New York Giants set a dismal record that has never been matched. Grady managed to commit four errors—count 'em, four errors—on a single batted ball: (1) He bobbled an easy grounder so that the batter was safe at first—error number one. (2) Then, much too late, he threw to first, only to sail the ball far over the head of the first baseman, allowing the runner to continue to second—error number two. (3) As the runner rounded second and headed for third, the first baseman pegged to Grady in plenty of time to cut down the runner, but Grady let the ball go through him—error number three. (4) Then as Grady retrieved the ball, the runner headed for home and Grady cut loose a heave that sailed right into the grandstand—error number four. Grady landed in the record books for letting a batter score a four-error homer on a simple ground ball.

Vanishing Paycheck

Baseball players at the end of the last century could consider it the "Ungay Nineties" when it came to their pay, which didn't approach the millions-of-dollars contracts of a century later. Future Hall of Famer Hugh Duffy had hit .438 in 1894, to this day a major league record, but the following year the Boston Beaneaters (later the Braves) at first refused to offer him a salary increase. Finally, after Duffy threatened to sit out the season, the club granted him a niggardly raise of $12.50 a month. And there was a zinger to that: For that whopping increase Duffy had to take on the chores of team captain. That was not the high honor it seemed to be, as there was a clause in the captain's addendum that made him responsible for all lost equipment.

At season's end such losses came to more than the increase Duffy had won, so he ended up losing on the deal.

BASKETBALL

What Game Is This Anyhow?

When Hamline College of St. Paul, MN, defeated the Minnesota State School of Agriculture in the first college basketball game, the final score sounded more like one of today's football or baseball games— 9–3. The tally did not really reflect the ineptness of the teams but rather the rules of the game at the time. Each team had nine players on the floor instead of the present five. As a result, the defense was much more powerful and could keep the offense far from the basket. The following year sports officials had enough of that, and the number of players was cut to five.

1896

OLYMPICS

Running in Style

When the first modern Olympics were held in 1896 in Athens, the Greek nation was determined to win one event over all others, the marathon. The race commemorated the run in 490 B.C. by the soldier Pheidippides from Marathon to Athens to announce the Athenian victory over the Persians. He cried out, "Rejoice, we conquer!" and then dropped dead.

Hysteria gripped Greece as people demanded victory by their national athletes. It was announced that not only would a victorious Greek receive the gold metal but 365 restaurant meals as well as the hand of a Greek millionaire's daughter. During the race messengers on bicycles and horseback brought word to the stadium on the progress of the race to the 100,000 spectators in the stands and the surrounding area. At first, to the dismay of the crowd, foreigners were in the lead, but late in the race came the electrifying news that Greeks had stormed to the front. Finally, a 24-year-old postman named Spiridon Loues appeared in the marble entrance to the stadium. As he made the final victory lap, the crowd was in ecstasy. Seven minutes later a second Greek, Charilaos Vasiklos, crossed the finish line. Then came yet another Greek, Dimitries Velokas. The fourth finisher was Gyula Kellner of Hungary. The Greek triumph was complete as they swept all three medals, but then consternation set in as Kellner lodged a protest against Velokas. The Hungarian claimed he had seen Velokas ride up toward the stadium in a horse carriage, then get out and resume the race on foot. Velokas admitted his deception and confessed to having hidden a carriage in a park to provide him with a respite during the grueling run.

Velokas was disqualified, his shirt and singlet with the Greek colors stripped from his back, the first of a number of cheaters who have haunted marathon competition ever since. The bronze medal was awarded to the Hungarian Kellner. For his services as an informer King George ordered that Kellner be given a gold watch as a reward. (As for gold medalist Loues, he was not able to accept one of his prizes, the hand of the millionaire's daughter, since he already had a wife.)

1897

BASEBALL

Missing Pitcher Dept.

Bill "Brickyard" Kennedy was one of the flakiest Brooklyn pitchers of the 1890s, although he had natural skills good enough to win 177 games for the Dodgers in that period. He derived his nickname from his hometown of Bellaire, OH, a brick-making center, but there were many who insisted that the sobriquet reflected the composition of his cranial regions. Kennedy was frequently lost in the Big City and once left his home in Brooklyn for a game at the Polo Grounds and wound up in the Midwest. Brickyard had instructions for taking an elevated train across the Brooklyn Bridge and then transferring to an uptown train. When Kennedy found these instructions too mind-bending, he asked a policeman, unfortunately mentioning he was from Ohio and not too familiar with New York transit. The officer promptly sent Brickyard off to a railroad train bound for Ohio.

On the field Brickyard was as easily misdirected. In a game at Eastern Park he held a 2–0 lead into the ninth inning, when the Giants rallied and scored three runs and had George Davis on second base. According to the *New York Times*: "On the field the New York players were turning handsprings and acting like a lot of maniacs." In the chaos one New Yorker kept his cool and cunning—George Van Haltren, who was coaching at third. Van Haltren broke for home as though he were a base runner. At the time Dodger catcher Johnny Grim was arguing with the umpire about the last scoring run and was not looking at Van Haltren. But Brickyard was. He fell for the trick and pegged to the plate. The throw went past Grim and bounced all the way to the backstop, allowing Davis, the genuine runner, to race in all the way from second. That made the score 4–2, and proved to be the winning run as the Dodgers came up with a run in the bottom half of the ninth. The *Times* reported that Kennedy was fined "for his stupid work."

1898

BASEBALL

Sending a Wire

Ever since the start of baseball the art of signal stealing has used whatever technology was available at the time. In the late 1890s the Philadelphia Athletics enlisted telegraph technology, and for a time they were quite successful with it. A wire was laid underground from the center-field clubhouse to the third-base coaching box. Utility catcher Morgan Murphy would survey the opposing catcher's signals with the aid of binoculars and pass the information in Morse code on to the third-base coach, who received the message through a steel plate in the ground. The coach then hand-signaled batters what the next pitch would be. The arrangement worked just dandy until Tommy Corcoran, a third-base coach for Cincinnati, accidentally caught his spikes in the wire. He dug it out of the dirt, pulled it free, and followed it all the way out to the center-field clubhouse.

Mighty technology had struck out.

1899

HORSE RACING

See How They Shouldn't Run

At New York's Morris Park a 1¾-mile event attracted only a field of three, but that was more than enough to produce a ton of confusion.

As the *New York Times* reported: "It was to have been run over the Withers course, and when the first quarter had been run, Slack, on Julius Caesar, who was in front, sent his mount off the Withers course and showed the way up the course that led over the hill. Wilson, on the favorite Maid of Harlem, knew the course he was to ride, and went over the Withers. But Odom, on Spurs, followed Julius Caesar blindly until he had traveled a quarter of a mile on the wrong course, and then realizing that a mistake had been made, he went back and took his mount over the proper course. Spurs got second money . . . but Julius Caesar ran on over the hill course and was not given third money."

The two errant jockeys were hit with hefty fines for their miscues, as were the trainers of the mounts for failing to have made certain the riders had some idea where they were to go.

c. 1900

HORSE RACING

Last Is First

Plagued by fixed races, a number of western rodeos and fairs took to running races in which the nag that finished *last* was the winner. Happily, such a race could not be fixed, because jockeys were switched to another horse before going to the post. As a result, all the jockeys rode their new mounts as fast as they could, as in regular races, to ensure that they stayed ahead of their own horse and did not endanger its chances of coming in last—and winning.

1901

BASEBALL

If You Can't Beat 'Em, Pick 'Em Off

Baseball pitchers are a superstitious lot, perhaps none more so than Nick Altrock. Before he made the big leagues, he played for an "outlaw" team, in Los Angeles. One day he became convinced there was no way he was to get the opposing batters out, and he proceeded to walk the first seven men he faced in the first two and one-third innings. Yes, he walked them all and then neatly picked every single one of them off base. After that, Altrock settled down and pitched brilliantly the rest of the way—and straight up to the Chicago White Sox, for whom he became a 20-game winner.

BILLIARDS

Toast to a Lady

At the beginning of the century Miss Frances Anderson was the toast of the billiard world. The tall, comely midwestern maiden was so good at pocket billiards that she made a standing offer of $5,000 for any female who could defeat her. No woman ever collected, and Miss Anderson received huge sums for exhibition tours of the United States and Europe. There were constant speculations that the lady could defeat many top male billiard experts, but she would hear nothing of that, declaring it would be most unfeminine. Actually it turned out that Miss Anderson might not have been either that good or all that ladylike. After a quarter of a century as the queen of the billiard tables, Frances Anderson confessed that her real name was Orie Anderson. Mr. Orie Anderson.

FOOTBALL

Football's Hidden-Ball Trick

Glenn ''Pop'' Warner introduced football's hidden-ball trick after noticing two of his players at Carlisle Indian School horsing around and one of them concealing the ball from the other by stuffing it under a third player's shirt. Later that year, when Carlisle played Harvard, Pop had his team well schooled in a new deception. On the Harvard kickoff Carlisle's Jimmy Johnson caught the ball on his 5-yard line. The Carlisle players shifted into a form of huddle but with the players facing upfield. Behind this wall of teammates, Johnson stuffed the ball under the jersey of lineman-blocker Charlie Dillon. Carlisle charged forward in a wedge formation, seemingly protecting Johnson. Meanwhile the true ball carrier, Dillon, seemingly couldn't keep up with the wedge and trotted to the far sideline and then took off for the end zone, scoring unmolested while Johnson was being buried by a swarm of tacklers. Harvard protested the play but to no avail, since there was nothing in the rules specifying that the ball had to be carried in a player's arms.

1902

BASEBALL

Errors Wholesale

Ball players, even premier fielders, are notorious for having occasional bad days and committing errors in wholesale lots. However, Al Selbach of the Baltimore Orioles managed to commit five errors in a single game—still a record for an outfielder. In the game against the St. Louis Browns, Selbach managed to glove three fly balls—and drop each of them. On two other occasions, he went to field routine singles but let the ball skip through his legs, allowing the hitter to gain an extra base.

Two years later Selbach was playing for the Washington Senators, having been dumped by Baltimore. And once again he established a record that holds to this day, committing three errors in one inning as an outfielder. Selbach was playing against the New York Yankees and (1) pegged wild trying to cut down a base runner, (2) fumbled a single so that a base runner and the batter each took an extra base, and (3) dropped an easy fly ball. Selbach was soon gone from Washington as well and in a couple of years wrapped up his rather undistinguished career.

Wrong-Way St. Vrain

Jimmy St. Vrain of the Chicago Cubs was one of the most amazing nonhitting pitchers ever. It was a major challenge for a manager to find a way for him to get his lumber around somehow to meet the ball. Jimmy was a southpaw pitcher but batted right-handed. One day against the Pittsburgh Pirates Jimmy came up twice and struck out twice, never getting as much as even a weak foul on either at-bat. Exasperated manager Frank Selee took him aside after the second strikeout and said, "Jimmy, you're a left-handed pitcher, why don't you turn around and bat from the left side, too? Why not try it?" It was a suggestion born of desperation on the manager's part, but he was faced with a batter who couldn't possibly do worse than strike out regularly.

On his next at-bat, St. Vrain came to the plate, and after a moment's contemplation, he crossed to the left side. And he actually hit the ball! It was a grounder toward shortstop Honus Wagner, so slow that Jimmy actually stood a good chance of beating it out for a hit. He took off, running hard, doing what he knew he was supposed to do after hitting the ball—cross the plate and head up the baseline full speed. Unfortunately, Jimmy forgot he had switched to batting left-handed and he raced for *third* base.

Everyone on the Cubs was screaming at Jimmy that he was going the wrong way, but he heard nothing, so excited that he had made contact with the ball. Head down, his spikes flying, he made it to third before the ball got there. Then he figured out why. Later on Wagner said he had been tempted to throw to third: "I'm standing there with the ball in my hand, looking at this guy running from home to third, and for an instant there I swear I didn't know where to throw the damn ball. And when I finally did throw to first, I wasn't at all sure it was the right thing to do!"

Embarrassing Score

The score that came across the telegraph lines was that Corsicana had beaten Texarkana in a Texas League baseball game 51–3. Around the country large numbers of telegraph operators supplying newspapers with scores assumed the score report was inaccurate and changed it to 5–3. The following day corrections had to be sent out, when the blowout score of 51–3 was established as genuine. Incidentally, Nig Clarke set a standing professional baseball record in the game by hitting eight homers in eight trips to the plate.

BOXING

Follow the Bouncing Boxer

It was the greatest "bouncing boxer" match in history when in a bout at Hot Springs, SD, Oscar "Battling" Nelson and Christy Williams decked each other a total of 47 times. Nelson, the winner, hit the canvas 5 times while Williams went down 42 times.

HUNTING

True Story of the Teddy Bear

On a famous hunt in Mississippi, Theodore Roosevelt's servants cornered a young black bear, which awaited its fate trembling in the crotch of a tree. When the president was handed his gun, he indignantly declared the situation "unsporting for a gentleman" and refused

The famous Berryman cartoon of Teddy Roosevelt "drawing the line" at killing a young bear made the "teddy bear" a national institution, but hardly comported to the facts.

to shoot. The story went over the wires coast-to-coast and made both Roosevelt and the quarry famous, the latter becoming a national mascot—and the original Teddy Bear. Enterprising toy manufacturers cashed in on the "teddy bear" craze that swept the nation.

Researchers later reported, however, that, while Roosevelt refused to shoot the bear, he ordered his servants to dispatch the creature when reporters left the scene.

1903

BASEBALL

Field of Nightmares

There has never been a "defensive" struggle to match that of a game between the Detroit Tigers and the Chicago White Sox. The two American League teams set a league record for errors in a nine-inning game with a total of 18—12 by the White Sox and 6 by the Tigers.

FOOTBALL

Helping Arms

In a tournament in the second "World Series" of pro football, Franklin (PA) Athletic Club was stopped cold twice by opposing Orange (NJ) Athletic Club on the 5-yard line from going in for a score. On third down the ball was snapped to Doc Roller, a physician, who wore kid gloves to protect his hands and thus seldom got to run the football. Doc went wide before the Orange tacklers realized that he had the ball, but now they came thundering in at him. But his teammate, 260-pound Franklin guard Herman Kerchoffe, came to the rescue, picking Doc up in his arms and bulling their way through tacklers for a touchdown. Franklin won the game and the series, and Doc Roller kept his precious hands in fine working order.

1904

BASEBALL

World Series—Take It Away!

Although the first World Series was held in 1903, there was no Series the following year—because New York Giants manager John McGraw held a near-pathological hatred for the Boston Beaneaters and their fans. The ill feeling went back to 1894, when McGraw was a third

*New York Giants Manager
John McGraw killed the
second World Series by
refusing to let his team
appear in Boston.*

baseman with the Baltimore Orioles and they were playing in Boston
against the Beaneaters. McGraw got into a fistfight with his opposite
number at third base, and soon both benches emptied and a melee
ensued. Boston fans found it impossible merely to watch the action,
and soon there were fights among the spectators as well. Then the
fans sitting in the 25-cent bleachers, well away from the action, began
getting hot. They had to bolt their seats because some Beaneater partisans had set the stadium ablaze. Before overworked firefighters could
douse all the blazes, the entire ballpark had burned to the ground and
the conflagration had spread to destroy 170 other buildings, with
$300,000 worth of property losses and some 2,000 persons left home-
less.

The memory of the incident still burned brightly in McGraw's memory, and now as the manager of the Giants he steadfastly refused to
allow his team to play against the Beaneaters. The Giants players

backed their skipper, and after considerable maneuvering, the two leagues decided to cancel the World Series for that year.

The Animal Cracker Contract

One of the most storied batteries in baseball was that of Waddell and Schreckengost with the Philadelphia Athletics from 1902 to 1907. Both, pitcher Rube Waddell and catcher Ossee Schreckengost, were colorful characters with their own special eccentricities, and it was said that no other players could have been roommates with either of them. Their hotel room activities on the road—which in those management pennypinching days meant sharing a hotel double bed—were devoted to partying, drunken bouts, and food-gorging contests. Then during the 1903 season Philadelphia Manager Connie Mack heard that Waddell would not sign another contract with the Athletics. Mack asked the brilliant if wacky hurler what the problem was. Was he not satisfied with his pay? "Got nothing to do with that," Waddell said, an aggrieved look on his face. "It's that damn Schreck and his eating at night. I don't even mind them Limburger and onion sandwiches, but the only way I'll sign a new contract is if that Schreck stops eating them animal crackers!"

Mack could only listen in astonishment as Waddell explained his woes. Schreckengost, it seemed, always took a box of animal crackers to bed with him every night and munched them down before going to sleep. Schreckengost could sleep, Waddell complained, but the crumbs drove him crazy. "I ain't signing no more contracts unless I'm guaranteed in writing that the animal cracker eating stops." To pacify his ace pitcher, Mack made out his 1904 contract with a clause that stated his roommate would be ordered to stop eating the animal crackers and, if it happened ever again, Waddell would get a change of quarters. The contract became celebrated in baseball circles as the "animal cracker contract."

Baseball's Clay Pigeon

There are a number of baseball batters who have been notable as beanball targets, but among them was Chicago Cub Frank Chance of the famed double-play combination of Tinker to Evers to Chance—who was pretty much in a class by himself. A notorious "plate crowder," Chance had so many balls bounce off his skull during his career that after his retirement he suffered hearing impairment and

In a doubleheader against the Cincinnati Reds, Cubs first baseman Frank Chance, a notorious plate crowder, suffered a black eye, a brutal headache, and bruised arms and ribs—after being hit five times by pitched balls, including one smash to the face that left him unconscious for several minutes.

nagging headaches, and he finally had to undergo brain surgery. Chance's worst day for taking hits by the pitchers occurred during a doubleheader against the Cincinnati Reds. In the first game Cincinnati hurler Jack Harper practically stuck one in Chance's ear, the ball smashing into his face and knocking him out for several minutes. As the *Chicago Tribune* noted, "If the blow had been an inch further back it would have killed him.'' However, the beanball was not enough to force Chance out of the game. He shook the cobwebs from his brain and was ready to play as soon as everything fell back into a single image. On his very next at-bat, Harper nailed Chance in the arm. On his third at-bat, Chance took a hard pitch to the ribs from Harper.

It was little different in the second game, as Reds pitcher Win Kellum twice caught Chance with wicked fastballs. Despite this, Chance provided the key hits (as well as getting on base twice as a hit batsman) that produced a Chicago victory and a split in the double-header. He ended up with a black eye, a vicious headache, and a bruised arm and ribs. Just an average day at the ballpark for baseball's clay pigeon!

Boosters, Inc.

Apparently no fledgling ball player had as many boosters as did the young Ty Cobb. Folks who'd seen him play in and around Royston, GA, were absolutely sure he had the potential to be a fine player. They wrote dozens of letters to managements in the South Atlantic (Sally) League, advising the various teams to offer Cobb a tryout. Nothing much came of that, but finally the Reverend John Yarborough gave him a letter of introduction to the Augusta club. Cobb made the team but lasted only two games before being fired for failing to follow the manager's instructions.

More letters followed, Cobb got a new tryout with the Anniston, AL, team, and performed well enough to make it back to Augusta in the Sally League in 1904. He batted only .237, but this didn't stop his letter-writing boosters, who kept peppering sportswriter Grantland Rice of the *Atlanta Journal* with epistles of praise. Taking note of the letters, Rice mentioned Cobb in a number of columns and wrote, ''This Cobb has great talent and may be one of the coming stars of baseball. Cobb hits well and has speed on the bases.'' Based on Rice's well-regarded opinion, the Detroit Tigers brought Cobb up to the American League the next year. Cobb clearly owed his start to the letter written by Rev. Yarborough but hardly to anyone else, since all the other notes to the Sally League clubs and to Rice were penned by Ty Cobb himself—or people to whom he dictated the messages.

FOOTBALL

Touchdown Swim

There never was a windier or wetter touchdown in college football history than when Oklahoma A&M met the University of Oklahoma on a neutral field in Guthrie, OK. Backed up to the 6-inch line, the Aggies were forced to punt. But the kicker, faced with a fearsome Sooners rush, got off a punt that went too high, and the stiff wind whipped the pigskin back out of the A&M end zone and into the swollen Cottonwood Creek, some 20 yards beyond the goal line. Under the rules of the period any loose punt belonged to whichever team recovered it, within bounds or without. Five players for both teams charged into the creek's icy water, all trying to capture the slippery ball. It squibbed away farther into the creek until Sooner halfback Ed Cook finally got control of it. He swam upstream to avoid Aggie tacklers, then made for relatively dry ground and cut back to the end zone, where he downed the pigskin for a touchdown. It was just that kind of a day for A&M, which went on to lose 75–0.

OLYMPICS

The Long-Riding Runner

American Fred Lorz was the early leader in the 1904 Olympic marathon held in St. Louis, but with the temperature in the 90s, he started to wither before the halfway point and dropped out at the 10-mile mark after developing a cramp. He hitched a ride with a truck that was heading in the direction of the stadium. As the truck overtook the competitors still in the running, Lorz waved to them. The truck broke down about 5 miles from the stadium, and Lorz, his cramp gone, decided to keep his muscles loose by resuming running. His ride had put him in the lead, and that was the way it appeared to officials and spectators when he entered the stadium to deafening cheers. The president's daughter, Alice Roosevelt, was getting ready to loop the gold medal around his neck when the other runners converged on them. They'd seen Lorz riding in the truck, and they angrily exposed him. Lorz confessed, insisting he had meant it only as a practical joke but had been carried away by the crowd's adulation. The gold medal was presented to Thomas Hicks of the United States.

AAU (Amateur Athletic Union) officials were deeply angered by Lorz's hoax and slapped him with a lifetime ban from performing in

Contemporary cartoon, somewhat inaccurate in details, depicts how U.S. marathoner Fred Lorz went from first to last and, with assistance, back to first.

any amateur contest. Oddly, the very runners who had been so enraged by Lorz's act now felt compassion for him and petitioned for the suspension to be lifted, as they had known he'd simply been playing a joke. Hard-nosed officials acceded, and Lorz resumed his marathon career, winning the Boston Marathon in 1905—completing that race entirely on foot.

Sentimental Journey

At the 1904 St. Louis Olympics, the crowd favorite in the marathon was, surprisingly, not an American but a plucky little Cuban postman named Felix Carvajal, whose story of his ordeal before the race made him the sentimental choice. Lacking funds to make the trip from his native Havana, he staged a number of exhibitions in the town square to scrape together enough money for his passage to New Orleans, with enough left to make it to St. Louis if he took odd-job chores along the way. However, when he got to New Orleans, Carvajal tried to fatten his kitty in a dice game with seasoned gamblers who took his entire poke in quick fashion.

Relentlessly, Carvajal pressed on, washing dishes and hitchhiking his way up the Mississippi until he got to St. Louis, where members of the U.S. weightlifting team allowed the 5-foot Cuban to stay in their quarters and share their food. However, Carvajal had no money for proper running gear or handlers to help him during training and the running of the race. He showed up at the starting line in long pants, a long-sleeved shirt, and heavy street shoes. Officials held up the starting gun for the race while American discus thrower Martin Sheridan cut off the Cuban's shirt sleeves and his pants at the knees.

Without handlers, Carvajal had to invent ways to obtain sustenance during the running, once filching a couple of peaches off one of the officials' cars and another time detouring into an orchard to grab some green apples—which ended up giving him cramps. If fantasy required that Carvajal win the gold medal, reality proved otherwise, although the plucky Cuban came in a very respectable fifth (fourth after a disqualification against the apparent winner). If Carvajal had financial woes on his way to St. Louis, he did not on his return to Cuba. Public collections raised the money for him to travel back in decent style, the most celebrated nonmedalist of the games. He was greeted as a hero in Cuba.

TENNIS

Tiebreaker

In a Wimbledon match between S. H. Smith and F. Resely the score stood tied at two sets each. Since Smith and Resely were partners in an upcoming doubles match, they wished to maintain their strength for that play and decided to settle the singles match by flipping a coin. Resely won the toss.

1905 _____

BASEBALL

Tinker to Evers to Chance—Silently

"Tinker to Evers to Chance" is nowadays synonymous with the double play, and it has been claimed (inaccurately) that the trio of slick fielders invented the play. They were immortalized by Franklin P. Adams in his poem "Baseball's Sad Lexicon," which appeared in the *New York Mail* in 1910:

> These are the saddest of possible words,
>   Tinker to Evers to Chance.
> Trio of bear cubs and fleeter than birds,
>   Tinker to Evers to Chance.
> Ruthlessly pricking our gonfalon bubble,
>   Making a Giant hit into a double,
> Words that are weighty with nothing but trouble,
>   Tinker to Evers to Chance.

It was amazing that the trio, who played together from 1902 to the eve of World War I, functioned as smoothly as they did, since they seldom got along. Frank Chance ignored the other two at every opportunity, especially second baseman Johnny Evers, who was a constant irritant on the field to both the opposition and his own teammates. Chance often said he wished Evers was "an outfielder so I couldn't hear him." But the real friction involved Evers and shortstop Joe Tinker. They had a cool but not unfriendly relationship until one afternoon in 1905 when Evers left the ballpark after a game and hopped in a taxi. Although he knew Tinker was just behind him, he did not offer him a ride. Later the pair had words several times about the slight and finally turned to fisticuffs at second base during the course of a game.

For the next three years the pair did not say a word to each other; yet they continued their fielding wizardry and were largely responsible for the Cubs winning the National League pennant in 1906, 1907, 1908, and 1910. It was Evers who saved the 1908 season for Chicago when he spotted Fred Merkle's famous bonehead play of not touching second. Evers called for the ball and stepped on second, wiping out a New York Giants victory that would have given them the pennant. Tinker did at least nod to Evers for his brilliant move, and after that the boys did occasionally exchange temperate words, if not actual

Although they were the most famous keystone combination in the game, Tinkers (left) and Evers (right) never liked each other and even engaged in fisticuffs on the field during a game. For three years they spoke not a word to each other while executing double plays.

pleasantries. In 1930, a quarter century after their celebrated falling-
out and long after they had left baseball, Tinker and Evers reconciled,
and they are still remembered for their brilliant on-field harmony.

Warming Up

A couple of hours before a game between the St. Louis Browns and
the Philadelphia Athletics, Rube Waddell was about to start warming
up as the starting pitcher for Mr. Mack's A's. But Manager Jimmy
McAleer had a strategem to try to unload Rube's cannon by having
a couple of his hurlers engage him in friendly banter. The boys lured
Waddell into a throwing contest to see who could heave a baseball
farther. Waddell was the sort always ready for any kind of challenge.
The boys adjourned to the far reaches of the outfield, and a Brownies
pitcher uncorked an impressive throw. Waddell snorted, "That's good
for a school kid, not for a big leaguer," and he let loose with a throw
that traveled several yards farther. The Brownies pretended they were
not impressed, claiming Rube had merely had a lucky throw. "Bet
you can't do it again." At the talk of money, Waddell's competitive
instinct rose several notches. He cut loose a heave that topped his
previous one, and then faced a rotation of Brownie hurlers trying to
beat him. Waddell won five or six times for every loss, but he also
won bets that he could outdistance one of his more outstanding efforts
three times out of five.

After well over an hour of such throwing, the Brownies hurlers
returned triumphantly to their own dugout, even though they were out
several dollars. They reported to McAleer that there was no way Rube
would be able to go a full nine innings. They were of course very
wrong. Waddell shut out St. Louis and fanned 10 batters in the process.
As he was leaving the field, Waddell paused to greet Manager McAleer
and, having not the slightest suspicion that there had been any ulterior
motive in the pregame happenings, asked him to thank his pitchers
for helping him have such a fine warm-up.

When Matty Set the Odds

Technically it was the second World Series, but it was the first played
under official rules. That meant the players would get 60 percent of
the gross receipts for the first four games, while the winners got 75
percent of that and the losers 25 percent. However, in this era when
top stars were fortunate to get $3,000 a year, a 75–25 gamble seemed

rather high stakes. The players of the two teams involved, the New York Giants and the Philadelphia Athletics, decided on a special arrangement. In another era this might be considered a "fix," but in those low paydays it did not seem unreasonable to those in the know. The players agreed that they would split the money 50–50, win or lose. Since they could hardly do it on an organized basis, the players agreed to pair off in twos and let each pair make their own agreement for the 50–50 split. Perhaps the only player who thought otherwise was the great Christy Mathewson, New York's brilliant 31-game winner. It could be said that Matty was a stickler for the rules in general, but even more than that he always hated to give up any money needlessly.

Matty was teamed with Philadelphia's rookie pitcher Andy Coakley, an ex-collegian who had enjoyed a 20-game season. "How are we going to split it, Matty?" Coakley asked. Matty pursed his lips and said, "Well, I'll tell you," in the purr of a cat cornering a mouse. "Why don't we just wait till after the first game and kind of see where we stand." Coakley, fresh out of Holy Cross, viewed Matty just as did most athletes, with unadulterated awe. It did not occur to him to challenge the master's decision.

Matty of course pitched the first game and efficiently shut out the Athletics 3–0, and Coakley knew exactly where he stood. Philadelphia won the second game but that didn't matter, as Matty was pitching game three. His opponent was his pool partner Coakley. Matty hurled another shutout, besting Coakley 9–0. The Giants took game four as well and then Matty took the mound again for game five. Yep, he pitched another shutout, 2–0. The Giants won the Series, and all the players split their cuts even-up. Matty and Coakley had never exactly come to any specific agreement, and as Coakley recalled many years later, "And of course when it was over, we split 75–25, just like the rules said. In fact, he beat me twice—9 to 0 and $1,143 to $381. I guess it was worth it to watch him."

"Yer Out and I'm Outta Here!"

In the early days of baseball, an umpire was judged not necessarily by how well he saw a pitched ball or a play but rather how well he stood by his decision. Timothy Hurst was a tower of strength in such matters. There were those who said Hurst sometimes did not call them the way he really saw them—he frequently had other matters on his mind—but it seldom paid to argue with him. One day Tim was working a Friday game in Philadelphia between the Athletics and the New

York Highlanders (later the Yankees) when he was suffering one of his distractions. Besides umpiring baseball he refereed boxing matches, six-day bike races, foot races, and marathons. These were attractive assignments because they paid extremely well. On Saturday he was slated to officiate a New York marathon run with an early-morning start. With train schedules in mind, Hurst needed a fast game to permit him to catch the late train to New York, but the contest proved tediously long. Finally the ninth inning rolled around with Philadelphia clinging to a one-run lead. New York's Kid Elberfeld made it to second base with two outs, and the next Highlander batter came through with a sharp single to center. A relayed throw came to the plate just a mite after Elberfeld slid in, and poor Hurst had visions in that instant of a tied game, extra innings, and a missed marathon assignment in New York. "Out!" he shouted, apparently seeing or at least believing Elberfeld had not touched the plate. Elberfeld, shocked at the call, charged at the umpire. "I said out," Hurst snapped. "That means you're out."

The irate Elberfeld pushed him. It was not something that Tim Hurst tolerated. Spotting the catcher's mask nearby, he picked it up and brought it down full force on Elberfeld's head, knocking him unconscious. Then Hurst calmly strolled off the field, changed clothes, and caught the train for Manhattan. League President Ban Johnson fined Hurst $100 and suspended him for a week, but since Hurst picked up $500 for his marathon duties, he ended up with a $400 profit with which to enjoy a week's holiday in the big city, proving yet again that the umpire is never wrong.

BOWLING

Almost Perfect

In a tournament in Seattle, WA, bowler James Blackstone had a perfect game going into the last frame, and then he made what seemed to be the final strike. However, one pin cracked in half and, while the top part flew off with the other nine pins, the bottom of the pin remained standing. After long deliberation, officials decided the only thing to do was give Blackstone a score of 299½. At first he felt he'd been robbed, but he then discovered his unique score brought him far more fame than a pedestrian 300.

1906

BASEBALL

No Help Wanted

Since they didn't have the technology in the early part of the century to measure a pitcher's speed accurately, George Edward "Rube" Waddell may or may not have been the fastest southpaw pitcher ever. But his major league strikeout total of 2,316, compared to only 803 bases on balls, indicates that batters frequently just came up, took their whiffs, and sat down again. Rube was a stellar attraction on the exhibition circuit throughout the season, since fans in smaller cities were dying to see major leaguers compete against their hometown heroes. Waddell was a hot drawing card because of his strikeout abilities, and the Rube had a way of really entertaining the fans. When a game reached the last inning, Rube would call in his infielders and outfielders, send them to the bench, and face the foe with only a catcher. He would then proceed to strike out the side. Decades later, oldtimers would insist that Waddell had done it in the majors, but that never happened. When Waddell was with Philadelphia, Connie Mack would never have stood still for such clowning. But, Mack told his biographer, Fred Lieb, "Waddell used to do it quite often in exhibition games, and it worked—most of the time."

One occasion that the Rube was to rue occurred, said Mack, "in Memphis when for some reason Mike Powers caught Rube instead of Ossie Schreckengost, his regular catcher. Harry Davis was managing the club for me that day, and we had a 6–0 lead in the ninth when Rube called in his infielders and outfielders. He fanned the first two batters and struck out the third, too, but Powers dropped the ball on the third strike and the batter reached first.

Pay no mind, Rube indicated, hand upraised to the crowd, much in the style immortalized in "Casey at the Bat." Rube figured he'd just do it again. Unfortunately "the next two batters hit little pop flies behind Rube and his tongue was hanging out chasing them," Mack said.

Rube looked imploringly at the Athletics' dugout and called, "Well, boys, I guess you'd better get back out here and give me a hand."

Acting manager Davis was too busy rolling in the dirt, convulsed in laughter, to comply. "You're doing great," he cried between giggles. "All it takes is one more, Rube."

The record shows that, although staggering in the Tennessee heat,

Rube Waddell was so confident of his pitching prowess that he entertained fans on the exhibition circuit by sending his infielders and outfielders to the bench in the final inning and then striking out the side. But then there was the game that Rube rued.

Waddell struck out the next batter—in self-defense, as another pop fly would have meant the stretcher bearers. As he stumbled to the club-house, Rube considered the high virtue of using a bat on seven of his teammates, but relented when handed a much-needed beer. After gulp-ing down a half dozen more, even Waddell allowed his horror inning had not been without its humor.

Slow Steal

The slowest steal of a base—in fact, a triple steal—occurred in a game between the Pittsburgh Pirates and the Chicago Cubs with the bases loaded. Pittsburgh's player-manager Fred Clarke was on third with the count 3 and 1 on the batter. On the next pitch, the umpire said nothing. Clarke, failing to hear strike two called, decided the umpire was indi-cating ball four by his silence and slowly trotted home while the batter moved slowly toward first. Meanwhile the catcher returned the ball to the pitcher. Just as Clarke touched home plate, the umpire barked, "Strike two!" The embarrassed umpire swallowed hard and explained, "I had a frog in my throat—I couldn't say a word."

The late call brought the batter back from first base with a count of 3 and 2. However, when the Cubs demanded Clarke go back to third and the other runners to second and first, Clarke protested. The Pittsburgh manager insisted he had stolen home fair and square, even if in slow motion. Since there was simply no other way of scoring it, the run stood.

HOCKEY

One-Man Gang

Fred Brophy of the Montreal Westmounts had already won fame in Canada as one of the most aggressive goalies in hockey, frequently punishing opposing players who stormed too near his net, with or without the puck. He also became the first goalie to go the length of the ice and score. He caught the opposing Quebec team out of position, tore straight down the ice, and slapped a vicious shot past goalie Paddy Moran. Two years later Brophy proved the play had not been a fluke—he did it once more.

TRACK AND FIELD

Don't Let Him Get Away

Walking races are among the most difficult for competitors, who have to worry about breaking stride as well as keeping up with the competition. At the 1906 Intercalated (or Interim) Games held in Athens, two walkers, Richard Wilkinson of Great Britain and Eugen Spiegler of Austria, were regarded as cofavorites in two events, the 1,500-Meter Walk and the 3,000-Meter Walk. In the 1,500, Wilkinson and Spiegler went right to the front and finished close together in that order, but both were disqualified for illegal technique. The following day in the 3,000, once again the two star walkers moved to the front and were walking neck-and-neck until they were 50 meters from the finish line. Each eyed the other fearfully, and suddenly both broke into a run. Again they crossed the finish line one-two, and once more they were both disqualified.

1907 _____

BASEBALL

Little Big Inning

It left famed Manager John McGraw raving to himself. His Giants had a less than memorable inning in a game against the Boston Braves, in which they scored the absolute minimum number of runs they could have under the circumstances—and that took some doing. *Question:* How many runs can a team score in an inning if they get one hit, three walks, five stolen bases, while the opposition commits an error, pulls no pickoffs, catches no one stealing, and doesn't get a double play? *Answer:* A grand total of one, and that takes some doing.

　　Sammy Strang started off the Giants fifth with a single, and he was stranded there as the next two batters popped out. With two out Strang stole second and moved to third on a throwing error. Then Cy Seymour walked. Next the pair worked a double steal with Seymour going to second and beating the peg as Strang scored. Roger Bresnahan walked, after which the two base runners pulled off another double steal, moving to third and second. Dan McGann loaded the bases on another walk, but Art Devlin struck out to end the inning. Try as they might, Giants fans tried to work out a scenario in which New York would not have scored at all, but anything they came up with was bound to produce at least one run—which is exactly what New York got (and lost the game).

FOOTBALL

Detour

Al Exendine, the premier pass receiver for Pop Warner's Carlisle Indian School, was generally covered by two defensive backs whenever he broke downfield on an apparent passing play. On a play against the University of Chicago, right-end Exendine raced down the sideline and suddenly veered sharply out of bounds and backtracked. The defensive men then shifted their coverage to Carlisle's left end, who was still on the field of play. Meanwhile, Exendine remained out of bounds, cutting behind the Chicago bench, and ran right into the end zone. On the Chicago bench only Coach Amos Alonzo Stagg seemed to be watching Exendine—and realized what was happening. He yelled to his players but not in time, and Carlisle quarterback Pete Hauser, scampering around in his backfield, cut loose with a perfect 50-yard touchdown spiral.

Today such a pass would be ruled incomplete, as any receiver who so much as steps on the sideline stripe is immediately ruled ineligible for a reception. In the early years of the game, however, variations of the Exendine move were pulled very often. It may have violated the code of good sportsmanship but not the rules as written.

1908 _____

BASEBALL

When Will You Take Me Out to the Ball Game?

While "Take Me Out to the Ball Game" is virtually the national anthem for baseball, it was not written by any devotee of the sport. Lyricist Jack Norworth was sitting in a New York subway car in 1908 when his attention was drawn to an advertisement for the New York Giants. As he thought about the popularity of the game of baseball, he started scribbling some lyrics on a scrap of paper. By the time he got off the train 30 minutes later, "Take Me Out to the Ball Game" had been completed.

The song, with music by Albert von Tilzer, became a tremendous hit, probably Norworth's most-played work, even more than "Shine on Harvest Moon" and "Meet Me in Apple Blossom Time." Ironically, when he wrote the lyrics, Norworth had never seen a baseball game, and in fact he didn't get taken out to the ball game until 34 years later, in 1942. Norworth hardly saw his absence from the baseball stadium as of any consequence. "So what?" he said. "Harry Williams wrote 'In the Shade of the Old Apple Tree' and I am sure he never saw a blade of grass. If he ever got three blocks off 26th Street in Manhattan, it was a big occasion."

And what of composer von Tilzer? He got taken out to the ball game for the first time about 20 years after writing the music.

Merkle's Boner

Today there would be no doubt that 19-year-old first baseman Fred Merkle committed a bonehead play, one that cost the 1908 New York Giants the pennant. But was it a bonehead play then? The fans and the press said it was, and Merkle was subjected to vilification that would continue for years thereafter. The *New York Times* said he was guilty of "censurable stupidity" and the *New York Mail* declared, "Merkle lost his head." The facts can be presented simply. It was a crucial game between the Chicago Cubs and the New York Giants for possession of first place late in the season, with the score tied 1–1 in the last of the ninth at the Polo Grounds. After the first Giant made an out, Art Devlin singled to center and the next batter, Moose McCormick, forced him at second. That brought up Merkle, who rifled a single to right field that sent McCormick to third. Up came shortstop Al Bridwell, who slashed a drive to center, bringing McCormick home with the apparent winning run. Merkle, seeing the runner score, stopped short of second base and made a mad dash for the center-field clubhouse, the custom of the day by players seeking to get clear of the field before fans poured out of the bleachers. Meanwhile, the alert Cub second baseman, future Hall of Famer Johnny Evers, kept calling for the ball. Allegedly he got it and stepped on second, which technically forced Merkle and wiped out the run that had already come in. There was bedlam on the field with jubilant fans by the thousands celebrating the Giants' supposed victory.

The whole scene then degenerated in controversy. Where did that ball that Evers had come from? The throw from center definitely was way off course, getting by Evers and shortstop Joe Tinker. Floyd Kroh, a Cub reliever, ran out of the dugout and tried to grab the ball, but Joe McGinnity, coaching at third for the Giants, blocked him and

Forever labeled "Bonehead Merkle" for his play that cost the Giants the pennant, Fred Merkle actually was given a raise after the season by Manager John McGraw to boost his confidence. He rewarded McGraw's faith by playing stellar ball for many years.

heaved the ball into the stands. According to Evers, Kroh and third baseman Harry Steinfeldt jumped into the stands and wrestled the ball away from the spectator who had caught it, Kroh mashing the hapless fan's derby in the struggle. The fact was that no one knew for sure whether the ball that Evers got was the one Bridwell had hit, or simply one of the Cubs produced for the dramatic play.

Nevertheless, Hank O'Day ruled Merkle out, the inning over and the score still tied 1–1. However, the game could not continue because of the thousands swarming over the field (and besides, no one was about to tell them their team had not won the game). In fact, some early newspaper reports listed a Giants 2–1 triumph.

The decision of what to do about the game was tossed into the lap of National League President Harry Pulliam, who ironically had upheld Umpire O'Day when he made the exact opposite decision under the same circumstances just a few weeks earlier. In that game, between the Cubs and the Pittsburgh Pirates, the third team involved in the tight pennant fight, the Pirates had men on first and third in a 0–0 game in the bottom of the ninth. The next batter got a hit, and the runner on first, Warren Gill, left the field without touching second. In that game also Evers appealed for a force-out, but umpire O'Day ruled against him and let the Pirates' win stand. In that case President Pulliam declined to issue a ruling, since an out had never been called in such circumstances, but he allowed that the Cubs had a legitimate beef. It was a stand that represented towering indecision and an opinion that did not gain much currency, certainly not to Fred Merkle. Now Umpire O'Day ruled the other way, and President Pulliam, an unstable man who hated McGraw (Pulliam would commit suicide the next year), supported him as he had when O'Day had ruled the opposite way before. The president ordered the game to be replayed at the end of the season if it would be a factor in the pennant race. It was, and as fate would have it, the Cubs won and Merkle's boner had cost New York the pennant.

To his credit, Manager McGraw never held it against Merkle. Instead of censuring him, he actually gave him a raise to encourage his downcast player. Merkle repaid McGraw's faith in him by playing stellar ball for many years, and he was recognized by fellow players if not the fans or the media as one of the most alert competitors in the game. McGraw appreciated that in a player. But he didn't appreciate O'Day's decision, and he refused to roll over and die while the dispute was raging. After the game he had sent Merkle into hiding in Coney Island and ordered his players not to talk about the play. He had even gotten his players to sign an affidavit that Merkle had indeed touched second, despite the fact that everyone else on the field knew he had not. McGraw, a scrapper from the old school, simply was trying every angle. The one problem he had in team support involved Christy Mathewson, who had coached at first base during the fateful inning. Mathewson balked at going along with the deception. Pitcher Mathewson was one of baseball's straightest arrows, and he agonized about signing such a paper when he had not seen Merkle touch second. Legend has it that to soothe Mathewson's conscience, McGraw returned to the Polo Grounds with Merkle and Mathewson and by lantern light had Merkle run from first to second. Then Mathewson signed the paper.

In the end, the ploy didn't work, and Merkle remained known forever in baseball history as Bonehead Merkle, the player whose blooper cost his team the pennant.

FOOTBALL

Seeing Red

In the college football wars of the early 20th century, two of the leading manipulators were "Pop" Warner, then of the Carlisle Institute, and Percy Haughton of Harvard. Early that season, when Warner's team faced Syracuse, the tricky coach came up with a gimmick that won the game for Carlisle. He had pads sewn on his players' pants and jerseys—all shaped and colored like a football. The trick gave Carlisle a huge edge, as the Syracuse team had a difficult time spotting the ball carrier.

When Carlisle came to Harvard for their big game, Coach Haughton noted that Warner's boys were practicing with the same confusing football uniforms. "That's not fair," he told Warner, to which Warner countered, "There's nothing in the rules that says I can't put anything I want on my team's jerseys."

At game time Haughton followed the standard custom of the home team supplying the balls for the game. When Warner reached into the ball bag he came up with a *red* pigskin. Warner reached for another one. Red again. The Harvard coach had colored all the balls.

"There's nothing in the rules that says I can't color a football any color I want," Haughton declared.

Warner saw red about the play but could do nothing about it. And Harvard rolled to a 17–0 victory.

OLYMPICS

Tape Tampering

One of the most controversial events in Olympic history was the 400 meters in London in 1908, marked with British anti-Americanism carried to comic proportions. The prerace favorite was Lieutenant Wyndham Halswelle, a 26-year-old London-born Scot. Facing him in the final were three American runners, W. C. Robbins, John Taylor, and J. C. Carpenter. The British officials were fearful that the Americans would run a "team strategy" against their man to keep him from winning, and they stationed their observers every 20 meters around the track.

Robbins went to the front early and by the halfway point held an 11-meter edge. In the last 100 meters the other three runners made their moves, and both Carpenter and Halswelle passed Robbins with Taylor gaining. Halswelle attempted to go to the outside to take the lead, but Carpenter ran wide, keeping the British runner from getting to the front. At trackside British officials were going wild, screaming "foul" and "no race." Then with the four runners all closely bunched, someone elbowed Halswelle. Carpenter pulled in front and raced for the tape. He crossed the finish line but did not break the tape, since an infuriated British official had snatched it away. Robbins came in next. Meanwhile, the enraged British yanked Taylor off the course so that he could not complete the race. By the time Halswelle hit the finish line, the tape was back in place, allowing him to make the traditional victory break.

Chaos ensued, quite naturally, and really no one could be declared the winner after officials disqualified Carpenter. In a compromise, Olympics officials ordered the race rerun two days later, this time with strings laid between the lanes to separate the runners. Taylor and Robbins rejected such conditions as well as the fact that Carpenter remained disqualified, and they refused to participate. As a result, Halswelle ran alone in a walkover without opponents, garnering the gold, but hardly stilling the controversy about the race, which continued for decades.

1909

BASEBALL

Yes, Dots Miller All Right

Sometimes there's less to a baseball player's nickname than meets the eye. In 1909 John "Dots" Miller joined the Pittsburgh Pirates as the team's second baseman alongside the illustrious Honus Wagner at shortstop. A reporter approached Wagner one day and inquired who was his new mate in the Pirate keystone combination. Wagner answered helpfully in his heavy teutonic accent: "Dots Miller"—the

Dots meaning "That's." The newspaperman took Wagner literally and used the nickname, which stuck, although Miller was baffled for some time where the darn thing had come from.

Those Three Umps: Messrs. Klem and Emslie

In his first full year with the New York Giants, Richard William Marquard soon got tagged with his nickname of "Rube" after he sat in the lobby of the team's hotel perusing the most important news of the day in the newspapers—the baseball box scores. He saw a standard line that read: "The umpires: Messrs. Klem and Emslie." Turning to a teammate Marquard said, "How long's this guy Messrs been up here? He was umpiring in the American Association when I was there."

BOXING

Pound Foolish

A century or so ago, black fighters enjoyed an easier time boxing in the British Empire than in the United States. True, Jack Johnson was at the time the heavyweight champion of the world, but with a black man holding the title, there was even less interest in advancing other blacks for American fight fans to root against. Thus it was that an exceedingly talented black boxer, Sam Langford, who Johnson showed a strong disinclination to fight, sojourned to England to do battle with Iron Hague, then the holder of the British heavyweight crown. The English promoters were paying Langford $10,000 and planned to have the winner challenge Johnson for the true heavyweight championship. When Langford, his manager Joe Woodman, and his trainer John Davis arrived in England, they watched Iron Hague in a tune-up match and chortled with glee. Hague, they decided, was a cream puff, a fighter with a good enough punch but the singular inability to take much of a punch. Even a run-of-the-mill club fighter who battled Hague managed to stand him up straight with some none-too-potent blows.

As fight time drew near, the Langford troupe were thrilled to find that English bookmakers were making the bout an even-money affair, and they told themselves they could readily risk their $10,000 purse money on Langford and double their take. Just before the fight, trainer Davis ventured forth and placed the "whole ten" on Langford, the money guaranteed by his purse money. Davis returned to the dressing room all smiles and waving his betting receipt. The boys all chortled until Langford glanced closely at the betting slip and, in his own words, "turned white." Langford couldn't speak for a moment and then gasped: "Look at this ticket," he whispered, handing the slip to his manager. It read that the wager for Langford to win was 10,000 *pounds*! At the then current exchange rate that meant Langford and company had bet $50,000, a sum they did not possess, on the outcome of the contest. "And," said Langford, his voice quivering, "this is a country where they jail you for welshing."

The boys had neither the time nor the money to bet the other way to cancel the bet, besides which the English authorities had this peculiar attitude on fighters placing bets against themselves.

Langford was still in a daze when he entered the ring. He barely noticed Iron Hague, seeing nothing other than images of himself behind prison bars. So preoccupied, Langford allowed himself to be battered around the ring for three rounds. Had not Iron Hague put him down for the last few seconds of round three Langford might never have been jarred out of his lethargy. When the bell sounded for round four, Langford was his old self, landing two blows to Iron Hague's jaw. That was all that was needed. The count could have gone to 150 or so before Hague would have been roused.

Langford and company thus ended up netting $60,000 instead of the $20,000 they had anticipated, and they took the next ship back to the States, but not before leaving behind close to $10,000 worth of their loot for spirits much needed to soothe their frayed nerves.

1910

BASEBALL

As the Wind Blows

The art of sign stealing, a time-honored one in baseball, was perfected by the old Philadelphia Athletics. However, stealing a sign was not enough since that fact had to be relayed to the batter, and there was the possibility that the opposing team might in turn steal that sign. The Philadelphians solved that dilemma by sending the signal not to the batter but to a spy on a housetop outside the stadium. He would simply turn a weather vane, readily visible from the batter's box, to describe the next pitch.

Evenly Matched

Without doubt the most closely matched contest in the major leagues was an odd game between the Brooklyn Dodgers and the Pittsburgh Pirates. The two teams belted out 13 hits apiece. Defensively the Dodgers had 12 assists and committed 2 errors. The Pirates did exactly the same. Both clubs sent 38 batters to the plate, had 5 strikeouts, and drew 3 bases on balls. The Dodger pitcher hit one batter, and the Pirate hurler did also. The Brooklyn catcher allowed one passed ball, as did the Pittsburgh backstop. With that set of statistics, what could the final score possibly have been? The game was called with the score standing 8–8.

Helping Hand

Larry Doyle was a slick-fielding second baseman for the New York Giants. Unfortunately, he was as good a fielder when the Giants were batting. One day Doyle was a runner on first when the next batter smacked a hard grounder to the shortstop, who fielded the likely double-play ball with aplomb and flipped to the second baseman, forcing Doyle. The second baseman wheeled and fired toward first to get the second out. It was then that Doyle, steaming down the base path, did what he did best. He caught the second baseman's throw, made a graceful pivot, and threw on to first himself in time for a lovely double play—for the wrong side. The play was ruled a completed double play, since far from interfering with the action, Doyle had aided the opposing team. Under today's rules both Doyle and the batter would have been automatically out, even if Doyle had not been such a flawless fielding base runner.

1911

BASEBALL

Outfielder's Triple Play

There have been several unassisted triple plays in baseball history, but only once was the feat accomplished by an *outfielder*. Walter Carlisle, playing for Vernon (Los Angeles) in the Pacific Coast League, was positioned in relatively short center field when a liner was hit to him. Carlisle took it on the dead run for the first out, did a remarkable flying somersault, and tagged second base for the second out and without breaking stride beat the runner from first back to that bag for the third out. Carlisle credited much of his lightning play to the fact that he was a former circus acrobat.

How to Pitch to Home-Run Baker

The 1911 World Series between the New York Giants and the Philadelphia Athletics was the first to employ a ghostwritten newspaper series by one of the star performers—pitching great Christy Mathewson. The story behind that story was related years later by news executive John Wheeler in his book *I've Got News for You*:

> I was traveling with the Giants in 1911 when I got a wire from the sports editor: "Sign Mathewson to cover the World Series. Offer up to $500, but try to get him for less." I offered Matty $500 and he accepted. I was to confer with him after each game, then turn out the masterpieces. All went well until Baker, the Athletics' third baseman, hit one out of the park off Marquard. Matty and I turned out a very informative piece, pointing out that Rube had pitched wrong to Baker, inside instead of outside.

Matty's ghosted words made papers from coast to coast as the A's pitcher-turned-scribe poured it on, making Marquard seem like one dolt of a hurler. This was in the second game of the series. Matty came back to pitch in the third game, having won the first game 2–1. The third game proved to be the most tense of all in the Series, with Matty clinging to a 1–0 lead into the ninth inning, when who came up but Frank Baker, the home-run hero of the second game, with one out. Some fans started edging toward the exits. After all, if the great Mathewson knew anything it was how to pitch to Baker. He'd said it in print, hadn't he? Matty got two quick strikes on Baker and sent in a sizzler, trying to strike him out. There was no way of determining if the pitch was going to be too high or too low or too much inside or too much outside. Baker cut loose with a savage swing and lofted the ball deep into the right-field stands.

As Wheeler recalled: "There was considerable razzing by the fans who evidently had read the article on the proper way to pitch to . . . Baker by Christy Mathewson. We had a tough time working out a story that night. Finally Matty decided the best way out of our embarrassment was to write that he had pitched wrong to Baker, too."

The Athletics had gone on to beat Matty in the 11th inning, 3–2, but the rest of the series was almost anticlimactic with the Athletics' bench constantly offering long, loud choruses of quotations from Mathewson. Even though Philadelphia won the series in six games, Matty survived the derision, as indeed did the high art of second-guessing in ghosted writings. Perhaps the man who achieved the greatest fame from the affair was the one who won the nickname that was thereafter indelibly inscribed in baseball history: Home-Run Baker.

Look Who's on First

One of the most creative—or flaky, depending on one's point of view—base runners in the game was Herman A. "Germany" Schaefer. In a game in 1911 against the Chicago White Sox, Germany, then with the Washington Senators, was on first base and a speedy teammate, Clyde Milan, was on third. Germany broke for second with the pitch, figuring the catcher's throw would permit Milan to race home. The only problem was that the catcher made no throw. Schaefer was most upset but still determined to find a way to bring the runner on third in to score. So he came up with a unique play never before seen on the baseball diamond.

On the next pitch, Germany started all over again by proceeding to steal *first* base! Germany figured such a play would rattle the White Sox receiver and force a throw. What the cunning Schaefer hadn't counted on was the fact that his action was so startling and outrageous that the Chicago catcher just held the ball and gawked. An argument ensued as White Sox Manager Hugh Duffy claimed that the theft of first was illegal. The umpires huddled to discuss the rules and decided there was nothing stated anywhere that barred Germany's bizarre move. They ruled him safe at first. Now the Chicago pitcher and catcher were completely rattled, and Germany was all set to try to steal second all over again. As the pitcher cranked his arm, Germany was gone. This time the catcher, so preoccupied with the crazy baserunning, totally forgot about Milan on third and pegged to second to try to cut down Germany. Schaefer slid in under the tag, and in the meantime Milan charged in from third to score. Later, a new rule was passed making the stealing of a previous bag an automatic out.

FOOTBALL

Booster

The game between Princeton and Dartmouth was a hard-fought affair, and it took a freak play to win the game and make Princeton the accepted national college champion for the year. Neither team could score until well into the final quarter, when Princeton's Hobey Baker recovered a loose ball on the Dartmouth 35-yard line. Two running plays picked up 4 yards and brought up then what was last down with six to go. Princeton's ace dropkicker entered the game and prepared to try a 45-yard field goal. The kick was straight but way too low and was clearly going to pass under the goal posts. But just before the ball was to sail under the cross bar, the line-drive kick hit a Dartmouth player in the back. The football spun higher in the air, plopped to the ground, and then, incredibly, bounced right through the uprights. Dartmouth assumed the field goal attempt had failed and that they had possession of the ball.

However, Referee Langford huddled with other officials and consulted his rule book for over eight minutes. Finally he shrugged and announced that the kick was good. The Dartmouth players were furious, but the referee stuck to his ruling, pointing out correctly that the rule book at the time was silent on the subject of a ball striking an opposing player or the ground and then passing between the uprights. All that was mentioned was that a ball that went through the uprights was a good kick. The freak kick caused the rule books to be made more explicit so that any ball that hit an opposing player or was tipped by him was still in play and was a good field goal or extra point conversion if it cleared the uprights.

1912

AUTO RACING

After Dessert, the Race

It was to be the slowest prize-winning time for the Indy 500. Ralph Mulford, driving a Knox, pulled up in the race 100 miles from the finish when his car developed clutch trouble. Meanwhile, nine cars— all the other entrants still in the race—crossed the finish line. That meant that if Mulford could somehow get his car going he could still place 10th. He eased his car off at 60 miles per hour, and kept circling the field until there were only 17 more laps to go. Then he stopped for a leisurely supper, after which he resumed the race. His car chugged across the finish line almost nine hours after the start, and Mulford earned his $1,000 prize money.

BASEBALL

He Pitched and Prayed

The oddest lineup ever offered in a major league game was fielded by the Detroit Tigers in a game in Philadelphia against the Athletics after Ty Cobb had been suspended by American League President Ban Johnson for going into the stands three days earlier and beating up a heckler. When the suspension was handed down, Cobb's teammates announced they would strike in support of their fellow player. Manager Hugh Jennings was in a bind and under pressure to field a team, or the Detroit club would face a fine, forfeiture, and possibly even the loss of its franchise.

With the help of Athletics Manager Connie Mack, Jennings was able to recruit some sandlot players as well as eight students from the St. Joseph's College of Philadelphia. Jennings himself and two of his coaches were also slated for emergency action in the game. The pitching chores were turned over to young Al Travers from St. Joseph's. The pickup team did not fare too well, although sandlotter Ed Irvin got two hits in three at-bats to end up with a lifetime major league average of .667. Pitcher Travers also set a record, but hardly one as impressive, in that he allowed all the Athletics' runs in the 24–2 defeat of the Tigers. This record for runs given up by a starting pitcher still stands. Actually, Travers had good reason to pray on the mound, since his studies were preparing him for the priesthood (which he achieved), and, frankly, he wasn't much of a pitcher, since he had even failed to make his college varsity baseball team. Amen.

FOOTBALL

Now See This!

It would be hard to find a more stupid football team than the Norfolk Blues, made up of collegiate all-stars, who took on Gallaudet, the college for the hearing impaired. Figuring that their opponents were deaf, the Blues saw no reason to huddle to set their plays, instead simply announcing them openly at the line. Presumably, the Blues were composed of players with more brawn than brains, as they never figured out the Gallaudet players were accomplished lip readers. Gallaudet romped to a 20–0 victory.

GOLF

Try, Try Again

In the qualifying round of the Shawnee Invitational for Ladies at Shawnee-on-Delaware, PA, a golfer's tee shot on the 130-yard 16th hole soared into the Binniekill River, the ball floating. Undeterred, the woman's husband got in a boat with her and she smacked away at the ball, finally beaching it 1.5 miles downstream. However, that was only part of her travail as she then had to play through a forest to the hole. Her score for the hole: 166 strokes. The lady's name is lost to posterity since she failed to qualify.

OLYMPICS

Royal Welcome

James Francis "Jim" Thorpe was named the greatest athlete of the half century by the Associated Press in 1950. The high point of the career of this Sac and Fox Indian from Oklahoma was the 1912 Olympics in Stockholm, where he became the toast of the entire world for his athletic prowess. First Thorpe won the pentathlon, and the next day, while the other pentathletes were recuperating, he competed in the high jump, in which he placed fourth. He made a respectable seventh in the long jump. Then came his greatest triumph, the decathlon, an event that lasted three days, with a huge number of competitors. Thorpe had never taken part in a decathlon before or even thrown a javelin until some eight weeks before Stockholm. Despite this, he won easily by an astounding 688 points, routing the best athletes from around the world in a performance considered by

The most celebrated athlete of the 1912 Olympics, Jim Thorpe won both the pentathlon and the decathlon. King Gustav V, giving him his award, said, "Sir, you are the greatest athlete in the world." Thorpe's reply: "Thanks, King."

some the greatest athletic achievement in history. Czar Nicholas of Russia gave Thorpe a jewel-encrusted chalice to go along with his gold medals. King Gustav V of Sweden presented him with a bronze bust for his pentathlon victory. King Gustav could not contain his admiration of Thorpe, telling him, "Sir, you are the greatest athlete in the world."

Thorpe, a man of few words, replied, "Thanks, King."

1913

BASEBALL

Paycheck Punishment

The much-storied baseball Manager Connie Mack could at times be a stern disciplinarian, but his anger generally stopped short of rank meanness. Certainly Mack had a right to be mean toward his star pitcher, Chief Bender, for his aberrant behavior in 1912. Mack's Philadelphia Athletics won the pennant in 1910, 1911, 1913, and 1914, and they should have won in 1912, but for the misbehavior of Bender and Rube Oldring, who broke training. In mid-August Mack had sent them ahead of the rest of the squad from Washington to New York for the team's upcoming series with the Yankees. Oldring and Bender went on a bender of their own and didn't show up for days. Their disappearance ruined the Athletics' chances, and the club faded to third place for the season. The next year Mack determined to discipline Bender. He sent the star pitcher a contract for a puny $1,200. "Goodness gracious," Mack recalled years later, "but that was mean of me. His wife tore it up so he couldn't sign it."

A few days later a chastised Chief Bender came to see Mack. "I don't know anything but baseball," he practically sobbed. "I'll sign and I'll behave." Mack made him sign for the $1,200, but in the end he couldn't hold himself to it. When the team made it to the World Series, Mack asked the pitcher, "How much of a mortgage is there on your house?" Bender said $2,500. "Okay," Mack said, "if you beat the Giants I'll pay it off for you." Bender won both games he pitched. Mack paid the mortgage. "In fact," he said, "I gave him something like $12,000 instead of the $1,200 he signed for. The Chief had kept his promise and had been outstanding."

Fence-Clearing Grounder

In an era, alas, before we had instant replay, hard-hitting George "Doc" Cutshaw of the Dodgers came up to bat in the last of the 11th and hit a vicious ground-ball smash down the first-base line at newly opened Ebbets Field. The ball zipped down the right-field line, and the Phillies right fielder, seeing he could not get to the ball, positioned himself to play the carom off the wall with the hope of holding Cutshaw to a single or at most a double. It was not to be. The hard-hit ball struck the embankment that abutted the wall, but did not ricochet.

Instead, it soared upward along the fence and into Bedford Avenue. Since at the time any ball that cleared the fence in any manner in fair territory was considered a home run, Brooklyn won the game on history's only fence-clearing ground-ball homer. Ah, for the videotape!

"Boo" to the Ump

There is general agreement that Bill Klem was the greatest umpire in baseball history. Not that he wasn't capable of having a short fuse, or even being wrong from time to time. And like most umpires there was almost no way that he would reverse a decision, especially not an ejection of a player. But Klem did have the capacity to admit error once in a great while. Once he was plate-umpiring in a close game between the Pittsburgh Pirates and the New York Giants when both teams got on him, seeking to get whatever edge they could. Klem felt certain that the Pirates especially were trying to put him on the defensive by riding him hard—until he warned them he would clear the bench unless they desisted. At a key point in the contest Pittsburgh Manager Fred Clarke sent up a rookie pinch hitter to bat. Never having seen the kid before, Klem asked him his name. The youth's first response was inaudible, so Klem snapped, "Out with it, kid."

The rookie gulped and said "Boo!" That response was enough to send Klem into orbit, and he immediately thumbed the rookie out of the game. Manager Clarke bounded to the plate in an instant, but Klem cut him off, declaring firmly, "No smart rookie is going to say 'boo' to me!"

"You'll have to make an exception in this case," Clarke told him. And Klem did. It turned out the rookie's name was Everitt Booe. Klem then canceled the ejection. It was something akin to the Red Sea parting.

The Dirtiest Trick

Somehow the legend grew up that Connie Mack was the courtliest man in baseball, a paragon of virtue. Usually he was, but he was also capable of the dirtiest of tricks if that would help his team to victory. Mr. Mack determined that if they were going to consistently beat the Chicago White Sox, they had to find a way to beat Big Ed Walsh, probably the game's best spitball pitcher in an era when the pitch was legal. In 1908 Walsh won 40 games and in a couple of other years 27 each, and over the years he consistently haunted Mack's Philadelphia

*Ace spitballer Ed
Walsh's pitching career
was effectively ended
after Connie Mack
pulled the "Great
Manure Caper" on
him.*

Athletics. His technique for pitching the spitball was to rub the baseball against his tongue and lower lip and then lick the horsehide all
over so that it was about as moist a spitter that any hurler could
deliver. Mack studied Walsh's style and thought up his very dirty
trick. He sent the ball boy to a nearby stable to procure a bucket of
horse droppings.

Mack rubbed all the balls down with the manure, which he could
do since the home team was required to supply all the balls used in
a game. In the bottom of the first inning, Walsh prepared for his first
splitter and licked up the ball. Right there on the mound he gagged
and threw up. Somehow Walsh stuck in the game getting sicker and

sicker, but by the third inning he had to abandon his most effective pitch and was driven to the showers after allowing Philadelphia to score 10 runs. Three days later Walsh returned to the mound for the final game of the four-game series. He still hadn't figured out what Philadelphia had done, but it was the same routine—Walsh heaving up, losing his effectiveness, and being victimized by the Athletics' again-potent bats. Naturally it did not take long for Mack's dirty tricks to make the rounds of the league, and everywhere Walsh was greeted by manure-doctored baseballs. It got so there was no way he could work up the nerve to lick up a ball without throwing up.

Walsh's confidence was gone on the road without his spitter, and he even found he was unable to lick up a horsehide even when at home, where he knew the balls were safe. He was finished as a top pitcher, and from then until his final year in the majors, 1917, he won a grand total of 10 more games. Even despite his lost last years, Walsh, thanks to his premanure state, still ended up with 190 career wins to 125 losses and an ERA of 1.82, which is still a record. He was inducted into the Hall of Fame in 1946. Of course, if Mack had come up with his dirty trick a few years earlier Walsh may never have been anything but a run-of-the-mill hurler.

FOOTBALL

Final Blow

Indiana University punter Clair Scott attempted to kick out of his own end zone in a game against the University of Iowa, but a 50-mile-per-hour wind blew the ball right back into the end zone, where Leo Dick of Iowa ran under the ball and caught it for a touchdown. It was that kind of day for the Hoosiers, who lost 60–0.

GOLF

Short Whiff

It was the shortest-blown putt to decide the U.S. Open. Harry Vardon merely had to sink a 6-incher to end up in first place. But he lost concentration and his careless stab at the ball caused it to ring the hole. And after that Vardon lost out in a three-way play-off won by Francis Ouimet.

1914

BASEBALL

Inside-the-Infield Home Run

When the second umpire failed to appear for a Federal League game between the Brooklyn Feds and the Chicago Whales, Bill Brennan was forced to work the game alone and stationed himself behind the pitcher's mound. This meant that Brennan had to make frequent long treks on a sweltering day to replenish his supply of baseballs. In the fifth inning a Brooklyn batter fouled away 20 baseballs, forcing the frazzled umpire to keep going for more horsehides. Desperately, Brennan decided to get a goodly supply, which he brought behind the pitcher's mound and stacked in a neat pyramid. The next batter was Brooklyn catcher Grover Land, who smacked a line drive straight at Brennan's prize pyramid of balls and sent the horsehides flying in all directions. In the mad scramble, each Chicago infielder came up with a ball. The first baseman stepped on his bag, but batter Land kept on running. The second baseman tagged him out, as did the shortstop and the third baseman. When Land reached the plate, the Chicago catcher also nailed him.

Land had been tagged out five times, but Umpire Brennan was not satisfied. He ruled that there was no putout since there was absolutely no way of telling if any of the Whales had used the batted ball. Chicago Manager Joe Tinker protested the game and took his argument to league President James A. Gilmore. Gilmore ruled he would not throw out the game unless the result affected the pennant race at the end of the season. It did not, so Grover Land went into the record books for clubbing the only inside-the-infield home run!

BOXING

The Freebie Championship Fight

Imagine a heavyweight championship bout in which both contestants fought gratis. It wouldn't happen today, but it did in 1914. Heavyweight champion Jack Johnson was at the time living in Europe, not eager to return to the United States to face conviction on Mann Act sex charges. As a result, Johnson was in dire financial straits and needed a fight to keep afloat. The champ jumped at an offer to fight a journeyman boxer named Frank Moran for the title. The bout was

On the run from U.S. authorities, heavyweight champion Jack Johnson was forced to defend his crown in France—and never collected a centime for his efforts.

promoted by Dan McKetrick, who was Moran's manager. McKetrick saw the bout as a real opportunity for his boy to board the gravy train if he could put away the out-of-condition Johnson. Then McKetrick was shocked to learn that Moran was planning to dump him as manager if he happened to take the crown. McKetrick went to his fighter and demanded he sign an extended contract. Moran look skyward and mumbled something about the two of them sort of getting along on trust. Livid with rage, the manager stormed, "To hell with trust, Frank.

If you don't sign with me now, I'll make sure no one makes a dime from this fight—not you, me, or Johnson.''

McKetrick got a French lawyer and tied up all the profits from the projected fight by claiming Moran had unpaid loans with him. He set up measures to have the money impounded in the Bank of France. By the time the bout rolled around, there never were two more dispirited fighters than Moran and Johnson, both of whom knew they were not getting any money for the match. The cash-short Johnson wanted his cut of the purse and announced he wouldn't fight unless he got paid. Such threats didn't go down well in Paris fight circles, long noted for underworld involvement. A big French gangster-type showed up in Johnson's dressing room, poked a gun in his ribs, and said, "Please." With his gun wrapped in a towel, the gunsel escorted Johnson all the way to his corner.

The fight was 20 rounds, and neither fighter was particularly interested in throwing punches. Still it was no contest, as Moran laid his gloves on Johnson twice, in the words of one observer, "when they shook hands before and after.'' Johnson won as he pleased. After the fight, McKetrick informed the contestants that the profits of $36,000 were being tied up and would remain so until he signed a release document—"and that will be never!''

Probably Johnson would have gotten his money in a year or two, but in the meantime World War I broke out, there was a bank moratorium in France, and McKetrick's lawyer died at the front. After the war, they never found the lawyer's records of the impounded money, and bank records failed to turn it up. So the boys really did fight for what could be called the Freebie Heavyweight Championship of the World.

HORSE RACING

Disqualified in a One-Horse Race

It is a rare event in horse racing when only one horse is entered in a race. The horse runs the course alone and wins the purse money, which because the thoroughbred faced no competition, is reduced to one-half the winner's usual amount. There have been over 30 walkovers in U.S. racing history. But in one case the horse was disqualified in his first attempt at a walkover. In the Autumn Stakes at Belmont Park, Roamer did his walkover run. However, because of a starter's error, the horse ran the wrong course. That run was disallowed, and

Roamer had to rerun his race against himself before his owner could claim the purse.

1915

BASEBALL

One for the Grapefruit League

It was Casey Stengel who set up Dodger Manager Wilbert Robinson for one of the more delightful hoaxes in baseball. During spring training in Florida, Stengel, the manager's favorite player and clown, and Robinson were watching a small airplane circling the Dodgers' Daytona Beach camp. Piloting the plane was a pioneer aviatrix named Ruth Law. This particular day she was air-chauffeuring a representative of a sporting goods company, who dropped his firm's golf balls along the beach as a publicity promotion. As Robbie watched the stunt, he mused to Stengel, "I bet I could catch a baseball dropped from a plane." What had been sticking in the manager's craw was that a few years earlier Senators catcher Gabby Street had caught a baseball dropped from the Washington Monument 500 feet above the ground. As a former catcher, Robbie considered himself superior to Street, and he saw this idea as the perfect way to top him. Stengel told the manager, "Leave everything to me." He arranged everything—and then some.

Aviatrix Law was eager to take part in the stunt, and Frank Kelly, the Dodgers' trainer, was dragooned into going up in the biplane and dropping a baseball to Robinson in position below. The plane took off and swooped down to about 525 feet and circled. Robbie, his concentration at a peak, saw a tiny speck drop from the plane. He moved under it, his mitt set for the catch. The missile hurtled downward, its speed accelerating geometrically, just as Newton had reckoned. The object slammed into Robbie's mitt, and the force knocked him to the ground. The object went right through Robbie's hands and rammed into his chest. The manager felt something burst. Robbie, flat on his back, was drenched in liquid—his chest, face, and stomach. "Jesus Christ," he screamed, "I'm killed! It broke open my chest! I'm all blood! Help me!"

Vaguely Robbie became aware of his players doubled over in laughter. And there was a funny scent in the air. Grapefruit! Finally the bewildered Robinson figured it out. He had been set up, most probably by Casey, with a grapefruit substituted for the baseball.

Robbie got shakily to his feet. "If it was a baseball," he announced, "I'da caught it. I had my hands on the damned thing until it blew up."

Stengel never did own up to masterminding the hoax. And although Robbie finally joined in the laughter, he announced he was considering firing trainer Kelly. Kelly's defense: A baseball might have killed Robbie, while a grapefruit could only have dampened his spirits.

Rookie's Indoctrination

It has been a given in the national pastime that rookies must be tested to see whether they have a high gullibility factor that an opposing team can take advantage of. Such was the indoctrination of Brooklyn's rookie pitcher Ed Appleton when he faced the St. Louis Cardinals. St. Louis loaded the bases, and Miller Huggins, a dedicated conniver coaching third base for the Cardinals, shouted out to Appleton a demand to have a look at the baseball. Unwittingly, young Appleton complied and tossed the ball toward the enemy coach. Huggins made no effort to catch the ball, simply moving out of the way and letting it roll toward the stands. Two men crossed the plate, and St. Louis had conned the hapless rookie into giving up the wining runs. It was a diamond dirty trick, and the rules were subsequently changed so that coaches were barred from causing a ball in play to be thrown to them by the opposing team for any reason.

1916

BASEBALL

Booting a Homer

It was one of the strangest home runs ever kicked. The Brooklyn Dodgers were leading the Philadelphia Phillies 4–2 in the eighth inning when Philadelphia got two men on base with hard-hitting Gavvy Cravath coming to bat. Cravath belted a long line drive toward outfielder Zach Wheat, who saw he had no chance of catching it on the fly. Wheat played for it on the first bounce, but the ball took a crazy hop and hit Wheat's right foot. While Wheat and the crowd stared openmouthed, the ball bounced way up in the air, over Wheat's shoulder, and landed in the bleachers. Since in those days a home run didn't have to clear the fence in the air, the hit was ruled a three-run dinger.

FOOTBALL

Slight Mismatch

It was Cumberland College's big chance to get into big-time college football with powerhouse Georgia Tech, but unfortunately things started going wrong for Cumberland even before they got to Tech's home turf. Several of the players slated to start detrained at a stopover in Nashville, got lost, and didn't make it to the game in time. This meant some scrubs had to start. The contest was pure disaster, as Tech scored every time it got possession of the football, which was very often. In one case a Cumberland player fumbled the ball and, spotting the huge Tech linemen storming at him, yelled to a teammate, "Hey, pick it up."

"You pick it up," came the response. "You dropped it."

Tech quarterback Leo Schlick scored 100 points on his own, and by midway in the third quarter Tech's lead stood at 122–0. Taking pity on Cumberland, the referees called the game.

Years later, Cumberland fullback A. L. Macdonald could at least lay claim to having made his team's nearest thing to a gain, saying "I lost 5 yards around right end."

1917 _____

BASEBALL

No-Hit, No-Luck

No pitcher who ever hurled a nine-inning no-hitter had more bad luck than Jim "Hippo" Vaughn. For nine innings Vaughn of the Chicago Cubs and Fred Toney of the Cincinnati Reds were locked in a pitching duel with the score knotted 0–0. Vaughn had not allowed any hits. Then in the top of the 10th he got the first man out, but Reds shortstop Larry Kopf singled for Cincinnati's first hit of the game. Kopf was able to move to third when Chicago's center fielder dropped an easy fly ball hit by Reds' first baseman Hal Chase. Jim Thorpe, the Cincinnati right fielder and football great, hit a slow bouncer for a single that brought in Kopf with the only run of the game. Meanwhile Toney retired the Cubs easily in the bottom of the 10th. Actually Toney was as much responsible for Vaughn's tough luck as anyone since amazingly he too pitched a no-hitter over nine innings and completed his no-hit stint in the extra inning. Hippo Vaughn's hard luck was that he happened to have taken part in a *double no-hit game,* and fortune ran out on him while smiling on Toney. It was the only double no-hit game on record.

Ruth's Imperfect Start

In an odd fashion, Babe Ruth was responsible for a Boston Red Sox teammate pitching a perfect game, albeit with an asterisk alongside the entry in most record books. In 1917 the Babe was still regarded as more of a pitcher than a slugger, and he was a good one. His main problem was baiting umpires, and he did so with the first batter he faced against the Washington Senators in a game at Boston's Fenway Park. Ray Morgan, the Washington leadoff man, worked Ruth for a base on balls, with Ruth disputing a number of the calls made by home-plate Umpire Brick Owens. In fact, Ruth protested the walk so vehemently that Owens thumbed him out of the game. Ernie Shore took over the hurling, and immediately Morgan was out trying to steal second. Thereafter Shore mowed down the Senators inning after inning, completing a perfect game, never allowing a base runner. Of course, Shore never would have gotten the opportunity had not Ruth gotten thrown out of the game. Shore was credited with a perfect game, although some purists argue that this should not be the case, since the leadoff batter had reached first base, albeit before Shore entered the game. Most authorities insist that Shore is entitled to the perfect game, though—after all, he'd faced just 26 batters and gotten 27 of them out!

How Not to Do It

One of Casey Stengel's favorite stories about "Uncle Robbie," the engaging Wilbert Robinson, who managed the Brooklyn Robins (later the Dodgers), involved his throwing a rare tantrum about the poor hitting exhibited by Brooklyn batters during spring training in Florida. With one player after another in a horrendous slump, Robbie called a special hitting practice session. He grabbed a bat and charged out to the plate snorting, "Here, you clowns! I'll show you something!" Unfortunately, Robbie had been out of practice for years, since he retired from active playing, and he took a half dozen futile swipes at the ball. "See," Robbie said triumphantly, "that's the sort of thing you guys have been doing. Now, I want you to get in there and slug the ball!"

The Three Goats

One of the most undeserved bad raps in baseball was making Heinie Zimmerman of the New York Giants the goat in the final game of the 1917 World Series against the Chicago White Sox. Zimmerman in following years was remembered as the man who chased base runner Eddie Collins across the plate in a botched rundown. Zimmerman could later also be accused of many faults, including fixing games along with the notorious Hal Chase, but he was clean in the '17 Series, and three others richly deserved the goat mantle. In the Chicago fourth, the Sox scored three times in a then 0–0 contest, for the margin of victory, the key play being Zimmerman's supposed faux pas. With Collins on third base and Joe Jackson on first after two Giant errors, Happy Felsch grounded to pitcher Rube Benton. With Collins trapped off third, Benton pegged to Zimmerman, who ran Collins toward the plate, but catcher Bill Rariden moved up too far on the line, so that Collins slipped by him and kept on going. With Rariden out of position and pitcher Benton and first baseman Walter Holke standing there gawking instead of covering the plate as sound strategy required, Zimmerman had no choice but to try to catch Collins on his own. As he said later, "Who the hell was I to throw to? [Umpire] Bill Klem?"

Zimmerman couldn't catch up to Collins, and there went the game and the Series to Chicago. Zimmerman rather bizarrely was dubbed the goat for "running the run home," although in reality there had been three actual goats—Rariden, Benton, and Holke—who all pulled boners on the same play.

1918

BASEBALL

AWOL

In 1918 pitcher Henry Heitman made it to the major leagues—and in the end the nation's defense was strengthened. In July the right-hander started a game for Brooklyn against the St. Louis Cardinals. It was

his first mound duty ever in the big leagues, and the first four batters
he faced banged out hits. Heitman was banished to the showers. He
was still fuming the next day when he went to Manhattan and enlisted
in the U.S. Navy without bothering to inform management. That concluded what was probably the shortest career ever in the majors, and
Heitman never again attempted to play big-league ball.

FOOTBALL

Wrong-Way Dowd

In a way Lehigh halfback Raymond "Snooks" Dowd deserves to be
more remembered for his boner run in the wrong direction than ill-
famed Roy Riegels (see 1929—Wrong-Way Riegels). However, in
Wrong-Way Dowd's case all ended well.

Dowd's play started off in bizarre fashion. He took a handoff and
scampered 15 yards into the end zone—his own! The opposing Lafayette players stood stunned by Dowd's bonehead move and let up for
a moment. This gave Dowd time to think about the play, and he
smacked his hand on his helmet, realizing what he had done. Fortunately, no Lafayette player had gotten to him, and Dowd took off like
a man possessed. He circled wide in the end zone and shot forward
at cannonball speed, rampaging down the sidelines, cutting back to
the center of the field to pick up blockers and then cutting back again
to the sideline. According to some accounts, every Lafayette player
had a shot at Dowd, but none could put him down. He bounced off
tackler after tackler and went the entire length of the field—a distance
of more than 100 yards, although technically all he had done was
score on an 85-yard run.

It was a magnificent moment for Wrong-Way Dowd and brought
him accolades at the time. But when Roy Riegels did his whacky
backward romp 11 years later, Dowd's exploit drew mention in only
a few accounts of the day.

1920s

BASEBALL

Too High a Price

No baseball team had more outrageous, unusual, or colorful fans than the Brooklyn Dodgers. There was the Dodger Sym-phony, Hilda Chester and her cow bell, and Jack Pierce, a Cookie Lavagetto fanatic, but back in their days as the Daffy Dodgers the team had to contend with an infamous fan known as Abie the Iceman. In the 1920s Brooklyn fans turned out at Ebbets Field not only to ride the competition but the Dodgers as well. Brooklyn manager Wilbert (Uncle Robbie) Robinson would carry on constant diatribes with them from the dugout, holding his own most of the time.

However, there was one kibitzer who was the bane of Robbie and the entire Dodger team, Abie the Iceman, who ensconced himself in the upper tier behind third base and heaped abuse on the team—win or lose. Finally, the story goes, an exasperated Uncle Robbie summoned Abie and made him an offer he couldn't refuse, a season's pass with the stipulation that his jeering would end. Abie agreed, and for a few days peace reigned in Ebbets Field. Then one afternoon Abie returned to the Dodgers' offices and turned in his pass. Keeping silent was more than poor Abie could bear. He went back to being a paying heckler.

FOOTBALL

Baiting Papa Bear

The stories of Chicago Bears Owner-Coach George "Papa Bear" Halas' baiting of referees are legendary, but his battles with Jim Durfee in the 1920s were in a class by themselves. The two actually were friends; perhaps Halas admired him because Durfee generally gave better than he got in their exchanges. Once Halas was riding Durfee fiercely in a game, and the referee marched off a 5-yard penalty against him. Halas blew a gasket. "What's that for?" he screamed.

"Coaching from the sidelines," Durfee shouted back. (Under the rules of the era coaches could not give instruction to their players on the field.)

Halas chortled, "That just proves how dumb you are. That's 15 yards, not 5."

"Yeah," replied Durfee, "but the penalty for your kind of coaching is only 5 yards."

In another game Durfee hit the Bears with a 15-yard penalty. Halas screamed at him, "You stink!" Durfee promptly marked off another 15 yards and called back, "How do I smell from here?"

1920

BASEBALL

The House that Grove Built

In 1920, the Martinsburg, WV, team in the Blue Ridge League was so in need of cash that it couldn't even afford a center-field fence. The Baltimore Orioles, then in the International League, allowed that they might well install a fence for Martinsburg, in exchange for the contact of a promising rookie pitcher. Martinsburg jumped at the good deal, which was how the great Lefty Grove started his rise to the big time. Baltimore later sold its $3,500 steal to the Philadelphia Athletics for $105,000, and fence-maker Grove went on to become a career 300-game winner.

GOLF

If the Ball Fits

In the Southern Amateur Tournament in New Orleans, the incomparable Bobby Jones found himself in a bizarre situation when his drive landed inside an old shoe on top of a workman's wheelbarrow. Rather than take a penalty for dropping the ball out of the shoe, Jones played the shot. He slammed the shoe out of the wheelbarrow and the ball flew out of the shoe, rolling just short of the green. The cool Jones then chipped to the green and holed out, managing to make par!

1921

BASEBALL

Heady Assist

Following the beanballing death of Roy Chapman by pitcher Carl Mays in 1920, ballplayers were haunted by the fact that they participated in a dangerous sport. Hard-hitting batters like Babe Ruth and Rogers Hornsby became concerned of the chance they might kill someone with their batted balls. Of the two, Hornsby had a swing that was much more straight-on and thus more potentially lethal. In a St. Louis Cardinals game against the Philadelphia Phillies, Hornsby lined a shot off the forehead of Philadelphia right-hander Bill Hubbell, the crack of which could be heard throughout the stadium. The ball bounded high in the air and was caught by third baseman Russ Wrightstone. The petrified Hornsby had frozen after barely leaving the batter's box for fear that he had gravely injured Hubbell, around whom his concerned teammates gathered. Miraculously, Hubbell soon bounded to his feet and in his Colorado cowboy drawl commented gloatingly, "Well, fellers, I found a way to get that dude out."

No Runs, No Hits, No Appearances

Few prospects got as much fanfare as young Claude Noel, who while pitching for Marshfield of the Wisconsin Valley Baseball League, threw two no-hit games over a four-day period. The St. Louis Browns beat out a number of other teams to ink him to a major league contract. Noel never proved good enough to make it to the majors.

BOXING

Selling Good News

There's been a theory in sports journalism that if you give the readers what they want, they'll buy any kind of a rag. All of French-speaking Europe was worked up when Gorgeous Georges Carpentier met Jack Dempsey in the United States for the heavyweight championship. In Geneva, Switzerland, a "pirate" newspaper, *Les Nouvelles Sportives,* appeared for its maiden edition with the first account of the results of the fight. It told in vivid detail how Carpentier had knocked out Dempsey within the first 30 seconds of round one. The newspaper sold like

French crepes as rejoicing crowds in hotels and cafes read and reread every stirring detail. When about an hour later the reliable Swiss newspapers hit the newstands with the actual results, a fourth-round knockout by Dempsey, most French-speaking citizens of Geneva refused to believe the sad news, and in some cases the legitimate newspaper offices were stoned. Needless to say, *Les Nouvelles Sportives* never appeared again, but its shrewd backers had garnered a fortune not only from the sale of the newspaper but apparently by collecting on a number of wagers on Carpentier and collecting before the facts appeared.

1922

BASEBALL

Fence Busters

While Babe Ruth is credited with ushering in the "lively ball" era in 1920–21 when he hit an astounding 113 home runs, baseball purists saw what they regarded as the end of scientific baseball—old-fashioned, low-scoring, defense-minded games—in a horrendous contest between the Chicago Cubs and the Philadelphia Phillies. Everybody and his uncle smacked the ball as the two teams racked up 51 hits—and practically battered Wrigley Field's fences to kindling wood. The Cubs barely nosed out the Phillies 26–23, after leading by 17 runs going into the eighth inning.

Seeing the Light

In one of the strangest decisions in World Series history, umpires George Hildebrand and Bill Klem called the third game between the New York Yankees and the New York Giants on account of darkness after 10 innings with the score knotted 3–3. Protests were lodged by both teams, who insisted it was still light enough to play. The fans showered the field with seat cushions and soda bottles at the announcement, and a group of infuriated spectators charged baseball Commissioner Kenesaw Mountain Landis' box and hurled insults at him, on the assumption that it was his decision. Actually, Landis played no role, and was himself surprised and angered by it. After about 45 minutes the sun did actually set and genuine darkness resulted. To placate the public, Landis ordered the entire receipts of $120,000 for the game be donated to military hospitals for disabled veterans.

Boobytrap Ball

Al Schacht, the future "Clown Prince of Baseball," ended his not-too-illustrious career in the big leagues in 1921, but continued for a few years in the minors, while honing that future baseball act that would eventually take him to most baseball stadiums in the country to put the fans in stitches with his wacky routines. While playing for the Reading, PA, club, Schacht started doing his act before the start of the game, bringing in quite possibly as many fans as the contest did itself. One of his best routines involved using a light fungo bat and a 10-cent sawdust-filled baseball with which he played "baseball golf," driving the ball off a tee with the bat and then "putting" toward a hole that wasn't there. After his act, Schacht returned to the dugout in case he was called on to relieve the pitcher later in the game. One day Reading was playing the then-minor-league Baltimore team, which was in the process of staging a late rally. Schacht was sent into the game in the ninth, and remembered he still had the dime sawdust ball in his back pocket. He switched balls and conferred with his catcher, advising him to throw the ball back immediately after each pitch so that the umpire couldn't get a good look at it.

The first batter took a mighty swing at the trick ball and lofted an easy pop fly right back to Schacht. Before pitching to the next batter Schacht massaged the ball well since it had been knocked lopsided by the hit. The result was exactly the same for the next batter, as Schacht again took the pop up directly in back of the mound. After this out, Schacht really had to work the ball over, as it was completely out of shape. Next up was the pitcher, Rube Parnham, a rather effective hitter in his own right, who really laced into Schacht's first serving and stared in disbelief that all he had done was give Schacht a third popper to handle and end the game.

Parkham protested to the umpire, demanding he take a look at the ball. The umpire cornered Schacht before he could get away and examined the ball. Thinking fast, Schacht whispered to the umpire that he had used the trick ball "but only against Parkham because he's such a pain in the butt." The umpire had to agree with that evaluation of Parkham, who was exceedingly unpopular with the arbitrators as well. As for Schacht's claim he was just having fun with Parkham but had retired the two previous batters fair and square, the umpire had to take him at his word, since the plays were over and there had been no protests at the time.

Schacht then made the umpire an offer he couldn't refuse: "Tell you what, since I used the trick ball just on Parkham, I'll have another go at him."

It was actually the only thing that could be done. Parkham batted over and, incredibly, popped a legal ball back to Schacht. The waggish pitcher walked off the mound with a contented-cat smile, indicating he'd not merely swallowed a canary but a whole chicken as well.

The Lost Week and a Half

It is little understood about baseball back in the early part of the century that the competition to break into the major leagues was much more intense than today, despite the present potential for multi-million-dollar contracts. By comparison, in the 1920s, as Hall of Famer Paul Waner recollected for writer Lawrence S. Ritter: "I was playing ball on amateur and semipro teams all the while I was in high school and college. In those days, you know, every town that had a thousand people in it had a baseball team. That's not true anymore. But in those days there were so many teams along there in the Middle States, and so few scouts, that the chances of a good player being 'discovered' and getting a chance to go into organized ball were one in a million. Good young players were a dime a dozen all over the country then."

Could a great talent like Paul Waner have been missed? The shocking answer is yes. In fact, it is no exaggeration to say that the only reason he was discovered was that a certain baseball scout was a lush. His name was Dick Williams, and he'd come to Oklahoma in the summer of 1922 to scout a prospect named Flaskamper for the San Francisco Seals of the Pacific Coast League. After sending in his report, Williams had gone on a monumental bender and did not sober up for 10 days. When he caught a train back to California he had no idea how he was going to explain his lost week and a half to the club. On the train he got to talking to the railroad conductor and identified himself as a baseball scout. It so happened the conductor, named Burns, knew a crackerjack prospect, one Paul Glee Waner (who happened to be keeping company with his daughter, a point that was not mentioned), and he waxed enthusiastic about Waner's prowess. Actually he was not lying when he said Waner was the greatest line-drive hitter he'd ever seen. Whether Scout Williams would have taken the spiel so seriously were it not for the fact that he was in desperate need for an alibi for those 10 missing days was another matter.

When he got back to San Francisco, management wanted to know where the devil he'd been. Williams got very confidential, saying he had been scouting out a ballplayer in Ada, OK, all that time. He played it quiet because he didn't want some rival scouts who were in the area to find out about him. "The kid's only 19," Williams enthused, "and there's no way he can miss."

Having conned his way out of a tough spot at least for a time, he wrote a letter to Waner, telling him that a conductor had told him about how great a prospect he was. He told Paul he'd informed management he'd seen him, so he should mail all pertinent information about himself, such as his weight, height, leftie or rightie, speed at running the 100, and so on. The scout emphasized that Waner should send the material to his home address, rather than to the Seals' office.

Scout Williams kept promoting young Waner out of a need for survival, and could only hope for a miracle. Thus there was a lot riding on it when Waner was invited to come to San Francisco for a tryout in 1923. The rest is baseball history. Waner started belting out 360- or 370-foot line drives. Soon he became a starter for the Seals batting around .370. Scout Williams walked around with his chest swelled, icy fear no longer gripping his heart. The following year Waner repeated around the .370 mark, and in 1925 he smacked out 280 hits and had an average of .401. In 1926 the Pittsburgh Pirates bought his contract for a then-whopping $100,000. Paul Waner was made, and Dick Williams gained a reputation as a brilliant scout. It was said he got a juicy bonus out of that $100,000 sale, and that he then went on a monumental bender. The Seals thought he was entitled to it.

FOOTBALL

Bad News

Because the rules of football were constantly being fine-tuned in the early 1920s, coaches frequently contacted the rules committee for clarifications. Southern Methodist University coach Ray Morrison did so during the course of a game, sending a wire to get an accurate ruling on an out-of-bounds play. He was rather annoyed not to get a response. Well after the game, Morrison got a telephone call from Western Union that he had a death message, which under the company's rules could not be read over the phone. Morrison went to the Western Union office and picked up the wire, which read: "Ball is dead."

1923

BASEBALL

Self-Destructing

"Climax" Blethen, a 30-year-old pitcher for the Boston Braves, had lost all his teeth and had false teeth that he carried in his back pocket whenever he played. Getting on first base one day with a single, he steamed hard for second when the next batter hit a likely double-play ball to short. The shortstop tossed to the second baseman, and Blethen tried desperately to take the infielder out with a hard slide to prevent a good relay to first. Unfortunately, the hard-running Blethen forgot all about his teeth in his back pocket. He was out at second and out of the game as well, a bloody mess. He had managed to painfully bite himself in his backside with his false teeth.

BOXING

Haymakers

When Canadian flyweight boxing champion Gene LaRue fought challenger Kid Pancho, both uncorked vicious lefts to the jaw, the blows hitting simultaneously, and sending both fighters to the canvas. The referee counted both of them out.

Amateur's Lesson

As a cub reporter Paul Gallico was often accused by other sportswriters of not having quite the feel for the subject. In boxing, for instance, he had described boxers' little punches to the neck and ribs as mere "love taps." Finally, to determine what it was really like inside the ring, Gallico asked heavyweight champion Jack Dempsey to spar a round with him. Dempsey was at the time in training at Saratoga Springs, NY, for his title defense against Luis Firpo, and felt he could use all the sparring partners he could get. Gallico later described his terrified reaction to being in the ring with the Manassa Mauler and

Sketch that accompanied writer Paul Gallico's account of getting in the ring with champion Jack Dempsey and absorbing what he had previously described as "love taps."

being "stalked and pursued by a relentless, truculent professional destroyer." Then Gallico suddenly became aware of an explosion in his head and lying flat on the canvas. He had never seen the punch that put him down. Gallico got to a sitting position and somehow climbed to his feet. He finished the round, Dempsey apparently not wanting to put him down again. Instead, the champion simply peppered him with those "love taps," blows that Gallico now found excruciating.

1924

BOXING

The Great Foul Act

French heavyweight Georges Carpentier had a boxing career dotted with both high and low points. One of his bravest performances was going four rounds with Jack Dempsey, a bout for which he earned much respect, although he was no match for the Manassa Mauler. On the other hand, Gorgeous Georges hit a low—in more ways than one—in his 1924 match with Gene Tunney and was to leave the big-time ring a laughing stock. There were different styles of fighting in Europe and in America. In England and Ireland, for example, the

technique was the classic style of the upright position. It was different
in France, where boxers fought out of a crouch, and in Carpentier's
case crouching and clutching the groin. In fact, Georges Carpentier
was the father of the European prizefight technique of foul-claiming.
He found it especially useful when he seemed to be losing his battle
to sink to his knees, his face etched in agony, and clasp his groin or
abdomen and moan to the referee, "I am betrayed." Continental referees apparently fell for such thespian appeals and frequently would
stop the bout and award Carpentier the victory by disqualification. The
records are imprecise on the subject, but it has been estimated that
Carpentier won at least a half dozen fights with such claims.

When Carpentier came to America in 1924 after a trove of dollars
such as he had garnered in his brief encounter with Dempsey, he was
to discover that American boxing officials seemed to have precise
knowledge of where a fighter's waistline was and allowed only claims
of foul for blows south of that border. To his credit, Carpentier put
up a good fight at the Polo Grounds, although he was hopelessly
outclassed by a Tunney whose sights were already set on the heavyweight crown, a goal he would achieve two years hence. For 14 rounds
the two traded punches, unfortunately for Carpentier at a rate of two
by Tunney for every one by the Frenchman. Near the end of the 14th
round it was evident to Carpentier that he was going to have to do
something very dramatic if he hoped to pull out a victory. He was
not going to win on points, and he was in no condition to score a
knockout, so he decided no other course was left other that his foul
swan dive routine. Tunney scored a solid body punch, and Carpentier
fell to his knees, clutching instinctively for his groin, about 12 or 13
inches lower than where Tunney's blow had landed. Carpentier rolled
the whites of his eyes at the referee, the highly competent Andy Griffin. Griffin knew both his boxing and anatomy, and he waved off
Carpentier's dishonest belt-line hoax. Griffin started his 10-count,
which was cut short by the bell ending the round.

Carpentier made no effort to regain his feet, instead crawling on all
fours to his corner while his manager François Descamps threw a
Gallic tantrum, clutching his own private area to demonstrate where
his boy allegedly had been struck. Griffin again waved off the performance, now a two-men-in-mortal-agony revue. When the bell sounded
for the 15th round, Carpentier came out but made no effort to raise
his gloves. Since it was obvious to him that he had lost the fight already,
he felt he might as well persist in the foul act. Referee Griffin declared
Tunney the victor by a technical knockout, pushing the supposedly reeling

Carpentier back into the arms of his chattering manager. Descamps tried to pull down his fighter's trunks to show off his putative injury, but he was restrained by boxing commission officials since the contest had been licensed as a prizefight and not a striptease. (Later medical examination found no evidence of any sort of a low blow.)

But Carpentier's act did at least win one supporter, an anonymous blonde who climbed through the ropes while the fighters were still in the ring and tried to scratch out Tunney's eyes. Just about everyone else in the place gave Carpentier the boos he so handsomely deserved. Carpentier's career went into rapid decline thereafter, and he had no more major fights, as his great foul act suffered its own form of disqualification.

FOOTBALL

Endorsements—But He Didn't Inhale

Today it goes with the territory. Top professional athletes endorse anything in sight, from gymnast shoes, beer, soft drinks, breakfast cereals, and coffee makers to cameras, automobiles, and even batteries. The first athlete to cash in on endorsements in a major way was football great Red Grange, thanks to his newfound manager C. C. Pyle, the later mastermind of the Bunion Derby. In a brief time, Pyle lined up Grange for a then-unheard-of sum of $50,000 to hawk such products as a soft drink, shoes, sweaters, hats, and even some dolls. Some said the C. C. in Pyle's name stood for "Cash and Carry," as he negotiated the cash and Grange carried it away. Then Pyle set up the biggest deal of all, for Grange to endorse a cigarette. The trouble was that Grange didn't smoke and wasn't about to. Pyle is supposed to have moaned that Grange would have been the perfect football athlete if he would only learn to inhale.

HOCKEY

Iced

The 1924 Winter Olympics held in Chamonix, France, proved to be an embarrassment to Switzerland as far as ice hockey was concerned. The Swiss hockey team had a defense as porous as a sieve and lost to Canada 33–0, giving up 18 goals in the first period alone. While this was an incredible score for a hockey game, the Canadians similarly embarrassed Czechoslovakia 30–0 and Sweden

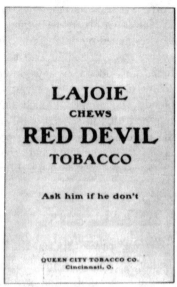

*The Galloping Ghost—Red
Grange—became the first athlete to strike
it rich on the endorsement circuit,
although Grange passed up a fortune
because he didn't smoke and was not
about to say he did. By contrast, earlier
athletes got only penny-ante rewards for
their endorsements. Legend has it that
Nap Lajoie got "10 chaws" and Joe
Wood either got a free pair of shoes, or a
reduction to half price.*

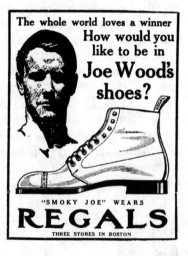

22–0. Great Britain was only slightly more respectable, going down
to defeat 19–2. In the final Canada knocked off the United States
6–1. The best individual performance was turned in by Canada's
Harry Watson, who could not be contained by Czechoslovakia as
he rapped in 13 goals.

1925

BASEBALL

Take 'Em with You, Burleigh

Throughout his career Brooklyn Dodger Burleigh Grimes abused the privilege of a pitcher not having to be much of a hitter. As such he may have produced the absolutely worst case of batting ever in the national pastime, being responsible for eight outs in four times at bat. In a game against the Chicago Cubs, Grimes hit into two double plays in a row, and that was merely a warm-up for his next at-bat in which he smacked into a *triple play*. It should be noted that in his final time at bat Grimes improved immensely, making a simple out and not taking anyone else with him. Still, his production of eight outs in four trips to the plate greatly contributed to the loss of the game by a score of 3–2.

Bragging Rights

Although he was generally considered an excellent fielding shortstop, Roger Peckinpaugh of the Washington Senators committed eight errors in the team's loss to the Pittsburgh Pirates in the World Series, 4 games to 3. This was a new record, eclipsing the previous mark of six miscues set by Honus Wagner, often regarded as the best fielding shortstop of all time. Peckinpaugh took his role as the goat of the series in good grace, and did not complain as much as some others, who felt that some of the errors were "stinko calls," as they put it, by the official scorer. Unfortunately, Peckinpaugh never made the Baseball Hall of Fame, many say because of his 1925 performance.

If Peckinpaugh could be philosophical about it, not so Max Carey, a member of the champion Pirates. A half century later Peckinpaugh and Carey ran into each other in Florida and Carey was still steaming about the error calls. Carey felt that two errors Peckinpaugh made on his batted balls were rightfully hits. He had been the hitting hero of the Series with a .458 batting average, but had not Peckinpaugh been charged with errors on those two plays, the Pirate slugger would have registered a phenomenal .543 average.

Peckinpaugh tried to soothe Carey: "For goodness sakes, Max, that's 50 years ago." But Carey could not be pacified. "All the same they should have been base hits," he kept insisting.

Spitballer Burleigh Grimes was famed for not being able to do spit as a batter. Once he outdid himself by causing eight outs in four at-bats, hitting into two double plays and a triple play.

Peckinpaugh always had reconciled himself by remembering that the great Wagner had previously held the Series' record. As he put it to baseball historian Don Honig two years before his death in 1977: "I tell people that I once broke one of Honus Wagner's records, but I don't tell them what it was!"

Did He or Didn't He?

It was a disputed catch, and apparently the truth was not established until almost a half-century later. In the third game of the 1925 World Series, the Washington Senators were leading the Pittsburgh Pirates 4–3 with two out in the eighth inning. Pittsburgh's Earl Smith hit a hard drive to right center and Sam Rice dove over the wall, the ball in his glove, and disappeared from view. When he reappeared, he still had the ball in his glove, and Umpire Charlie Rigler ruled it a catch despite Pittsburgh's claim that he'd lost the ball and it had been handed back to him by a Washington fan. The argument about Rice's catch went on for years, and whenever Rice was asked about it, he smiled and said, "The umpire said I did."

Eventually, Rice said he would tell the true story after his death, and he left a letter at the Hall of Fame Museum in Cooperstown, NY, in 1965. It was opened after Rice died in 1974. It read:

> It was a cold and windy day and the right-field bleachers were crowded with people in overcoats and wrapped in blankets. The ball was a line drive . . . and I turned slowly to my right and had the ball in view all the way, going at top speed.
>
> About 15 feet from the bleachers, I jumped as high as I could and back-handed the ball. I hit the ground about 5 feet from a barrier about 4 feet high in front of the bleachers with all the brakes on, but couldn't stop. So I

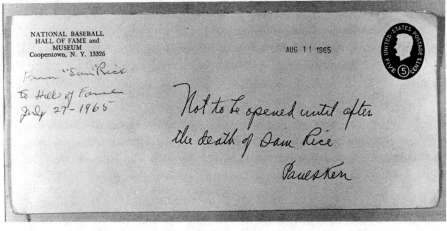

Cover envelope of Sam Rice's revelation about his disputed catch in the 1925 World Series. The letter was not opened until after his death.

tried to jump it to land in the crowd, but my feet hit the barrier about a foot from the top and I toppled over on my stomach into the first row of the bleachers.

I hit my Adam's apple on something which sort of knocked me out for a few seconds but McNeely [the Washington right fielder] arrived about that time and grabbed me by my shirt and pulled me out. I remember trotting toward the infield still carrying the ball for about halfway and then tossed it toward the pitcher's mound. (How I wished many times I had kept it.) At no time did I lose possession of the ball.

BOXING

The Three-Hour Champion

The official record books do not show Willie Stribling, better known as Young Stribling, to have ever been light heavyweight champion of the world. But he was, if only for about three hours. Why Joe Jacobs, the manager of champion Mike McTigue, ever agreed to the fight in the first place was something few, including his own fighter, could comprehend. McTigue understood the problem of fighting Stribling, a Georgia boy, in Columbus, GA. McTigue knew something about hometown fights, having himself won the crown from a French Senagalese, Battling Siki, on his home sod of Ireland—and on St. Patrick's Day to boot. "Do you think we should have this fight, Joe?" McTigue asked Jacobs. The manager had considered the fight in the bag. He had it on good authority that Stribling was not much, a clincher rather than a real boxer. Besides, the promoters down in Georgia were offering top dollar for the fight, and Jacobs was not the sort to pass up allegedly easy pickings. But as insurance, Jacobs had forced the southern promoters to accept his referee, Harry Ertle, a good northerner with a reputation of knowing how to take orders. The George promoters had to bow to that condition or it was no fight.

When McTigue and company hit Georgia, Jacobs nosed around the Stribling camp and discovered that his boy's opponent was no pushover. He tried to cancel the fight, but to no avail. Then he tried to remove the "world title" label from it, but that didn't wash either. As the Georgia promoters, no dummies themselves, pointed out, if Stribling beat McTigue he would be recognized as champion whatever the bout was labeled. Jacobs was hooked, and so was McTigue, in the match itself. To most of the crowd and to sportswriters covering the fight it appeared that Young Stribling had gotten the better of it, enough so perhaps to get the decision, even though boxing had already developed a strong preference that a defending champion be knocked out, or at least outpointed by a wide margin. At the conclusion of the bout, Jacobs could only hope that Referee Ertle, the sole judge of the contest, would see it that way, especially since Ertle already understood what was required of him. The problem was that the referee was not a man of strong character. What he noticed about the Georgia crowd was the heavy concentration of firearms. By quick estimate he had it that something in excess of half of the good old boys in the arena were armed. They wanted a local boy to make good.

The more Ertle thought about all those guns the more he figured he could not give the decision to the champion. He also had the feeling that Jacobs would decapitate him if he gave the nod to Stribling. The worried referee made a big show of toting up his scorecard and checking and rechecking his figures. He then approached the fight's chief promoter, a fellow named John Paul Jones, and asked him to announce the decision. Jones asked what it was. Ertle gulped and said, "A draw."

With an expression befitting a hog seller, Jones said, "If that's your decision, get back out and tell it to the folks."

Referee Ertle turned several degrees more pale as he went to the center of the ring and gazed out at the tense crowd. He raised Young Stribling's arm in victory. The arena was fairly buffeted by the wild cheering. Only Jacobs and McTigue were outraged. Whatever happened to honor? They had to wonder. Ertle was supposed to have been bought and paid for. Ertle made a quick dash for the train station to the cheers of the crowd, but McTigue and Jacobs were in close pursuit. The boys headed north together, and Ertle, safe now from Georgian wrath, learned the errors of his ways—according to some in the train's washroom. At the next stop, Ertle sent a wire north that his official decision was a draw, which meant McTigue retained his crown. That became the official verdict everywhere save Georgia. And in Georgia the folks there viewed McTigue, Jacobs, and Ertle as the combined living embodiment of William Tecumseh Sherman. Poor Stribling never did become a true champion as he might have, dying as he did in a motorcycle accident while still in his twenties.

1926

BASEBALL

Protective Punch

Miller "The Mighty Mite" Huggins was the New York Yankees' first successful manager, which made him popular with fans and players alike. A second reason the players held enduring affection for Huggins was his obvious interest in their welfare, although he sometimes expressed it in an unusual manner. Lou Gehrig was only in his second complete season with the Yankees and not yet making big bucks, although he certainly considered the money big by the standards he was used to. One day Huggins stormed into the dressing room in search of Gehrig. Spotting the tall first baseman, he said, "You big, stupid clown!" With that he slammed his fist into Gehrig's face. Gehrig was stunned but could do nothing but laugh. Huggins stood only 5'4" and weighed 140 pounds, and had to fairly leap to land the blow. Gehrig later recollected, "I stood there laughing and he glared at me. 'Here I've been trying to teach you some sense and you go out and spend a year's salary on an automobile.'" Then, as the little manager cooled down, Gehrig could tell him the truth. He was at the time under contract for $6,000, and someone had told Huggins that Gehrig had just laid out $5,000 for a new car. Actually Gehrig had spent $700 for a used Peerless. Hearing this explanation, Huggins permitted his balled fist to open and he waved a finger under Gehrig's chin. He said, "Well, let that punch be a lesson to you; that's what will happen to you if I ever hear you're throwing your money away."

Three Men on Third

For over three decades, until the Brooklyn Dodgers deserted that borough for the sunnier climes of Los Angeles, there was a famous joke that originated when a fan had to leave Ebbets Field before the completion of a Dodgers game. As he entered a cab, the driver asked him how the contest was going. "Pretty good," the passenger replied. "The Dodgers have three men on base." The cabbie responded, "Yeah, which base?"

In their later years, the 1940s and 1950s, the Brooklyn Dodgers took their baseball seriously. Before that time they were known as the Daffiness Boys, and the daffiest of them all was Babe Herman, who besides being a great hitter and a dreadful fielder was a genuine eccentric when

Lou Gehrig faced the wrath of Yankee Manager Miller Huggins after it was reported that he spent $5,000 of his $7,000 salary for a new car.

negotiating the base paths. The Babe was the sparkplug for the crazy time the Dodgers ended up with three men on base—the same base.

The game with the Boston Braves was tied 1–1 in the bottom of the seventh with the bases filled and one man out. Hank DeBerry was on third, Dazzy Vance on second, and Chuck Fewster on first, with Herman at bat. Herman hit a hard drive to right, and the runners held up a

*The ability of Babe Herman, the daffiest Dodger of them all, to perform
awesomely stupid plays at bat, in the field, and on the base paths was best
typified by his central role in the notorious "three men on third" caper.*

moment to see if the ball would be caught, an eventuality the Babe had
never seemed to take into consideration when running the bases. The ball
banged against the fence. DeBerry came in to score and Vance rounded
third and headed for the plate. Fewster was between second and third
when he was shocked to see a steaming Herman bearing down on him,

also on his way to third. Mickey O'Neil, coaching at third, also spotted Herman making his mindless headlong dash. "Back, back," O'Neil screamed. Vance, almost home, stopped, thinking the frantic instructions were meant for him, and turned back for third. Fewster, running for his life, got to the base standing up just as Vance came sliding in from home and Herman from second. It was a miracle Fewster was not spiked coming and going. Needless to say there were three confused Dodgers there, while coach O'Neil slammed his cap to the dirt.

The Boston third baseman got the ball after it had been thrown home and tagged Vance and Herman but actually missed the tag on Fewster, who just sort of wandered off the bag in a daze. In point of fact, the Boston third baseman had not actually tagged a soul. The lead runner Vance was entitled to the base, so the tag on him was meaningless. There was also no need to tag out Herman, since he was out automatically for passing Fewster. Meanwhile, Fewster simply decided a double play had ended the inning. He started for behind second base to pick up his glove on the short outfield grass and take up his fielding position there. Finally Doc Gatrea, the Boston second baseman, called for the ball and slapped the tag on Fewster, who would have been safe if he had simply gone back to second. With the tag, the umpire yelled, "Fewster, you're out." Fewster said, "I thought I was out five minutes ago."

That ended the confusing inning with one run in. Babe Herman never could understand why he was subjected to so much abuse about his running on the play, and for years he chafed that the description of the play was botched over the years. True, as he contended, he had not tripled into a triple play as some said, but had merely doubled into a double play. And he observed years later: "Only time I can think of when a fellow drives in the winning run and the press makes him a goat instead of a hero!"

Herman was technically correct, but there remained just one way to describe the daffiest Dodger of them all: Good hit, no field, insane run.

1927

BASEBALL

Disturbing the Peace

There have been any number of ballplayers, managers, coaches, and even umpires who have gone into the stands to engage in fisticuffs with spectators deemed to have gone beyond the proper limits of booing and jeering. The venerable Connie Mack, on the other hand, was much more restrained in dealing with obnoxious fans—he took them to court. Once in 1927 Mack had a fan named Harry Donnelly taken into custody for heckling his Philadelphia Athletics at Shibe Park. Mack testified at a hearing for the arrested fan that he had so rattled outfielder Zack Wheat and infielder Sammy Hale that each committed errors that caused Philadelphia to lose their games. Mack was most irate about Donnelly's cruelty toward outfielder "Bustin' Bill" Lamar who, he said, actually became worthless to the Athletics and had to be released. Donnelly was fined $500 for disturbing the peace, Mr. Mack's word being regarded as beyond dispute. And it turned out Mack had not exaggerated about Lamar. His ego had been so shattered he never played ball again.

"Batting for Wellington ..."

Famed sportswriter Grantland Rice knew full well of the perils of doing radio interviews of athletes, and most especially of Babe Ruth, without a prepared script, and therefore typed out in advance the answers the Bambino was to give on his weekly show. In response to one question Ruth pontificated, "Well, you know, Granny, Duke Ellington said the Battle of Waterloo was won on the playing fields of Elkton."

After the disastrous show the exasperated and mystified Rice moaned to Ruth: "Babe, the Ellington for the Duke of Wellington I understand. But how did you ever read Eton as Elkton? That's in Maryland, isn't it?"

The Babe's ready response: "I married my first wife there, and I always hated the goddam place."

Keep Your Eye on the Middle Ball

Pittsburgh Pirate right fielder Paul "Big Poison" Waner was not a premier home-run hitter—at 153 pounds and 5'8½" he did not lambast the ball out of the stadium with the consistency of a Ruth or a Gehrig—but he may well have been the finest line-drive slugger. In this, his sophomore year in the majors, Waner won the National League batting championship with a .380 average, one third of his hits being for extra bases, and he drove in 131 runs. He was deservedly named Most Valuable Player. Already in his mid-20s, Waner also gained

Although generally regarded as the gentleman baseball manager, Connie Mack (here signing an autograph for a youngster) was actually a stern disciplinarian with his players—and the fans. He was noted for having hecklers arrested and in some cases having them fined $500 for disturbing the peace and rattling his players.

another distinction as one of the majors' most dedicated guzzlers of what he called "happy juice." It was said he never came to bat when he did not see the pitcher uncork what seemed to be three baseballs at once. Nonplused, he readily solved the dilemma of which was the real ball and which were mere delusions. "It's simple," he said. "I swing at the middle ball."

During that year Pirate management sought to protect their batting treasure by trying to keep him off the juice. The campaign proved a failure as Waner learned a standard Prohibition-era gimmick, carrying around several phony fountain pens, which he could unscrew and take a snort of John Barleycorn. Once Warner attended a revival meeting in St. Louis and was so moved he took the pledge. Immediately, he went into his first batting slump. It was enough to drive him to drink, and it did. Some baseball experts insist that Waner could not have come to the ballpark consistently plastered and possibly hit as well as he did. Hung over, perhaps, but not totally smashed. The opposition thought otherwise. In Ebbets Field one afternoon Waner had been held in check by Dodger pitching, as even the middle ball seemed to be jumping. Then he came to bat in the ninth inning with the bases loaded and the Pirates behind by two runs. He promptly tripled off the right-center-field wall. As Waner slid into third base, Brooklyn Manager Wilbert Robinson came out of the Dodger dugout, yelling, "Damn you, Waner, why'd you have to sober up with men on?"

Babe Herman—Almost Sane

It happened about a year after Babe Herman pulled the goofiest of all his baserunning blunders (see 1926—Three Men on Third). By then Babe's zaniness at bat, on the base paths and off the field, had clearly established him as the intellectual leader of the Daffiness Boys that were the Brooklyn Dodgers. Even Babe began to suspect all this was not giving him good press. One day he approached a newspaperman in a hotel lobby and complained about the scribe's stories, which consistently made him out to be a clown. "I wish you would lay off'n me. I don't mind so much on my account, but I make a living playing ball and I got a wife and kids to support. If you keep making fun of me, it's going to hurt me." The writer had a conscience, and then and there he announced he would write no more humorous barbs about Herman. The Babe was pleased to have won the journalist over and reached into his pocket and came up with a slightly used cigar. As Herman started to draw on it, the writer went for his matches, but Herman motioned him off. "Never mind, it's lit," he said and puffed away to produce a perfect glow. The writer was now incensed at himself for even considering taking the Babe seriously. "It's all off," he shouted in near hysteria. "Nobody who carries lit cigars around in his pocket can tell me he isn't a clown."

Years later Herman was still mystified about the writer's reaction. After all, he explained, "just the tip of it was lit."

FOOTBALL

The Golden Imitation

A star lineman in college for Southwest Oklahoma State, Perry Jackson was invited to try out with the Providence Steamroller of the National Football League. Unfortunately, Jackson was seriously ill at the time, but, not wishing to waste a golden opportunity, he sent his teammate and buddy Arnold Schockley to take his place. Schockley (using the name Perry Jackson) impressed the Providence coaches, made the team, and was a key figure in the Steamroller winning the championship in 1928. That same year the real Perry Jackson was fully recuperated and eager to make the pros. The phony Perry Jackson recommended him (using the name Arnold Schockley) for a tryout. The real Perry Jackson finally got his big chance but failed to impress and was cut from the roster. Nevertheless he remained in the NFL record books—even if in name only.

Little Big Horned

George Halas, the celebrated Papa Bear of the Chicago Bears, liked to tell this story although he was the butt of it. Halas was playing defensive right end against the New York Giants and Joe Guyon, a full-blooded Indian who had played with Carlisle and other teams with the legendary Jim Thorpe and was himself a future Pro Football Hall of Famer. As Guyon faded back to pass, Halas broke through the line and bore down on the quarterback, who was facing in the opposite direction. It was a glorious opportunity for a blind-side hit that could cause a fumble. However, Guyon got rid of the pass a split second before Halas' arrival, and he wheeled sharply with an upraised knee that poleaxed the flying defender. As Halas rolled on the ground moaning with several broken ribs, Guyon said, "Come on, Halas. You should know better than to try to sneak up on an Indian."

TENNIS

Comeback Kid

Probably no tennis player in Wimbledon history ever dug himself into so many holes and then pulled back from the precipice of certain defeat than Henry Cochet of France. After being down two sets to none in the quarter-finals, Cochet rallied to beat Frank Hunter of the

United States. Next came the great Bill Tilden, and he repeated the process, going from two sets down to a 3–2 victory. The Frenchman moved on to the finals against fellow countryman Jean Borota. In the fifth set Cochet was trailing 5–2, and all his opponent had to do was win one more game to become the men's singles champion. Borota had six match points, but Cochet fought him off each time. In a miraculous court comeback, Cochet swept the next five games for his victory, winning adulation as France's greatest hero since Marshal Foch.

1928

BASEBALL

Cure

The stories of Hack Wilson's capacity for drink are legion, as are the efforts of his various managers to cure him or at least temper his intemperance. Joe McCarthy, his manager with the Chicago Cubs, came up with a vivid demonstration to show Hack the evils of the rotgut gin that he imbibed regularly, usually between every inning of a game. Finding his lectures were failing to lure Wilson to less potent libations, the manager had a groundskeeper dig up a worm from the field and bring it to his clubhouse office.

"Look, Hack," McCarthy said, "I want you to see what happens to this worm." He took the worm and dropped it into a glass of water. The wiggly creature swam happily in the liquid. Then McCarthy asked for Wilson's ever-present gin flask and poured some of the rotgut into another glass. McCarthy fished the worm out of the water and dropped it into the glass of gin. Wilson watched open-mouthed as the worm immediately shriveled and died.

"Look what's happened to that worm," McCarthy said. "Now, Hack, do you see what I've been telling you?"

Wilson thought very hard, and then a knowing smile broadened his face. "Now, I get it," he said. "If I drink gin, I won't get worms. Thanks a lot, boss."

Only the Noggin Counts

The daffiest of all the Dodgers, Babe Herman, is most renowned as the player who doubled into a double play, a horrendous misadventure that culminated in the fabled situation of three Dodgers ending up on the same base and arguing over the rights of possession (See 1926— Three Men On Third). However, Herman perpetrated plenty of other famous boners as he patrolled right field in his own inimitable style. *Collier's* magazine once profiled Herman under the title of "The Great Hoiman" and related the situation that would arise when a fly ball wafted Babe's way:

> It was an even bet that Babe would either catch it or get killed by it. His general practice was to run up when the ball was hit and then turn and run back and then circle about uncertainly. All this time the ball was descending, the spectators were petrified with fear and Mr. Herman was chewing gum, unconcerned. At the proper moment he stuck out his glove. If he found the ball there, he was greatly surprised and very happy.

Legend has it that Herman actually got hit on the skull trying to gather in a simple fly ball, but researchers have never found the incident. What did turn up was a time in 1928 in which Herman was pulled late in a game for defensive purposes and his place taken by a young player named Al Tyson. Tyson lost a line drive in the sun, and the ball hit him on the top of his head and bounced to the wall. Herman was far from the scene of the crime, but as the word spread of the miscue, blame, with considerable logic, was placed on Babe.

Herman was frequently annoyed when the incident was told and retold and angrily informed interviewers that if he ever took a fly ball to the noggin, he would quit baseball.

"How about on the shoulders?" he was asked.

Babe judiciously considered the situation and proclaimed: "On the shoulders don't count."

The Ump Kept Him In

To baseball sluggers there is nothing quite like the pressure of a title competition going down to the last game of the season with a couple of hitters neck and neck so that the day's final box score will crown the king. Quite a few players wilt under the pressure, and some who are ahead by a couple of points have even opted out of the last game entirely to shift the pressure to their opponent. The batting duel in the American League in 1928 was a sizzler between Washington's Goose Goslin and St. Louis' Heinie Manush.

For much of September the unofficial stats were so close that unofficial record keepers such as the Associated Press were themselves unsure whether their figures identified the actual leader. Fittingly, the last game pitted the two teams together in Sportsman's Park, with Goslin unofficially ahead .379 to .377. Manush came up with a strong effort to overtake the Goose by going 2 for 4 while Goslin was 1 for 4 going into the ninth inning. Goslin sat in the dugout trying to figure out if he was still ahead and reckoned he was by a hair. If he simply did not bat as scheduled, he told his teammates, he would have the title wrapped up, since the Senators were behind and unless they tied or went ahead Manush would get no more times at bat. Goslin's fellow Senators were not so sure of the Goose's mathematical skills and insisted he go up and bat like a true champion and win or lose the title with his lumber, the way it should be decided. Goslin sighed, and when his turn came, he strolled to the plate. However, the Goose still had a mind to get out of batting. He could get a base on balls or . . . The second alternative interested him. What if he got the umpire to throw him out of the game? He would not be charged with a time at bat. He started arguing with Umpire Bill Guthrie on the first pitch and kept up a steady diatribe with him. The shrewd Guthrie knew exactly what Goslin was angling for, and he was not buying. "Forget about it, Goose," the umpire said sternly. "No matter how nasty you get, I'm not going to toss you out."

Goslin swallowed hard. It was not a just world when a ball player could abuse an umpire with impunity. With resignation, Goslin eyed the next pitch. A sharp crack of the bat. A single . . . A batting championship. (As it turned out, Goslin could have not batted and he would have won the batting title by .000279. Instead he took the crown by .00164—the fair and square way.)

Bon Appétit

Although he was a potent hitter for much of his career with the Detroit Tigers, experts to this day agree that Bob Fothergill was prevented from gracing the Hall of Fame because of his girth. His belt line was enormous and by contrast made Babe Ruth, with his overlapping waist, look like a stringbean. In fact, Fothergill was so gigantic that he was often referred to as the William Howard Taft of the Diamond. Even hard-willed Ty Cobb, who took over managing the Tigers, could do nothing to get Fothergill close to ideal playing weight. Slightly more successful was the next Tiger manager, George Moriarty, who got the outfield dinosaur down to 256 pounds. To press the good works, Moriarty introduced a system of fines and suspensions without pay if Fothergill's weight ballooned above 260. This forced Fothergill to diet with the grimmest of attitudes, converting the generally easygoing outfielder into a snarling beast and eventually giving the coup de grace to the manager's master plan. Batting one day with Umpire Bill Guthrie behind the plate, Fothergill was annoyed when he took one strike and then another. He growled and clutched his bat, but then took a pitch that he considered to have been off the corner. "Strike three!" Guthrie called. This was all the real or imagined injustice that Fothergill could take. He turned on the umpire, a savage look in his eyes, and took a bite out of the fleshy part of Guthrie's upper left arm.

If nothing else, Manager Moriarty saw that his weight-reduction plan was a total disaster. He announced, "A ballplayer who will eat an umpire must be hungry, or something." Thereafter Fothergill was permitted to eat what and whenever his appetite dictated. But no umps.

Switch Hitter Versus Ambidextrous Pitcher

All baseball fans know that a switch hitter who bats left-handed against a rightie pitcher and right-handed against a southpaw has a distinct advantage. Well ... how about an ambidextrous pitcher who can change his delivery depending on which side of the plate his opponent is batting? And better yet, what if a switch hitter came up against an ambidextrous pitcher? It happened in the Western Association minor league when ambidextrous Paul Richards of Muskogee faced Art Wilson of Topeka batting left-handed. Immediately, hurler Richards geared up to throw left-handed. But Wilson jumped to a right-handed stance. So Richards then set up to throw right-handed. Again Wilson switched positions—and Richards followed suit. This weird contest of nerves went on for several minutes without a single pitch actually being made. Finally hurler Richards broke the deadlock by going into an unusual windup with both of his hands in the air. However, the battle was won by batsman Wilson, who caused Richards to lose his concentration and issue a base on balls.

FOOTBALL

After the Gipper

The story has been told over and over, certainly not the least by Ronald Reagan, who played George Gipp in the movies. Notre Dame's star George Gipp was in the hospital in 1920, dying of complications from pneumonia. Notre Dame's Coach Knute Rockne visited him in the hospital, and Gipp told him, we are informed by both Gipp and Hollywood: "I've got to go, Rock. . . . It's all right, I'm not afraid. . . . Sometime, Rock, when the team's up against it . . . when things are wrong and the breaks are beating the boys . . . tell them to go in there with all they got . . . and win one for the Gipper. . . . I don't know where I'll be, Rock . . . but I'll know about it . . . and I'll be happy."

Eight years later, Notre Dame was playing a superior Army team, which had been undefeated while the Irish were 4 and 2. This was the biggest game of the season for Rockne's team, and 85,000 fans jammed Yankee Stadium for the traditional donnybrook. The Irish held the Cadets to a 0–0 tie in the first half, but Rockne knew his team was tiring and ripe to be taken in the second half. He gave his famous locker-room pep talk, relating Gipp's dying words. And Notre Dame did go out there and win one for the Gipper, topping Army 12–7. It was the upset of the decade. And it figured to be Notre Dame's best season, since their one remaining game was at home and hadn't been beaten on their own turf in 12 years. So they met a very mediocre Carnegie Tech team—and lost, 27–7. Some observers called that the upset of the decade.

TRACK AND FIELD

The Bunion Derby

Promoter C. C. Pyle came up with the idea of the longest footrace ever run. It was to start at Los Angeles' Ascot Speedway and conclude 3,422 miles later at New York's Madison Square Garden.

Entry fees were $100 a runner, who could be anyone from an Olympian to a neophyte. Pyle offered a total of $48,500 in prize money in what the media soon dubbed the Bunion Derby, and he hoped to take in a lot more from sales of programs and promotional fees from the cities along the route. In addition, the promoter was to handle product endorsements—for running shoes, foot powder, liniments, jock straps and bandages, among others—by the eventual winner. Pyle patterned his derby along the lines of the European nine-day bicycle races, with competitors covering a specified distance each day. The daily times were to be recorded and the accumulated times added up, with the lowest figure indicating the winner.

A total of 199 competitors were off at the starter's gun on March

4, but 76 dropped out within the first 16 miles. Others fell by the wayside as the race wended its way through New Mexico and Arizona, through the Texas Panhandle and into Oklahoma, Missouri, and Illinois. One runner was forced to drop out when struck by a hit-and-run driver. By the time the field got to Ohio, there were only 55 left, and these then "sprinted" for the finish. A part-Cherokee Indian from Claremore, OK, named Andrew Pyne took the $25,000 first prize, completing the race in 24 days, not counting nightly rest periods. He beat out the place finisher, one John Salo of Passaic, NJ, by 15 hours.

Promoter Pyle took a $15,000 bath on the first Bunion Derby, but he remained convinced he was onto a good thing. He upped the prize money for the following year, but neither competitors nor the public took much interest in the event, the former because it was too grueling and the latter because it was too drawn out to hold their interest. Pyle's promotional support dwindled, he lost $100,000, and the Bunion Derby was laid to rest.

1929

BASEBALL

"Oh, Those Bases on Balls"

Back before the 1914 season, Manager George Stallings said of his Boston Braves team: "I have 16 pitchers, all of them rotten." Nothing frustrated Stallings more—and many another major league skipper— than his hurling staff's penchant for giving up walks. But under former catcher Stallings' tutelege, the Braves moundsmen improved, and in fact became an integral part of that year's "Miracle Braves." On July 19 the team was mired in last place but then went on a tear, winning 60 of their last 76 games to make a shambles of the National League pennant race. The Braves beat out John McGraw's New York Giants by 10½ games and swept Connie Mack's Philadelphia Athletics four straight in the World Series. It was Stallings' glory year, and he became known as the "Miracle Man." That, however, was the first and only time Stallings managed a first-place winner. Most of his 13 years of managing the Philadelphia Phillies, Detroit Tigers, and New York Yankees and then eight years with the Braves ending in 1920, Stallings was plagued by poor pitching staffs than had trouble finding the strike zone.

George Stallings died May 13, 1929, a harried baseball man to the end. As he lay on his deathbed, he whispered his final words to his wife: "Oh, those bases on balls."

Telling It Like It Is

The greatest baseball player of all time? Some would say Babe Ruth or Ty Cobb and others Rogers Hornsby. Probably each of the trio would have agreed he deserved to top the list. However, only one would have been insistent about it—Hornsby. The Rajah never had the slightest doubt about his world-shaking abilities. There is much in the statistics to back him up. In 1929, for example, his first with the Chicago Cubs, Hornsby played in all of the club's 156 games, batting .380 on 229 hits, and he walloped 39 home runs and drove in 149 runs. That gave Hornsby the right to be arrogant, and he always exercised the right to the fullest. Asked by a sportswriter in awe of his performance if he had ever experienced batting slumps, Hornsby most surprisingly admitted, "Why, yes, I had one this season."

"Really," the reporter exclaimed, "how long did it last?"

"Oh," said Hornsby in total seriousness, never being noted for even the slightest exhibition of humor, "I must have gone to the plate at least six times without a hit."

Path of Least Resistance

Brooklyn Dodger Manager Wilbert "Uncle Robbie" Robinson was a sort of relaxed baseball man, appearing to operate in a loose fashion for which he was sometimes labeled a clown. His players knew this was not the case, that he was a very sound manager, one who could handle pitchers with the best of the field generals in the game. But Robbie did have his idiosyncracies and could alter his strategy for the weirdest reasons. In 1929 Brooklyn acquired a catcher named Val Picinich from the Cincinnati Reds, and Robbie informed him one afternoon to get his gear on, as he would be catching. As Robbie was filling out the lineup card, he turned to Babe Herman—of all people— and said, "Hey, Babe, how do you spell that new guy's last name?"

"Don't you know how to spell it, Robbie?" Herman said.

Robbie contemplated the situation for a minute and finally muttered, "Aw, the hell with it. I'll put DeBerry in to catch."

Thus Brooklyn had two men expecting to do the catching, and when the game was about to start both Picinich and DeBerry came out to home plate all geared up. They looked at each other until Robbie came out and declared DeBerry was catching. However, as soon as Robbie boned up on the spelling of Picinich's name, he got him into the lineup.

BOXING

Therapeutic Punch

A popular deaf-mute boxer, Danny London, lost a bout in Brooklyn after taking an explosive punch to the head. After shaking the cobwebs from his head, the elated loser discovered he could once again hear and speak.

FOOTBALL

The School That Never Was

As a moneymaker the football team of Massachusetts' Salem Trade School was without compare. In fact, other high schools in the state eagerly sought to have them on their schedules. What made Salem Trade so desirable was the fact that it operated on a restricted sports budget, had no home field, and thus had to play strictly as a visiting team. This meant that the other schools could save themselves quite a bit of traveling expenses—and as the host team they kept a major share of the gate revenues as well. And there was another compelling reason to want to play Salem Trade: Even though they fielded a team of very muscular jocks, they weren't that good, often blowing a lead in the fourth quarter, which made the home team very popular with its fans.

Salem Trade first started booking games in 1923, and it wasn't until 1929 that the awful truth came out: No, Virginia, there was no Salem Trade School. The institution had been a figment of the imagination of a group of husky lads in their twenties who came up with a novel way for picking up money every football season. They booked a dozen or so games each year, and after each game took enough of the revenues to earn the boys a dandy income. The dramatic losses were a stroke of genius; because it satisfied their foes with a supposedly dramatic comeback victory. "Wait till next year," the Salem Trade boys would say, and the opposing schools signed them up right on the spot. The hoax was discovered when a high school wrote to the

Salem Trade School to book a game, only to have the letters returned
"Addressee Unknown." It was the end of a seven-year con.

Wrong-Way Riegels

In the Rose Bowl game between California and Georgia Tech, a contest most pundits declared would determine the best team in college
football, defensive lineman Roy Riegels picked up a Tech fumble and
romped into gridiron history. The game was scoreless in the second
quarter when Tech halfback Stumpy Thomason fumbled the ball after
a 6-yard gain. The pigskin popped loose around the 34-yard line, and
Riegels pounced on it and started running, the star lineman's heart
thumping as he realized this was a rare chance for a defensive player
who hardly ever got his hands on the ball to score. Riegels headed
for the near sideline, but he spotted four Tech tacklers blocking his
way. He spun smartly to the left while giving ground and then saw
an opening. Riegels zoomed for the goal line. Unfortunately the goal
line he was heading for was his own.

It was a mad scramble that confused not only Riegels but his team-
mate tackle Steve Bancroft, who called out to guard Bert Schwartz,
"Boy, am I glad I didn't pick up that fumble. I'd have run the other
way." Up in the broadcast booth, a hysterical sportscaster Graham
McNamee yelled into the microphone, "What's the matter with me?
Am I crazy?"

He wasn't, but some of Riegels' teammates were as they even
started throwing blocks for him. Only teammate Ben Lom, the speedster of the team, sensed what was happening and took off after Riegels,
screaming, "No, Roy, no—not that way!" But the roar of the crowd
of 66,404 drowned out his pleas. Tears streaking down his cheeks,
Lom finally caught up with the rampaging Riegels on the California
10-yard line.

"Get away from me!" Riegels yelled, perhaps thinking Lom was
trying to get in on his glory. "This is my touchdown!"

Riegels pulled loose of Lom and got to the 2-yard line when Lom
grabbed him again. Lom spun his bewildered teammate around on the
1 and tried to get him going in the other direction, but several Tech
tacklers bowled both of them over. Riegels was downed on his own 1.

Dejected by his monumental skull, Riegels sat on the ground shaking his head. His teammates sought to console him, and on the next
play Cal tried to punt out of trouble but Lom's kick was blocked and

resulted in a safety. That proved to be the difference in the game as Tech went on to an 8–7 triumph.

Riegels' wrong-way run was the top newspaper story the next day. The misplay was the subject of an estimated 4,500 feature stories and about 250,000 column inches in newspapers from coast to coast. While Riegels went on to be named team captain for 1929 and made several All-American teams in that, his senior year, he never really lived down the nickname of Wrong-Way Riegels. Decades later he would still say, "I still don't understand how I did it."

GOLF

Fairway Hunting Dog

The Van Cortlandt Park course in New York City had suddenly turned into a golfer's nightmare. For a month frustrated players kept getting off beautiful drives, only to come to the spot on the fairway where the balls should have been and find nothing. Finally, the mysterious disappearances reached such epidemic proportions that it became a high-level police matter. Inspector Joseph Cleary went undercover in plus-fours and set out with two plainclothesmen, who were assigned to hide in a clump of trees down the fairway. Cleary teed up a marked ball and drove it away. When it rolled to a halt, the police spies in the woods spotted a bulldog bolt out of the underbrush, pick up the ball in its mouth, and dart back to its protective cover. Cleary drove a second ball, and the bulldog did his thing again. Cleary's third tee shot got the same reaction. Now the officers closed in on the under-brush. They did not find the canine golf snatcher, but came up with 24-year-old Frank Conroy, who just happened to have seven golf balls in his pockets, all with telltale teeth marks. It turned out that Conroy was a professional nurse newly arrived from San Francisco who was making extra money searching for "lost" balls.

Further investigation of Conroy showed he had a history in California of dog training and ball stealing, and a judge sent him to the workhouse for 10 days. The hunt for Conroy's dog continued at the time while the *New York Times* editorialized: "One cannot but ponder the career that would be open to such an animal if he were shown the evil of his ways and induced to lead an honest life."

1930 _____

AUTO RACING

Backward Derby

It was, some journalists would report, the first effort to establish a brand-new sport, backward auto racing. Two young men from St. Louis ran what may be considered the "maiden race" in a demonstration that, it was hoped, would produce a bevy of challengers for future events. Mechanic Charles Creighton and interior decorator James B. Hargis drove backward from New York to Los Angeles and back again in a vehicle doctored up with the headlights attached to the back and the gears locked in reverse. Driving virtually nonstop, with an average speed of about 10 miles per hour, Creighton and Hargis covered the course in 42 days. They experienced only one major accident throughout. They were wheeling out of New York when a befuddled taxi driver ran his cab into their radiator, damaging a fender and a running board. While the pair gained considerable notoriety for their backward exploit, there were to be no future "Backward Derbys" as many communities let it be known they would ban such tomfoolery as a menace to other drivers, who had their hands full contending with cars just going forward.

BASEBALL

Please, Fellas, Don't Force Me!

The year 1930 was a vintage one for disappearances in New York City. In August the police were saddled with the perplexing case of Judge Joseph Crater, who stepped into a taxicab on a Manhattan street and was never seen again. Then in September there was to be another strange and unsolved crime in the kidnapping of Charles Flint Rhem, an effective if flaky pitcher for the St. Louis Cardinals. Rhem had come to the big leagues in the mid-1920s and had some good years. Some dark ones as well. In fact, he had spent 1929 back in the minors at Minneapolis because of his unfortunate habit of mixing highballs and fast balls. The next year Rhem was back with the Cardinals, promising Vice-President Branch Rickey he was now off the happy juice.

Rhem had a six-game winning streak going when St. Louis breezed into Ebbets Field for a crucial three-game set with the Brooklyn Dodgers, whom they trailed in the standings by a single game. He was to pitch a game on September 17, when at warm-up time it was revealed that he had been among the missing for 48 hours. Manager Gabby Street was at his wit's end. While Rhem had been AWOL before, it had never been for 48 hours and never at such a key time. The next morning the New York papers announced a shocking tale. Rhem had finally turned up, pale and wan, late on the night of the 17th, with a terrifying tale to tell. It seemed he was standing in front of the Cardinals' hotel when two men in a taxi (just as in the Crater case!) hailed him. Rhem went over to see what they wanted and they forced him to get in at gunpoint. The pair and a few other confederates took him to a hotel room—he couldn't identify the establishment—and held him prisoner for the next two days and forced him to consume huge amounts of bootleg liquor.

"How could they force you?" reporters asked.

"They held a gun on me," Rhem replied.

"Do you think it was the work of gamblers, or a rival team or something?"

Rhem made no effort to sort out that question. "Reckon so," he said.

The newspaper headlines blazed: "RHEM KIDNAPPED—FORCED AT GUNPOINT TO DRINK LARGE QUANTITIES OF LIQUOR."

The New York Police launched an investigation. Meanwhile St. Louis survived the Brooklyn series and went on to win the pennant. Manager Street announced that since Rhem said he was prepared to forgive his unidentified abductors, the manager would forgive him. And Rickey declared sagely, "Rhem's story is both interesting and gruesome and cannot be disproved." It never was. Rhem himself said he was climbing back on the wagon and would in the future also beware of strangers in taxicabs. And the New York Police dropped their investigation of the player's alleged kidnapping to go back to not solving the disappearance of Judge Crater.

The Better Year

In 1930, while the Great Depression lay heavy on the land, Babe Ruth signed an incredible contract with the New York Yankees calling for a then-unheard-of sum of $80,000 for one season. Clearly Ruth's slugging and box office appeal justified his salary, but still many Americans were stunned at the size of the contract during such hard economic times. An aggressive reporter pointed out to the Babe, "Do you realize you are making more money than Hoover, the president of the United States?"

*Babe Ruth had a far better year in 1930 than did President Herbert
Hoover—and some said in more ways than one.*

Babe mulled that situation for a moment and replied, ''Well, I had
a better year than he did.''

While that was true, the fact remained that over the next couple of
years virtually everyone in the major leagues had to take cuts in pay,
from Commissioner Kenesaw Mountains Landis (reduction of $10,000 a
year) to managers, coaches, and players including Ruth (reported for a
similar reduction to the commissioner's). Still 1932 remained a better
year for Ruth than for Herbert Hoover. The president was fired from
his job.

Ford Frick, later commissioner of baseball, here pictured with Babe Ruth, made up phony action as a baseball broadcaster of re-created games whenever transmission problems cut him off from the action.

Filling the Dead Space

Before he became first president of the National League and later commissioner of baseball, Ford Frick was a sportswriter and wrote books and articles under Babe Ruth's byline. He also announced baseball games on the radio, in an era when live on-field broadcasts were not made of out-of-town games. Instead, the games were "re-created" by the announcer, who got his information from a telegraph wire and described the action in the present tense. Frick soon gained a reputation as the best in the business, carrying this off even when those inevitable gremlins interfered with the transmission. Years later his announcing partner, Stan Lomax, recollected:

> I'll never forget a game we were re-creating when the New York Giants were in Chicago to play the Cubs. During the course of the game, there was a fire outside Wrigley Field and the wires leading to the relay station caught fire. We were cut off from what was happening on the field. Ford had a batter fouling off the pitch about eight times. Then he followed with a lengthy argument between the umpires and the two managers. For 10 minutes he filled in with pure cleverness and imagination. He was an amazing person.

BASKETBALL

Sitting on the Lead

The lowest-scoring basketball game ever occurred when Georgetown High School in Illinois defeated neighboring Homer High 1–0. After scoring a free throw, Georgetown proceeded to freeze the ball. As a result, the Homer players got angry, then bored, and finally they simply sat down and gave up. The referee kept busy reading the newspaper until, mercifully for the fans, time finally ran out.

FOOTBALL

Tricky Tackle

By all logic he should not have made the squad, but Whittier College had no choice, since only 11 students tried out for the football team. So Richard Nixon played tackle his freshman year. The next three years he became largely a benchwarmer as more players made the squad, but he remained the most vocal and most excitable member of the team. And it was finger-crossing time whenever he did get sent into a game. As one former teammate noted later, he was so eager to win that he was offside on virtually every play.

The Unstoppable

In any list of the hardest runners in football, the name of Bronko Nagurski is, not without reason, generally at the top. Coach George Halas of Chicago discovered why during the Bronk's rookie year with

Richard Nixon played tackle for Whittier College as a freshman but was largely a benchwarmer the next three years. Reason: He was so eager to win that he was offside on virtually every play.

the Bears in a game at Wrigley Field. The Bears drove down to the 2-yard line when Nagurski got the handoff and, head down, legs churning, smashed into the line, bowling over two defensive men trying to bring him down. Nagurski burst right through the end zone, his head still down, and ran full-speed into the brick outfield wall. Bronko went down for a moment, then jumped up and raced to the sideline, where he commented to a shaken Halas, "That last guy really gave me a good lick, Coach."

HOCKEY

Got a Light?

In a Quebec amateur league game goalie Abie Goldberry was carrying a pack of matches in his pocket when the hard-driven puck scored a direct hit, igniting them. Goldberry's uniform caught fire and he suffered burns before players and spectators could smother the flames.

1931

BASEBALL

Race for Home

It was the "skull" baserunning play that cost a home-run batting title. Amazingly, it happened to one of the brightest players in the game, Iron Man Lou Gehrig. Early in the season, on April 26, Gehrig smacked a home run, and he raced around the bases—never noticing that he passed teammate Lyn Lary. Instead of being credited for a homer, Gehrig was called out. Gehrig concluded the year with 46 home runs and ended up tied with teammate Babe Ruth. But for his silly baserunning error back in April, Gehrig would have had the home-run crown all to himself.

You Can Take It with You

Dizzy Dean always considered himself the best pitcher in baseball, and he also allowed he was a right dandy batsman as well. While still in the minors with the St. Louis Cardinals Houston farm club, Diz was pitching against Fort Worth and in an early inning smacked out a home run, an accomplishment that swelled him with pride. Later in the game, however, Diz got in trouble and loaded up the bases. This brought manager Joe Schultz to the mound and got Diz a ticket to the showers. Instead of heading for the clubhouse, Diz strolled out to the scoreboard, climbed a ladder, and plucked out the one-run slat he had contributed to Houston's score. When he got back to the dugout, Manager Schultz demanded, "And just what was all that funny business about?"

The response was vintage Dean: "Twarn't no funny business. If I can't pitch, you can't have my run."

Diz was clearly ready for prime time, and he took his wackiness up to the big leagues.

BOXING

Dempsey's Short Count

Almost all boxing fans know that Jack Dempsey lost his chance to reclaim his heavyweight crown in his second fight with Gene Tunney in 1927 when he failed to go to a neutral corner after knocking down

Tunney. It was the famous "Long Count" that enabled Tunney to have about a 16-second respite before getting up from the canvas and outpointing the challenger. However, less well remembered is the Manassa Mauler's involvement in another 10-count imbroglio. This occurred in 1931 when Dempsey returned to the ring as a referee to officiate a match between Max Baer and Tom Heeney of New Zealand. Both were heavy hitters, a situation that virtually guaranteed a victory by knockout.

In the third round Baer waded in on Heeney with a brutal volley of punches to the head and body, forcing the New Zealander back to the ropes near his own corner. Another combination sent Heeney through the ropes, so that he thudded down on the edge of the apron. Three sportswriters shoved him back into the ring (much as was done for Dempsey in his classic battle with Luis Firpo) to keep him from falling on them. Dempsey picked up what he thought was the count while Heeney rested on one knee. However, at the count of eight, the official knockdown timekeeper, the reliable Arthur Donovan, brought down his gavel to signal that Heeney had been counted out. Heeney, Dempsey, and in fact the 8,000 spectators were stunned at the result. There was a roar of outrage as Heeney protested, but with no success. Donovan explained that the count had started at the moment Heeney had landed on the ring apron, and that the full 10 seconds had elapsed by the time the boxer-turned-referee got to eight. Ironically, Dempsey, the victim of a historic long count, had deprived another boxer of an opportunity to win, by victimizing him with a short count.

FACE SLAPPING

Slap Happy

A "sport" that enjoyed a short-lived rage in the Soviet Union was that of face slapping. The first such contest—and almost the last—was a match in Kiev between Michalko Goniusz and Wasyl Rezbordny in which the pair slapped away open-handed at each other for 30 straight hours, their faces turning to bloody pulp. The contest was finally broken up by appalled viewers when neither contestant would concede defeat. Not surprisingly, the unnatural sport soon died a natural death.

FOOTBALL

Pigskin Tripleheader

In an unusual experimental "tripleheader," the University of Alabama faced three different college teams for 20 minutes each in a charity exhibition held at Washington, DC. In the first "game" the Crimson Tide battled George Washington to a scoreless tie. Bama then took the second game, against Catholic University, 7–0. By the time they took the field against their final opponent, Georgetown, the Alabama players were showing definite signs of fatigue. Georgetown marched all the way to the one-foot line, but the Crimson Tide staged an amazing goal-line stand, stopping Georgetown on three scoring thrusts and forcing a field goal try. The kick sailed under the crossbar, and Alabama was able to complete the tripleheader unscored upon, ending up with one victory and two ties.

HORSE RACING

Slide, Horse, Slide

Perhaps the only race won by a horse in an upside-down position was the incredible victory by Brampton at Dargaville, New Zealand. The thoroughbred stumbled some 40 feet before the finish line and fell with such force that he rolled over several times and then actually slid across the line with jockey Joe Parson still clinging desperately to his mount. Brampton slid over the line just inches ahead of the next horse and was declared the winner.

TENNIS

Horror on the Court

Wimbledon tennis spectators were shocked when a female player, Lili de Alvarez, showed up for her match in short trousers rather than the standard knee-length skirt. While fans, competitors, and the press generally agreed the unusual outfit allowed for increased mobility for female players, all were positive that such costumes would never catch on, as most women would consider them too ugly to wear.

1932

BASEBALL

The Should-Be Home-Run King

Who should hold the record for the most home runs in a season? According to many experts, not Babe Ruth with 60 in a 154-game season, or Roger Maris with 61 in a 162-game season, but rather Jimmie "Double X" Foxx. The powerful Philadelphia Athletics' first baseman missed Ruth's mark when he bashed out 58 homers in 1932. He should have had more but, in the midst of a hot-hitting September, Foxx went home one night and did some household chores. While on a stepladder changing a lightbulb, he lost his footing and fell, spraining his wrist. Foxx continued to play, but for about a week his monstrous swing was tempered, as he could not come around hard to pull the ball. As a result, he failed to hit a single home run in the stretch, and Ruth's 60 remained safe.

The Mostest

It was a game that became known simply as "the mostest"—with some amazing stats and probably the worst (but winning) relief stint every hurled. It was a marathon 18-inning contest between the Cleveland Indians and the Philadelphia Athletics. Being of that length, it wasn't amazing that it provided the opportunity for shortstop Johnny Burnett of the Indians to set a record for the most hits in a game—nine. More impressive (or perhaps depressive) was the performance of Eddie Rommel, later an umpire but then in his final season as a hurler for Connie Mack, who took over in the second inning and pitched the rest of the way. The Indians lambasted him almost every inning as Rommel gave up 21 hits and 14 runs. Despite this horrendous bit of moundwork, which allowed Cleveland to move into the lead repeatedly, the Athletics kept rallying to tie the score and save Rommel for yet another inning. Finally, Wes Farrell, who had relieved for Cleveland in the 7th, gave up a bad-hop hit in the 18th to let the winning run score, and Philadelphia won the bizarre contest, despite Rommel's handiwork.

FOOTBALL

Shrink That Field!

The first playoff in the history of the National Football League was scheduled between the Chicago Bears and the Portsmouth Spartans (later the Detroit Lions). The two teams had finished in a tie for first place, and the playoff game was slated for Chicago's Wrigley Field. However, on the day of the game, December 18, a snowstorm battered the city and the temperature dropped to as much as 30 degrees below zero. Under the circumstances it was decided to shift the game indoors to the Chicago Stadium, an arena used mostly for basketball, horse shows, and other exhibitions.

There proved to be another problem. The field could only be 80 yards long instead of 100, and 10 yards narrower than the usual 53⅓ yards wide. To compensate, the teams agreed that the ball would always be put in play at least 10 yards from the sideline. In addition, the goal posts were moved from the end line up to the goal line to protect the players from running into the wooden wall that was erected to surround the makeshift gridiron. Despite this, no three-pointers were made, as the Bears won, 9–0, on a touchdown and a safety. For some reason the idea of the goal posts being on the goal line intrigued the NFL, and it stayed with the arrangement for 40 years.

OLYMPICS

Spaghetti to Go

The most colorful athlete at the 1932 summer Olympics held in Los Angeles was Italian cyclist Attilio Pavesi, who competed in the 100-kilometer race. Since the contestants were not permitted any outside assistance during the event, Pavesi set out well-fortified on his own. He carried a bowl of soup and a bucket of water on his handlebars, a dozen bananas, cinnamon rolls, jam, cheese sandwiches, and spaghetti in a bib tied around his shoulders. He also carried two spare tires.

The plucky Italian took the gold medal in the winning time of 2:28.05.6, more than 15 seconds ahead of the silver medalist. Pavesi had had no need for the spare tires but finished all the food. At the end of the race he was not exhausted—just a bit hungry.

Cheers

An unexpected complication occurred when the 1932 Olympic games were held in Los Angeles. At the time Prohibition still lay heavy upon the land, which meant no alcohol for the competitors. This was more than the French national team could bear, and that country officially protested that while alcohol might be illegal in the United States it was an essential part of the diet of most of the French athletes. As a result, the French team won permission to bring with them several thousand bottles of wine and champagne. The French athletes could of course imbibe during meals and after hours, but they drove officials batty by constantly wandering off the field into the tunnel leading to the locker rooms and there quaffing a quick one.

No Witnesses

In the 1932 Olympics in Los Angeles, Jules Noël of France made a discus throw in excess of 49.49 meters (162'4"), a new Olympic record, but for the most bizarre of reasons, he did not get credit for it. On his fourth of six allowed throws, Noël cut loose a magnificent heave that appeared to have landed just beyond the top throw made by American John Anderson, also a new Olympic mark. Incredibly, every one of the discus throw judges failed to watch Noël's performance, being distracted by a dramatic competition at the pole vault, where a Japanese athlete, winning the heart of the spectators, was unexpectedly threatening U.S. dominance. The chagrined officials could not accept the word of witnesses to Noël's super throw and instead merely offered him an additional throw along with the two he had remaining. However, the Frenchman was unable to match his enormous effort a second time and did no better than 47.74 meters and had to sail home with a fourth-place nonmedal finish.

1933

ACROBATICS

Leap of Their Lives

One of the most amazing escapes ever was that made by the seven passengers on a bus negotiating a sharp turn on a mountain road about 100 miles from Tokyo. The bus skidded and plunged over a cliff down the mountainside and crashed several hundred feet below. The driver was killed, but miraculously all seven passengers survived when halfway down the mountainside the bus hit a lone tree, which checked the vehicle's descent for a bare few seconds. The men realized they had one chance to survive and made a mass flying leap from the opened windows into the branches of the tree. No average persons could have executed this incredible feat of timing and agility, but the seven were aerialists who had performed together in a circus trapeze act.

BASEBALL

Hack's Revenge

For years Hack Wilson had been one of the mightiest of National League hitters, in 1930, whacking out 56 home runs, only 4 off Babe Ruth's record of 60 in 1927. But by the time Hack joined the Brooklyn Dodgers in 1932 for the last two and a half of his last three career years, his performance was in fast decline. In 1933 he batted only 360 times and hit only 9 home runs. Poor Hack was being tortured by pitchers who never could have contained him a few years earlier. They tossed him slow junk. Sidearmers were curving him to death. Above all, the great Carl Hubbell was victimizing him with screwballs. Hack was desperate.

One day Wilson was near the plate, bat in hand, waiting his turn. With a man on second, a teammate smashed a drive to left, and the base runner rounded third and headed for home as the left fielder uncorked a perfect peg to the plate. Then the truly weird happened. There was a mighty crack of the bat. Hack Wilson had smashed the thrown ball right over the left-field fence. The runner of course was declared out for interference, costing Wilson's team the run. Why had Hack done it? Red-faced with shame, but still with an air of justification, he said, "In thirty days, Skipper, that's the first fast ball I've seen. I just couldn't let it go by."

"Yer Out! Yer Out!"

In one of the weirdest plays in baseball, two base runners managed to get tagged out at home plate—on the same play. New York Yankee base runner Lou Gehrig started to run home but held up when he thought a fly ball would be caught. Meanwhile, base runner Dixie

Irritated that he got only slow junk to hit, Hack Wilson got his revenge while in the on-deck circle by slamming a throw to the plate right out of the ballpark.

Walker, starting from second base, came blazing for the plate behind Gehrig. The ball landed just in fair territory, and Goose Goslin fired it home to Washington Senators catcher Luke Sewell, who tagged out both the sliding Gehrig and Walker.

FOOTBALL

Prayer Protection

Late in a scoreless game between the New York Giants and the Chicago Bears at the Polo Grounds, the Giants attempted a field goal. The kick by Ken Strong was good, but it was negated by an offsides penalty. The ball was placed back 5 yards, and Strong once again successfully booted the three-pointer. As the Giants returned to the sidelines, Coach Steve Owen was livid with rage, not about the off-sides call but at his brother, Bill, who was playing tackle. The coach had observed his brother on both kick attempts, failing even to put a block on his man, Bears guard Joe Kopcha.

"Why didn't you destroy that Kopcha?" Steve railed at his brother. "He was just kneeling there at the line of scrimmage on both kicks, and you didn't do anything!"

"I couldn't," his brother pleaded. "On each kick Kopcha raised his eyes toward the heavens and said, 'Please, God, don't let him make it.' Gosh, Steve, I couldn't belt a guy when he was praying."

Reportedly, Coach Owen told his brother specifically where he could go.

HORSE RACING

One and Only

In a stunning upset in the Kentucky Derby a maiden—a horse that has never won a race—named Broker's Tip won the Run for the Roses at Churchill Downs. Besides never having won a race before, Broker's Tip never won another race in his life.

TENNIS

Streak-Buster

In the Wimbledon finals, Dorothy Round, although losing to Helen Wills Moody, wrote her name in the tennis record book. Since 1927 Moody had been undefeated, having taken five Wimbledons, four U.S. Opens, and four French Opens. That was amazing enough, but over that six-year period Moody *had never lost a set*! True, Round lost to her as well but by two sets to one, but that was a most commendable accomplishment that had the tennis world buzzing. Mighty Moody still couldn't be beaten, but she wasn't absolutely invincible.

1934

AUTO RACING

Guzzler

Charlie Tramison had a most embarrassing excuse for failing to qualify for the Indianapolis 500. His car exhausted its supply of fuel before the completion of the trial run. Tramison and his sponsor could be excused from trying to hide since the car's name was "The Economy Gas Special."

BASEBALL

What's Upstairs?

Whether Dizzy Dean was the greatest pitcher of all time can be argued, but hurling was not his only stellar quality. He was also a fierce competitor with a bat and especially running the bases. In the 1934 Series, Dean pitched the Cardinals to victory in the first game against the Detroit Tigers and then saw no action until the fourth game, when he was sent in to pitch run for Spud Davis, who had singled. The next batter hit a sure double-play ball to Charley Gehringer, who flipped to shortstop Billy Rogell, while Diz, determined to break up the play, came into second standing up so that Rogell would not get a clean shot to first. Rogell tried threading the needle, and his hard throw smashed Dean between the eyes. Dean teetered a moment and then went down for the count and was carried off the field on a stretcher, semiconscious. He was rushed to a nearby hospital for X-rays of his head. Released a little while later, Dean had good news, told in his own inimitable style, for the gathering of reporters: "They X-rayed my head and didn't find anything."

Even if Dean didn't quite say it right, he was back pitching the next day, but lost a heartbreaker 3–1. He made amends in the seventh and deciding game by shutting out the Tigers, getting two hits and scoring the first-run—all that was needed—himself.

Four At-Bats, Eight Outs

In one of the most inept examples of hitting, Goose Goslin of the Detroit Tigers batted into four double plays in a row. Despite Goslin's atrocious batting, the Tigers still managed to beat the Cleveland Indians 4–1. Otherwise, Goslin himself noted, his goose would have been cooked in Detroit.

Incentive

In one of the most remarkable pitching achievements ever, the Dean brothers of the St. Louis Cardinals pitched a double shutout of the Brooklyn Dodgers in a doubleheader at Ebbets Field. Dizzy Dean won the opening game 13–0, allowing only three hits, the first coming in the eighth inning. Then Daffy Dean topped his brother by hurling a no-hitter in the nightcap. The Diz was proud of his brother but still a mite peeved. "Effen you'd only a-told me you wuz gonna pitch a no-hitter," he growled, "I'da pitched me one, too."

Hairpin Power

It has long been believed by baseball players that finding a woman's hairpin is good luck for hitters. The superstition goes back to the late 1800s, but the origin of the belief is now lost. In fact, with the St. Louis Gashouse Gang of the 1930s, the search was dedicated and organized. Many of the players were true believers, above all Pepper Martin. Whenever he was mired in a slump, Martin would go out searching for hairpins. A good source he found was just outside the ladies room at the ballpark. When he could not find any pins, Martin turned morose, sure that his hitting would remain subpar. Once a sportswriter and Cardinals shortstop Leo "Lippy" Durocher decided to give Pepper the inspiration that he believed would goose up his batting average. Just before he was due to take his practice swings before a game, they littered the area around home plate with hairpins. Unfortunately future Hall of Famer Joe "Ducky" Medwick decided to take his swings ahead of Martin. Medwick was another believer in hairpin power. When he spotted the lovely horde of hairpins he let out a shout of joy and dropped to his knees to gather them up. An upset Durocher rushed to the plate to try to rein in Medwick. "Leave those pins be, Joe," Leo cried. "They're for Pepper."

Medwick never stopped his hairpin hunt, replying, "To hell with Pepper. These hits are mine!" For other hairpin-power advocates it should be noted that '34 was a vintage year for Medwick, but not nearly an outstanding one for Pepper Martin.

After Dizzy Dean (left) *hurled a three-hit shutout in the first game of a doubleheader, his brother Daffy* (right) *pitched a no-hitter in the nightcap. The slightly peeved Diz said, "Effen you'd only a-told me you wuz gonna pitch a no-hitter, I'da pitched me one, too."*

BOWLING

The Pressure Didn't Stop

There is nothing quite like the pressure that builds up in a bowling alley as a kegler seems to be on his way to a perfect 300 game. Competing in the Genesee Business Home League in Buffalo, NY, Barney Koralewski was knocking over the pins with stunning regularity. By the time he had rolled six perfect frames, the crowd started building up. After he had completed eight frames, all the other lanes were deserted, all eyes on Barney. With or without the spectators, Barney was feeling the tension.

Then suddenly all the lights went out. After a long wait the bowling management announced that all the wires had gone down because of an electrical storm, and that there was no way service would be restored for several hours, probably not until the next morning. It was announced that Barney would have to complete his game at the league's next date, March 29, one week later.

Buffalo bowling fans talked about nothing other than Koralewski's perfect game attempt. It didn't help Barney to have friends urging him not to be nervous.

When Barney returned to the alley, the talk circulated that he was very tense-looking. But his actions told a different story. Like pure clockwork he rolled four strikes, completing his perfect game. He won a gold medal from the American Bowling Congress—even if he had bowled the longest, most nerve-wracking perfect game ever.

FOOTBALL

"Sneakers Championship"

He wasn't a player; he wasn't a coach. Nevertheless he won the National Football League championship for the New York Giants. Abe Cohen was a tailor and a sports fanatic, and he served both the New York Giants and Manhattan College as a sort of Mr. Fixit on the bench and in the dressing room. He made his enviable mark in the memorable 1934 championship game against the Chicago Bears. The game was played on the frozen Polo Grounds with both teams skidding and falling all over the field. At the end of the first quarter Abe Cohen had seen enough. He left the Polo Grounds in a cab for Manhattan College. There was no one around the Manhattan clubhouse, and Abe used a master key to open the basketball players' lockers. He gathered up all the sneakers and headed back to the game.

By that time, play was well into the third quarter, and the Bears, winning the battle of the skids, had moved ahead 13–3. The desperate Giants quickly shed their cleats and donned whichever sneakers approximated their foot size. From his sideline Bear Coach George Halas screamed at his players, "Step on their toes!" The well-tractioned Giants managed to dance their feet out of harm's way and with sure-footed ease scored 27 points in the final quarter, giving them the victory in what became celebrated thereafter as the "Sneakers Championship."

Lew Burton of the *New York American* declared the following day: "To the heroes of antiquity, to the Greek who raced across the Marathon plain, and to Paul Revere, add now the name of Abe Cohen."

GOLF

When Things Go Bad

The 11th hole in the U.S. Open held at Merion Course near Philadelphia was a brutal par 4, with a creek cutting through the fairway and continuing along the side of the green. Scotland's Bobby Cruickshank was having a terrific Open and was right with the leaders when he hit the wicked 11th. On his second stroke Cruickshank tried to get over the creek but topped the ball, which headed straight for the water. Going into the brook would leave the Scot very much up the creek as far as the tournament was concerned. While Cruickshank watched in frozen horror, the ball plunged into the water—but miraculously bounced off a rock and up onto the green!

Elated with his sudden good fortune, Cruickshank celebrated by flipping his club into the air—and it came down on his skull. The good news–bad news golfer managed to regain his footing and par out for the hole. However, it turned out that his self-inflicted skull bashing definitely affected his coordination for the remainder of the match. He lost his concentration and faded to a third-place tie in a tourney he could easily have won.

Crow Hunting

One of the oddest outbreaks of golf-ball theft occurred at New York's Taconic Club. Superintendent Richard Baxter spotted 10 crows flying from the 4th and 15th greens, each with a golf ball in its beak. For a tournament held there a week later, it was declared, in what was probably a golfing first, that entrants could carry shotguns to protect their golf balls.

1935

BASEBALL

"Please, Ump, I Didn't Mean to Strike Him Out!"

It was a bizarre scene—a pitcher racing off the mound to protest a called third strike against a batter. It happened to Jim Walkup of the St. Louis Browns, who were managed by Rogers Hornsby. A stern disciplinarian, Hornsby had a firm rule that any of his pitchers enjoying a count of no balls and two strikes could not serve up a pitch the batter might hit. Hornsby hoped the batter would then swing at a ball for the third strike. Any pitcher who violated the instructions was hit with a $50 fine, a huge sum during the Great Depression.

Walkup delivered a pitch to the outside, but the umpire saw it nip the corner of the plate and yelled, "Strike three!"

The umpire and the fans in the stands were all slack-jawed as Walkup came toward home plate, screaming "No! No! That was a ball!"

Later Walkup would recall: "The ump looked at me like I was crazy. 'Whose side are you on?' he asked me."

Walkup was of course on his own side, but it did no good. The strikeout counted, and Manager Hornsby, even though he was an accomplished umpire baiter himself, listened to none of Walkup's alibiing. The $50 fine stood.

The Sliding Frenchman

Perhaps the zaniest of all base runners was Stan "Frenchy" Bordagaray, who played for five major league teams from 1934 to 1945. Whenever he was on base some misadventure was apt to occur, to drive Manager Casey Stengel nuts when he was managing the Brooklyn Dodgers. Once Frenchy managed to get picked off second base while tapping his foot on the bag. He habitually disobeyed instructions, running when he shouldn't and standing pat when the steal was on, his gut feeling being that he would be thrown out. Sometimes when asked why he hadn't run, he said, "I forgot." Once Casey was coaching at third and yelled to Frenchy not to move. Naturally Frenchy came on the next pitch. Only the fact that he was safe kept Stengel from fining him. Frequently Frenchy infuriated the manager by not sliding into a base. In one game he was tagged out at the plate without even trying to slide past catcher Gus Mancuso. Casey fined him $50 on the spot for that bonehead play.

Not long afterward, Frenchy got his revenge, having vowed he would slide every chance he got. Then Frenchy hit his first and only home run of the season. Charging to first base, he went in with a hard slide, and then hook slid into second and third. As he passed third, Stengel followed him down the line yelling, "Cut that out!" Frenchy went in with a beautiful head-first swan-dive slide. He looked up innocently at the enraged Stengel, who fined him another $50 "for showing me up."

BOXING

Do It Again, Jack

In 1935 former heavyweight champion Jack Sharkey was attempting a comeback with a big payday in mind—which in those days meant fighting Joe Louis. Sharkey did not have the best of reputations ever since he'd lost the heavyweight title in 1933 to Primo Carnera, the amiable but incompetent fighter promoted by gangland interests. The fight had lasted six rounds when Sharkey went down following "an invisible punch" that nobody in the arena noticed save for Sharkey himself. There was much talk of a gambling coup, and Sharkey did not attempt to return to the ring for two years.

However, before he could do battle with Louis and, win or lose, make considerable green, Sharkey had to rehabilitate himself by beating someone or other. Thus, his manager, the resourceful John Buckley, came up with Unknown Winston, whose very name spoke volumes about his pugilistic talents. The bout took place in Boston, and Sharkey, whose prowess had faded to the level of Unknown's, huffed and puffed and swung wildly at his opponent, who did all he could to offer encouragement by sticking out a cooperative chin. Then some sort of contact occurred, and Unknown Winston went down to the canvas, looking for all the world like a man who had departed the same, at least for 10 seconds. Sharkey's arm was raised in victory, but the fans weren't buying. They booed lustily and cries were heard, "We didn't see the punch!" and a bit more ominously, "Lynch 'em!" Boston fight fans of the period were an unruly lot and rather vindictive, but they probably would not have followed through on the lynching, if for no other reason than having lacked the foresight to bring a rope.

In their corner Sharkey and Buckley were worried, however. A hurried conference was held between the two fighters (Unknown Winston having recuperated nicely), their managers, and the officials. An announcement was made to the angry crowd that it had been decided to stage the match all over again, thus presumably giving ticket buyers double their money's worth. The bell rang, and the boys danced around for three minutes, Sharkey not even coming close to a damaging barrage, even though Unknown continued to lead with his chin rather than his left. In the second round, Unknown went down for the count after Sharkey hit him, how hard being a matter of conjecture. Unknown cared not: he went down emphatically and lay there defiantly in dreamland. After all, he had fulfilled his obligations, having suffered two knockouts for the price of one.

Still huffing and puffing, Sharkey surveyed the crowd along with Manager Buckley. It cannot be said the audience was completely pacified, but they did at least move sulkily for the exits. Sharkey went on to his payday against Louis (being put away with dispatch with a punch everyone saw).

Sportswriter John Lardner summed up Sharkey's two "battles" with Unknown Winston: "He is still the only fighter in history who has ever licked his man twice in a night without paying time and a half for overtime."

FOOTBALL

Soaking the Opposition

A torrential downpour hit the game between Kansas State and Oklahoma A&M, forcing the referee to use a large umbrella at his post near the sideline. Spotting this, Kansas caught the Aggies napping as their quarterback dropped back quickly to pass. Suddenly one of the Kansas halfbacks popped out from behind the referee and his umbrella, where he had been hiding in a brilliantly executed sleeper play. Wide open, State's receiver gathered in the pigskin and sloshed to the goal line unmolested.

Try, Try Again

In a game played in Welasco, TX, it took Welasco High almost 300 yards' rushing to produce a single touchdown. With the ball on Welasco's 15-yard line, Torres broke through the defense and scampered all the way to score. However, the play was called back because of an offensive infraction. On the next snap Matter ran more than 90 yards for a score—but again a penalty brought the play back. On the third try, Porter took the ball and cut wide, reversed directions once again, and romped the entire length of the field for a touchdown. This time, after three carriers totaling almost 300 yards, the play stood.

Cover-Up

An important aspect of football is the art of covering up an infraction that a team has committed. Susquehanna had a play in its playbook to accomplish exactly that when the team inadvertently ended up with 12 men on the field instead of 11. In a game against Pennsylvania Military College, the Susquehanna quarterback suddenly became aware that there were 12 men in the huddle instead of the allowed 11. Fortunately, the officials had not noticed it at the moment, and the quarterback immediately switched plays to a special end run to the side of the field with the Susquehanna bench. As the play developed in that direction, a designated offensive player casually slipped off the playing field and plunked himself down on the bench. By that time, the officials had awakened to the possibility that something was wrong, but a quick count of the players indicated that Susquehanna had just 11 men on the field. Thus, the offense made a few yards on a play that should have resulted in a penalty of 5 yards.

GOLF

Grabby Crabs

The fairways of Australia's fashionable Darwin Club were suddenly plagued by a rash of disappearing golf balls. The mystery was finally solved when a fast-moving caddy, following a ball sliced into the rough, spotted a land crab ambling into the mangroves with it. A new rule was immediately instituted, allowing a player to retrieve his shot from one of the many crab holes without penalty.

1936 _____

BASEBALL

One Fat One Coming Up

Dizzy Dean's confidence in his ability to spot the opposition a few hits and still get them out without damage was nothing short of legendary. Some batters enjoyed good hitting days simply because Diz happened to be fond of them and was willing to fatten their averages to ensure their worth to their own teams. Dean always had a special fondness for Burgess Whitehead, with whom he had roomed in the minors. When Whitehead was shipped to the New York Giants, Dean considered it his duty to see to it that the light-hitting Whitehead always got a few hits off him when he pitched against New York. He would call out from the mound: "Hey, little bitty buddy, I'm throwing it right over, so you get your hits. You got to get your hits off of Ol' Diz." In one game in St. Louis, Dean gave Whitehead a fat pitch and Whitehead slammed a line drive that caught Diz right between the eyes. Dean got up off the ground shaking the stars from his eyes and looked over at Whitehead standing on first base. He said, "Little bitty buddy, you got to start pullin' that ball."

Go, Go, Go!

In an exhibition game during spring training, Manager Burleigh Grimes of the Brooklyn Dodgers was coaching at first base and had set up a wink of the eye as the steal signal. During the course of the game, Grimes got a long-distance call from the front office. In the dugout, he ordered that someone be put out on the first-base line when the Dodgers came to bat. In Brooklyn's half of the inning, pitcher Max Butcher took the post. Butcher was a reasonably good pitcher, but he suffered from perpetual blinking. They used to say Max pitched between blinks.

Brooklyn's Gibby Brack was the first man up, and he got on base. He looked at Butcher's eyes. They were blinking away, and Brack took off for second on the next pitch, just as Grimes returned to the field. With nobody out and the Dodgers trailing in the game, Grimes almost had heart failure when he saw Brack run—and get cut down by a good 10 feet.

Somehow Grimes contained himself until the end of the inning and then confronted Brack. "What the hell kind of play was that? Who sent you?"

Brack was incensed. He jerked his thumb at Butcher. "He did," he protested.

"Max," Grimes demanded, "what the hell did you give him the go sign for?"

Butcher said, "I didn't give him the go sign."

Now Brack was on the point of hysteria. "You're giving it to me right now!" he screamed at Butcher, who was blinking away.

During the rest of the season due care was taken that Butcher never got near the coaching box again.

BOXING

Gourmand Knockout

The zaniest disqualification of any boxer from the Olympics can be claimed by South African lightweight Hamilton-Brown who became overweight only after he was officially eliminated from the competition. In the opening-round match, Hamilton-Brown lost a split decision to C. Lillo of Chile. Disappointed and no longer in need of staying in training, the morose South African went on an eating binge. While he was out stuffing himself on beer and sausage in Berlin beer gardens, officials discovered that one of the judges had inadvertently reversed his scoring of the two boxers and that the victory actually belonged to Hamilton-Brown. The results were immediately reversed, and the South African was declared the winner, eligible to move up to the next round.

But where was Hamilton-Brown? His manager, trainer, and other members of the boxing team went hunting him, but it took them several hours, until just after midnight, to find him—in very bloated condition. They put him on the scales and were horrified to see that he was 5 pounds over the allowable weight of 135½ pounds. The team trainer tried to boil the weight off, but it didn't work. At weigh-in time the next day Hamilton-Brown was still over the weight limit and was disqualified.

HORSE RACING

Miracle Finish

On May 8, leading jockey Ralph Neves "died" in a racing mishap at California's Bay Meadows Racetrack. Despite this, Neves was back riding mounts the next day and went on to be the leading rider at the track. This unlikely, and rather dark-humored, occurance started during the fourth race, when Neves was aboard Flanakins. As the field went into the far turn, the four horses running ahead of him went into a spill when one of them stumbled against another. All four horses and their riders fell to the ground. Neves tried to swerve his mount, but Flanakins reared and sent the jockey flying; then stumbled and landed on top of Neves. When three doctors reached the scene, they found no evidence of a heartbeat or pulse. The jockey was pronounced dead, and his body removed by ambulance to a nearby hospital, where it was placed in a cold-storage room to await removal to a mortuary. Meanwhile the 20,000 spectators at the track were informed by the track announcer that Neves was dead, and they joined in a silent prayer for him.

About 30 minutes after he was brought to the hospital, Neves stirred and awakened to find himself in a darkened room. He screamed for help, but his calls were unheard. Neves groped for the door and in the corridor light found himself naked except for his riding boots. He grabbed a sheet to cover himself and rushed outside the building and hailed a cab to take him back to the track. When he arrived there were still thousands of fans milling about, and in a panic Neves started running. He was seized by two fellow jockeys, who rushed him to the track first-aid station. There the same medical men who had pronounced him dead found him not only still alive but suffering from nothing more than a case of mild shock and some minor cuts and bruises. Neves was given thunderous applause from spectators when he appeared on his first mount the next day. He received the ultimate racetrack tribute of not being booed when his horse failed to win.

OLYMPICS

Eleanor's Non-Olympics

At the 1932 Berlin Olympics held in Nazi Germany, it was expected that Eleanor Holm, who had taken the gold medal for the 100-meter backstroke at age 18 in 1928, would be an easy repeater. It was a

Swimming star Eleanor Holm was forced to sit out the 1936 Olympics after her shipboard crossing to Germany, during which, plied with champagne by sportswriters Paul Gallico and Joe Williams, she engaged in several days of drinking, gambling, partying, "et cetera."

competition in which she had not been beaten in seven years. In the meantime, though, she had married and had performed in nightclubs, and there was some worry whether she had maintained the required discipline. On the S.S. *Manhattan*, which carried the 350-member U.S. team to Germany, Eleanor had a wild time. Among others, sportswriters Paul Gallico and Joe Williams got her loaded on champagne, and she engaged in several days of drinking, gambling, partying, "et cetera." Early one morning the team doctor found her "in a deep slumber which approached a state of coma." He attributed her state to "acute alcoholism." While still aboard ship, members of the American Olympic Committee voted to drop her from the team.

Stunned, Holm went to the stateroom of Avery Brundage, president of the AOC, and begged through a crack in the door for another chance. It got her nowhere. More than half the U.S. team signed a petition calling for her to be reinstated, but that too was ignored by officials. When the *Manhattan* docked in Hamburg, the Germans were fully apprised of the Holm situation, and the Nazi government sided with the AOC. Josef Goebbels' propaganda publication said, "She probably didn't believe they could disqualify her, but she thought wrong. It wasn't herself who mattered. It was the others—and discipline. For that no sacrifice is too great, no matter how many tears are shed."

Yet, later the Nazis apparently struck a more favorable attitude toward Holm, who seemed to have German public opinion on her side. The Nazis treated her as a very special visitor. Years later Holm told an interviewer:

> It was a *fantastic* Olympics, spectacular! I had such fun. You know, athletes don't think much about the politics of it all.... I enjoyed the parties, the *Heil Hitlers*, the uniforms, the flags. Goering was fun. He had a good personality. So did the one with the club foot [Goebbels]. Goering gave me a sterling-silver swastika. I had a mold made of it and I put a diamond Star of David in the middle of it.

The Gender Olympics

Probably the most divisive sex charge ever in the history of the Olympics followed the women's 100 meters, a story that was to reach a stunning conclusion 44 years later. The heavy favorite was the Polish entry Stanislawa Walasiewicz, who had come to the United States as a child with her parents and Americanized her name to Stella Walsh. Although living in America, Stella represented her native land in the Olympics. She won the same event in 1932 and two years before that had become the first woman to run the 100-yard dash in under 11 seconds. Now Stella was the overwhelming favorite to repeat as the gold medalist. A dark horse in the race was Helen Stephens of the United States. At the start, Stephens came off her mark fastest of all the competitors and took the lead. She ran Walsh into the ground, beating her by 2 full meters in a time of 11.5 seconds. The Poles were stunned by the loss and shrieked that Helen was not a woman but a male ringer. To settle the dispute Stephens had to undress and undergo a sex check. The unanimous decision: Helen was totally female. If that brought Stephens added notoriety, it left the Poles highly embarrassed.

There was to be an ironic twist to the dispute, one that did not surface until 44 years later. Stella Walsh continued running until she was well over 40, enjoying considerable success in track competition. On December 4, 1980, 69-year-old Stella Walsh went to a Cleveland, OH, discount store to buy some party supplies for a reception planned for the Polish national basketball team. A robbery attempt was under way, and Stella got caught in gunfire in the parking lot and was killed. The autopsy, required after any violent death, discovered that, while Helen Stephens had not been a male and did not have male sexual organs, Stella Walsh most certainly did. Thus, when she set 11 women's world records, 41 AAU titles, and a gold and a silver Olympic medal, she was actually a man.

RODEO

The Greatest Bronco

In his day Pete Knight was the best of the saddle bronc riders. As such he developed a great respect for the horses that so majestically resisted being ridden, grinding a would-be rider into the dirt. During his heyday on the rodeo circuit, Knight at one time or another got the best of every bronco he mounted save one, a great bucking horse named Midnight, 1,000 pounds of pure dynamite. Many others tried to ride Midnight as well—and had the broken bones to prove it. Knight did the best, once managing to stay on the horse in a rodeo in Cheyenne, WY, in 1932 for all of seven seconds before the powerful bronco whipped him into the dust. Knight vowed that someday he would beat that horse, but he never did. Only nature could beat old Midnight, whose legs began to go bad until he died in 1936. Knight and other rodeo riders to whom Midnight had never submitted resolved to give him a proper burial. They erected a monument to him in Plattsville, CO, and the verse on it told the respect for their animal adversary:

Underneath this sod lies a great bucking horse.
There never lived a cowboy he couldn't toss.
His name was Midnight, his coat black as coal.
If there's a hoss heaven, please God, rest his soul.

TENNIS

Never Give In

It was the most incredible rally in the history of tennis. In a match in Prague, Czechoslovakia, between Farcas Paneth of Romania and Alex Ehrilick of Poland, the competitors went at it for two hours and five minutes before scoring a single point.

TRACK AND FIELD

Cheating a Racehorse

One of the most idiotic athletic claims is that a human can outrun a horse, and a racehorse at that. In point of fact, two-legged humans cannot outrun many four-legged animals, save the more lumbering quadrapeds.

But after Jesse Owens won four gold medals at the 1936 Olympic games and was dubbed the "world's fastest human," the American public was ripe for the preposterous claim that Owens could beat a racehorse. And, amazingly, Owens went out and proceeded to beat good racehorses in 100-yard sprints.

Of course, the races were shams, with the poor animal cheated out of any chance of winning, as Owens would admit in later years. The key to the phony setup was that Owens and the promoters always chose high-strung thoroughbreds rather than run-of-the-mill plugs. The race would be run with the horse positioned next to the starter and Owens on the outside. The starter would deliberately hold the gun next to the horse's head so that the horse would invariably rear in terror at the gun blast.

Meanwhile, as Owens explained, "I would be off with a tremendous break and by the time he came down I was 50 yards down the track, and at that point even though he would be covering 21 feet for every 7 I covered, it was too late; I would win."

The Great Turtle Mile

In the 1930s it was predicted that if any runner could run a 4-minute mile, it would certainly be Glenn Cunningham, out of the cornfields of Kansas. Cunningham had overcome enormous odds to become a track star, having had both legs severely burned in a schoolhouse fire at the age of eight. Despite a toeless left foot, he established a world

Jesse Owens was dubbed the "world's fastest human," but could he really beat a racehorse without stacking the odds?

record in 1934 with a time of 4:06.7. But by 1936, Cunningham's star seemed to be in decline. When he entered the Knights of Columbus meet for the Columbian Mile at New York's Madison Square Garden, he was no longer considered the favorite. During that season Cunningham had been beaten a total of four times by two other runners, Joe Mangan of Cornell and Gene Venzke of Pennsylvania. In every case they had let Cunningham go out in a torrid pace and then come on to beat him. New York bookmakers did a land-office business on the Columbian, with money about even divided between Venzke and Mangan, while Cunningham got very little support.

Cunningham remained serene. As Joe Namath, the hero of the New York Jets victory in the 1969 Super Bowl, would do years later, Cunningham predicted a victory. "Maybe I'll even set a record," he added slyly. "I'll outsprint them tonight." And that is what he did, but not in a way anyone expected. When the starter's gun sounded, Mangan and Venzke, according to their previous plans, both broke slowly, looking for Cunningham to spring to the lead. But Cunningham wasn't there. He was a very distant third and practically walking. Puzzled, both Mangan and Venzke slowed down, virtually offering Cunningham the lead. Cunningham merely smiled at them and held to his crawl. As a result, the quarter-mile time that flashed on the board was pathetic: 1:32. Some among the 17,000 spectators started to boo. Mangan was in the lead and frustrated, and he threw up his hands in despair to the crowd, as though begging their forgiveness. Venzke would not move up on the front-runner, and Cunningham showed absolutely no intention of challenging them. The half-mile time was a drowsy 2:34, and the booing was now intense. By the end of the third quarter the runners had sleepwalked around the track in a pitiful 3:54.5, and the Garden echoed with wall-to-wall booing. Then, with 250 yards to go, the jeers were suddenly replaced by cheers. Cunningham, the Kansas Flyer, was living up to his nickname as his long legs stretched out in athletic beauty. He turned from turtle to jack rabbit and bounded past his shocked competitors. He crossed the finish line in the clear while Venzke and Mangan staggered in many yards behind.

But what of Cunningham's boast that he would not only outsprint his foes but that he would set a new record? The time was 4:46.8, more than 40 seconds off his previous best time. Ah, but it was a record, and it still stands to this day—the slowest major mile ever run.

1937

BASEBALL

Quota

It was always said that Dizzy Dean was the most cocky pitcher of all time, fully convinced that he could do anything he set his mind to. In a game against the Boston Braves, the brash St. Louis pitcher bet a teammate he would strike out Vince DiMaggio every time he batted. DiMaggio came up the first time and struck out, ditto the second and third time. On his fourth time at bat, the ace Cardinals hurler put across two quick strikes. But then DiMaggio lifted a pop foul that St. Louis catcher Brusie Ogrodowski could easily have garnered.

"Drop it or I'm dead!" Diz implored his catcher and Ogrodowski obligingly made a big act of misjudging the ball. A much-relieved Dizzy Dean then smoked across the third strike.

Diagnosis

In the 1937 All-Star game, Dizzy Dean was struck in the toe by a sizzling line drive by Earl Averill, a blow that would end his career a short time later. Informed the next day that the toe was fractured, Diz snorted, "Fractured, hell! The damn thing's broke."

BASKETBALL

One-Man Show

No basketball player ever found himself in such a predicament as did Pat McGee of St. Peter's High School of Fairmont, VA, or acquitted himself as brilliantly. All the other members of the squad fouled out in a game, leaving McGee alone to face a five-man opposition with the score tied 32–32 and four minutes left on the clock. McGee played frantic defense to keep his opponents from scoring and managed to sink a basket on his own and make a free throw. Final score: 35–32 in favor of McGee.

FOOTBALL

The Great Competitors

They frequently came close to blows, but the camaraderie between owners George "Papa Bear" Halas of the Chicago Bears and George Preston Marshall of the Washington Redskins is an enduring legend in professional football. In *My Life with the Redskins*, Corinne Griffith, the silent-film star who married Marshall, tells of a sidelines shouting match between Marshall and Halas during the 1937 championship game. Marshall had blown his stack when a Bear took a punch at Sammy Baugh, and he stormed down to the playing field to let Papa Bear have it:

> George stomped back to the box, snorted as he sat down and, of course, took it out on me [Corinne].
> "What's the matter with you? You look white as a sheep!"
> "Oh, that was awful!"

"What was awful?"

"That horrible language. We heard every word."

"Well, you shouldn't listen."

"Oh, you. And right in front of the ladies. . . . And as for that man Halas!" Every hair of George's raccoon coat bristled. "He's positively revolt—"

"Don't you dare say anything against Halas." George was actually shaking his finger under my nose. "He's my best friend!"

1938

BASEBALL

Waner the Unstoppable

No batter terrified Frankie Frisch when he was managing the St. Louis Cardinals in the 1930s more than Paul Waner of the Pittsburgh Pirates. Waner, nicknamed "Big Poison," was not a major home-run slugger, but he was something Frisch respected even more, a consistently successful line-drive hitter who would double and triple the opposition to death. In one game Waner was wearing out the Cardinals with his patented line drives, and Frisch slammed his cap to the ground in disgust and shouted, "Who on this ball club can get that Waner out?"

Of all the Cards' pitchers only Max Macon replied: "I can get him out." Macon was always a bit of a pop-off, but Frisch was ecstatic at having a volunteer, and he immediately sent Macon to the bullpen to warm up. When Waner came to bat, Frisch eagerly brought Macon into the game. Waner generally did not swing at the first pitch, but he made an exception in Macon's case, and rifled a line drive back to the mound that broke Macon's little finger. Frisch was helpless, lying down on the bench and laughing until the tears flowed.

Reprisal

Fiery Pepper Martin of the St. Louis Cardinals was a terror on the base paths, but he did not appreciate opposing runners working him over. Pepper especially hated to have to play third base, mainly because he detested fielding bunts. One time in Boston, Manager Frankie Frisch put him on third against the Braves. Before the game started, Pepper walked up to Casey Stengel, then manager of the Boston team, and said, "You'd better tell your guys not to bunt on me, because if they do I'm gonna hurt them."

Naturally, the Braves started bunting on him like crazy. Finally Pepper got so steamed up that when a batter laid down a bunt, he'd run in, pick up the ball, and throw it at the runner rather than to the first baseman. Several balls just zinged past Braves players. Finally Elbie Fletcher dropped a bunt that Pepper was able to pounce on quickly. When Fletcher saw that Pepper had the ball so early and was winding up for a murderous throw, he cut away, his head down between hunched shoulders, and headed for the Cardinal dugout. Martin cut loose with a bullet that almost nipped Fletcher's cap and smashed into his own team's dugout, sending his own teammates scattering for cover. By that time, the Braves got the message. There were no more bunts.

The Big Blow

If today's fans think San Francisco's Candlestick Park is baseball unfriendly, they can consider old Braves Field in Boston. Left-handed hitters simply hated the place, in which a terrific wind generally gusted in from right field. A towering drive to right that would be a four-bagger in almost any other stadium in the league would turn into a harmless pop fly that would bring in the right fielder for the catch. On September 21, 1938, the Boston Bees were playing the Cardinals, and the wind was kicking up a mite more than usual. The umpires ruled the game should continue. The infield dirt was whirling and then a big billboard behind the left-field fence toppled over. A fly ball to center ended up being caught out of bounds by catcher Al Lopez. As the wind velocity increased, balls were coming in from center and right and going out in left. Finally a batter hit a high popper that Boston's first baseman Elbie Fletcher called for in back of the mound. The wind lashed the ball out farther, and the shortstop called for it. Then the left fielder was calling for it. And finally the wind blew it completely out of the park. At this point umpire Beans Reardon threw in the towel and called the game.

Driving home after the game, Fletcher was stunned to see fallen trees littering the streets, and his car had a hard time negotiating through the winds. It turned out to be the killer hurricane of '38, the worst ever to ravage New England. "But that's how bad the wind was in Braves Field," Fletcher later recollected. "We were playing in a hurricane and didn't know the difference!"

GOLF

Positioning

In the PGA match-play tournament, golfer Sammy Snead reached the green on the first stroke of the par-three 13th green. His opponent, Jimmy Hines, fell just short of the putting surface. Then Hines pitched up, and his ball hit Snead's, which went right into the cup. Remarkably, Hines' ball followed right behind. Officials conferred and awarded birdie twos to both golfers, which was just dandy as far as Slammin' Sammy was concerned. He beat Hines by one stroke.

Nightmare Hole

It was called the most embarrassing golf hole in the history of professional tournament play. At the 16th hole of the U.S. Open, Ray Ainsley sent his ball into a stream. Rather than take a penalty, he waded in and swung and swung and swung trying to get the ball out. He finally did after 11 desperate strokes . . . but unfortunately the ball went into the bushes. Ainsley ended up taking a 19 on the hole.

1939

BASEBALL

Talking Contract

In the 1990s a rule of thumb on baseball salaries was that if a player whose contract was up saw his batting average crash 20 or 30 points below the previous year, to about .250, he would figure to get a "minimal" raise of at least a quarter million dollars. How different from the old days, especially when players had to dicker with Branch Rickey. Take the case of Johnny Mize, who racked up the top average in the National League in 1939, a hefty .349. Mize was eager to talk contract but didn't get much of an increase from Rickey, who kept noting, "Your home-run production stayed pretty much the same." The next year Mize solved that problem by walloping 43 home runs, a St. Louis club record, and leading the league in runs batted in. With that kind of slugging, not surprisingly, his batting average dipped. This time Rickey said, "Well, your batting average wasn't so good. Would you be willing to take a cut?"

Golfer Sammy Snead scored a strokeless birdie when opponent Jimmy Hines knocked both his own ball and Snead's into the cup so that each player was credited with a birdie. Snead ended up beating Hines by one stroke.

Years later Mize was still irate about Rickey's dickering, saying, "I led the league in hitting, then I led the league in home runs and runs batted in, and he wanted to know if I'd take a cut!" Mize married a St. Louis girl whose father was a good friend of club owner Sam Breadon. Breadon gave Mize $500 as a wedding present. The next year Mize talked contract with Rickey, who said, "Well, you made 7,500 last year." Mize corrected him. "I only made 7,000." Rickey replied, "Really? Where's that 500 that Breadon gave you?"

Nice Try

In an attempt to make the highest catch of a baseball, Joe Sprinz, a former big-league catcher then with the San Francisco Seals of the Pacific Coast League, positioned his catcher's mitt as a ball was dropped from an airship 1,000 feet over Treasure Island in San Francisco Bay. He managed to get the mitt on the ball but was unable to hold it, and the force of the blow jammed the mitt in his mouth, costing him four front teeth.

Ejections Wholesale

While American League Umpire Red Jones holds the record for the most players ejected in an inning at 14 (see 1946—Mystery Heckler), another American League arbiter, George Pipgras, bounced 17 men in one game. Pipgras had played 17 years and had never himself been thrown out of a game, and upon getting back to the majors in 1939 as an umpire, he set firm standards against players baiting umpires, especially himself. In a game between the Chicago White Sox and the St. Louis Browns, both benches got on him from time to time. Pipgras' thumb went into high gear, and before he was finished he had ejected 17 players. That night he got a telephone call from league President Will Harridge. "George," he said, "have you gone crazy?" "No, I haven't gone crazy," Pipgras responded. "They're going to let me alone out there, or I'm not going to be there."

"Don't you think you were a little bit rough on them?" Harridge asked.

"Not at all."

"But *17* men, George."

"All that yelling from the bench isn't necessary," Pipgras said. "I never read anything that said you had to yell at the umpire in order to play ball."

It was the law according to George Pipgras, and in time it stood up. As Pipgras told Don Honig in *Baseball When the Grass Was Real*: He made mistakes and he would admit it. And most players and managers would understand. "Bill Dickey was a great one for that. He'd say 'What was wrong with that pitch?' and I'd say, 'Nothing. I missed it.' And he wouldn't say another word." Once Manager Jimmy Dykes, noted for being tough on umpires, stormed out at Pipgras, who proceeded to cut him short: "Jimmy, I kicked it. Now let's get on with the game."

It worked. Most players and managers could understand an umpire missing a pitch since they were often fooled themselves. The fact that Pipgras was man enough to admit it satisfied them. They also understood that Pipgras was not going to reverse his call, no way, no time—ever. So it was time to play ball.

Time Marches On

Muhammad Ali was not the only athlete to believe that he was "the greatest." Baseball Ty Cobb fiercely held that he was the best the game would ever see. Years after his retirement, Cobb was not about to desert his faith in his own prowess. He was interviewed at the New York World's Fair by a reporter who asked, "Mr. Cobb, how do you think you would fare against the ballplayers of this day, and especially the pitchers?" Cobb pursed his lips a moment and said, "Probably hit about .320, maybe .325." The reporter was taken aback. "But Mr. Cobb," he said, "your lifetime average was .367 and you have always said the pitchers of today weren't nearly as good as those you faced in your time. How come you think you'd only bat .320 now?"

With a perfectly straight face, Cobb declared, "You've got to remember something, sonny. I'm 52 years old now!" (When Cobb turned 65 years old, he was asked the same question by another interviewer, and he now allowed he would only bat around .310.)

BOXING

Wrong Approach

Before his fight with heavyweight champion Joe Louis, Two-Ton Tony Galento launched what he thought would be an effective war of nerves against his opponent. He telephoned Louis and told him, "Hey, bum, get in shape. I'm gonna eat your eyes out for grapes." Louis TKO'd Galento in the fourth round of a brutal battle.

"I think that made him get in shape for me," Tony later reflected on his telephone campaign.

Two-Ton Tony Galento (left) *telephoned champion Joe Louis before their fight and said, "Hey, bum, get in shape. I'm gonna eat your eyes for grapes." After being TKO-ed in the fourth round after a fearsome lacing, Galento mused about his telephone campaign: "I think that made him get in shape for me."*

1940

BASEBALL

Stand-In

Leo "Lippy" Durocher was probably the most vicious "bench jockey" manager ever. His ability to invoke anger and frustration in the opposition was legendary, as was, amazingly, his ability to stay out of harm's way as often as he did. While managing the Brooklyn Dodgers he was riding Cub pitcher Claude Passeau in a game in Chicago. Passeau was one of the more volatile competitors himself, and he took exception to the repeated aspersions about his ancestry. Unfortunately, he could not tell who on the Dodger bench was lambasting him. He kept looking in the dugout trying to locate the culprit.

Then Leo cut loose with a particularly vile suggestion to Passeau. Claude had had it and, tossing aside his glove, stormed toward the Dodgers bench. He snarled, "The guy who made that last crack doesn't have guts enough to come out and back it up."

It was not a challenge Leo could let go unanswered, but with puckish cunning he turned to Joe Gallagher who had been so preoccupied he was not aware of what had been happening and said, "Joe, get out there and hit." Gallagher picked up a bat and strolled out of the dugout, suddenly face-to-face with the raging Passeau.

"You need a bat, your big son of a bitch?" the pitcher yelled and then punched the innocent Gallagher. "Claude," Gallagher said, "what's wrong with you?" Passeau hauled off and hit Gallagher again, but the blow had little impact on Gallagher, a good-natured but powerfully built man. "Claude," he said now in exasperation, "don't get me mad."

When Passeau wound up to let loose a roundhouse, Gallagher dropped his bat and wrapped his arms around the pitcher and started to squeeze. "Claude," the still mystified Gallagher said, "if you don't want to talk about this thing, I'm just gonna keep squeezing and squeezing."

The confrontation provoked ejection from the game for both scrappers, an effect Durocher found eminently satisfactory.

By the time the Cubs hit Brooklyn on a road trip, Passeau had discovered the villain of the piece and, winding up on the mound, he cut loose a pitch into the Dodger dugout, barely missing Leo's skull. It was said that Joe Gallagher was once more mystified. First he had been the victim of Claude Passeau's bizarre rage, and now Leo Durocher. Passeau was really strange.

Holy Alibi

It is the duty of baseball managers to see to it that their players abide by a curfew that gets them into bed at a reasonable hour. Dickie Kerr, managing in the minors in the St. Louis Cardinals chain, was a stickler for checking the late-night flings of his wards. Despite his own late regimen, Kerr was up, if bleary-eyed, at 7 one morning to see the young Stan Musial entering the hotel. "So you been doing batting practice all night?" Kerr snapped. "No sir," Musial replied, "I just came from mass."

The word went up the Cardinals' line of command thereafter: Don't bother making curfew checks on Musial.

Foul Breath

With Jersey City runners on second and third in a game against the Montreal Royals, a Jersey City Giant laid down a perfect bunt along the third baseline. As third baseman Bert Haas watched, hoping the ball would go foul, both base runners came around to score. Meanwhile, it was apparent that the ball was going to stay fair by about an inch. The ingenious Haas lay down on the ground and blew at the ball as hard as he could. His breath caused the ball to trickle into foul territory, and he immediately grabbed it. The two base runners were required to return to their respective bases.

The Correct Time in Washington, DC

Kidding rookies is standard in the national pastime, practiced by players and managers alike. The Cleveland Indians developed a joke about the clock in Washington's Griffith Stadium in the early '40s. During a night game with the Senators, one of the players sitting on the bench near a rookie would note, "I see that clock out there is a little fast." Everybody on the bench would chime in that was the fact, that the clock was fast. The only thing was there was no clock out there, but with so many signs and so many various colors on the outfield walls it would be hard to be sure. Naturally no rookie was going to admit he couldn't even see the clock, and for the rest of the game the Indians would watch him frowning at the fences looking for it. The Indians kept the hoax going for a few years, but as rookies came and went back to the minors they spread the word, "Remember there ain't no damned clock at Griffith Stadium."

FOOTBALL

"Fifth-Down Friesell"

The 1946 Cornell-Dartmouth game proved to be a real shocker in more ways than one. Cornell was considered the number-one powerhouse in the country, but underrated Dartmouth held its own against the Big Red and amazingly pulled ahead early in the fourth quarter with a field goal. Twice after that, Cornell mounted long drives but was stymied both times, once by an interception in the end zone. Then with two and a half minutes to go, Cornell was on the move once more. The Big Red Machine made a first down on the 6-yard line. With less than a minute left, Cornell ripped off plays at breakneck speed—and was stopped one, two, three, four times, the last play being a pass in the end zone, which meant Dartmouth should have gotten the ball on its own 20. Instead, Referee Red Friesell, a highly respected official with 22 years of experience, took the ball and marched back out to the 6-yard line and signaled that it was fourth down for Cornell. Some of the Dartmouth players were disconcerted, but there was no protest from Coach Earl Blaik of Dartmouth. In the excitement of the heated efforts to score or stop a touchdown, the Dartmouth coaches, like Friesell, had lost track of the downs, and the Dartmouth players were confused. Had there been a penalty of some kind that they hadn't noticed? On the extra down, left halfback Walter Scholl rolled to his right and lobbed a pass to right halfback Bill Murphy in the end zone for a TD. The extra point was added and Cornell won 7–3.

Friesell was in the officials' dressing room when the bombshell dropped. Howard Odell, then a Pennsylvania coach, there to scout Cornell, came into the room and told Friesell, a close friend, "It's a hell of a note, Red, but my figures show that Cornell had five downs on that last series." Friesell was dumbfounded. He did some checking of both the Dartmouth and Cornell charts. They also showed five downs. Friesell said, "Okay, I'll wait for the films. If they confirm the five downs, I'll reverse my decision."

On Sunday Dartmouth called. Its films showed five downs. Early Monday morning Cornell called with the same embarrassing intelligence. At noon Friesell announced to the world that he had pulled a boner, and that Dartmouth should have been the winner of the game 3–0. Then Friesell wrote letters of apology to Dartmouth, including one to team Captain Lou Young. "I want to be the first to admit my very grave error on the extra down," he wrote Young. "I assume full responsibility ... Lou, I am so sorry, for you were such a grand captain and leader."

Technically, Friesell's admission could not alter the 7–3 score, but Cornell President Edmund Ezra Day as well as Coach Carl Snavely agreed the result had to be changed. Cornell wired Dartmouth announcing it was "relinquishing claim to victory." That ended the Big Red's long unbeaten streak, and the official record books were changed to a Dartmouth win. Cornell, Friesell, and the entire Ivy League emerged from the incredible blooper with considerable honor.

Of course, Friesell did not escape being labeled "Fifth-down Friesell," and there was even a racehorse by that sobriquet named after him. Mail addressed to "Fifth Down, Pittsburgh, PA" was forwarded to him by the post office. Friesell went on to be a top official in the National Football League, and he was elected to the National Football Foundation and Hall of Fame. And he did not have to feel embarrassed in the company of either Cornell or Dartmouth people. In fact, he was an honored guest at reunions of both schools. Friesell's mistake had been monumental, but he proved a class act, and his frankness earned respect few "boneheads" ever achieved.

Save Those Pigskins

It became the largest margin of victory in National Football League regular-season or postseason play. The Chicago Bears destroyed the Washington Redskins by a score of 73–0 in the NFL championship game. Bill Stern, a top radio sports broadcaster of the day, noted, "It got so bad that, toward the end, the Bears had to give up placekicking the extra points and try passes instead because all the footballs booted into the stands were being kept by the spectators as souvenirs. And they were down to their last football."

1941

BASEBALL

Adorning the Throne

Few teams had as devoted—or as wacky—fans as did the Brooklyn Dodgers. One was a man named Eddie, the owner of a number of apartment houses in Brooklyn, who came to all the Ebbets Field games. In 1941, as the Dodgers were closing in on the pennant, Eddie managed to ride the Dodger train up to Boston for a big series, the one as it turned out in which they clinched first place. Eddie was ecstatic, and as Pete Reiser told Don Honig in *Baseball When the Grass Was Real*:

> Naturally he came back on the train with the team. Well, there was a big mob to meet us at Grand Central that night and the reporters are interviewing everybody who comes off the train. Somebody asks Eddie how he feels about it. He says, "I'm so happy about this I'm going to put all new toilet seats in my apartment buildings." There really was no place like Brooklyn.

Orders from the Bleachers

Hilda Chester was the most famous and certainly the loudest fan the Brooklyn Dodgers had in their zany years at Ebbets Field. Ensconced in her domain in the center-field bleachers, she bore a white banner proclaiming "Hilda Is Here" as she sounded off with a deafening truck horn and a cowbell. Those sounds, together with a voice that needed no amplification, made her a true Ebbets Field celebrity in the 1940s and 1950s. If Hilda dominated the sound waves, she also in

Hilda Chester was the loudest fan the Brooklyn Dodgers had in their wacky years at Ebbets Field. Here she attends team's pre-season camp at Bear Mountain, N.Y.

her own way could affect the course of a game. Pete Reiser recounted the wackiest situation of this type for Peter Golenbock's oral history *Bums*:

> I was going out to take my position in center field, and I hear that voice: "Hey, Reiser!" It was Hilda. There could be 30,000 people there yelling at once, but Hilda was the one you'd hear. I look up, and she's dropping something onto the grass. "Give this note to Leo," she yells. So I pick it up and put it in my pocket. At the end of the inning, I start heading in.
>
> Now, [Dodger executive] MacPhail used to sit in a box right next to the dugout, and for some reason he waved to me as I came in, and I said, "Hi, Larry," as I went into the dugout. I gave Hilda's note to Leo and sat down. Next thing I know he's getting somebody hot in the bullpen; I think it was Casey. Meanwhile, Wyatt's pitching a hell of a ball game for us. In the next inning, the first guy hits the ball pretty good and goes out. The next guy gets a base hit. Here comes Leo. He takes Wyatt out and brings in Casey. Casey got rocked a few times, and we just did win the game, just did win it.

Leo had this rule that after a game you didn't take off your uniform until he said so. Usually he didn't invoke it unless we'd lost a tough one. But this day he goes into his office and slams the door without a word. We're all sitting there waiting for him to come out. Finally the door opens and out he comes. He points to me.

"Don't you ever give me another note from MacPhail as long as you play for me."

I said, "I didn't give you any note from MacPhail."

"Don't tell me!" he yells. "You handed me a note in the seventh inning."

"That was from Hilda," I said.

"From Hilda?" he screams. I thought he was going to turn purple. "You mean to say that wasn't from MacPhail?"

I hadn't even looked at the note, just handed it to him. Leo had heard me say something to MacPhail when I came in and figured the note was from Larry. It seems what the note said was: "Get Casey hot. Wyatt's losing it." So what you had was somebody named Hilda Chester sitting in the center-field bleachers changing pitchers for you.

BOXING

The Dynamic Stance

During the heavyweight reign of Joe Louis, the greatest payday other fighters in the division could have was a bout against the Brown Bomber. It didn't offer much hope of triumph but the financial rewards in hard economic times were terrific—as was the competition for the role. It paid to have a gimmick, being super-sized like Abe Simon, nasty like Two-Ton Tony Galento, foreign and presumably exotic like Arturo Godoy or Tommy Farr, or hopefully something even better. When it came to a bizarre gimmick, none could beat Lou Nova for originality. Lou, he himself proudly declared, had the whole powers of the cosmos in his corner. "I cannot be hurt," he informed the press, "because I employ the Dynamic Stance. This faces me in the direction in which the world revolves. Thus, the man who hits me is bucking the earth's motion—a force that moves at 1,000 miles per hour." That also allegedly gave Nova great offensive powers as well, since his own punch always traveled in the same direction as the earth's rotation—giving his fists the speed of 1,000 mph, plus all the might Nova could add himself. Thus, the Cosmic Punch supplemented the Dynamic Stance. In his training bouts Nova took his Dynamic Stance against his sparring partners, his left foot firmly planted on his right foot. And his Cosmic Punch apparently sent them reeling. It

*Joe Louis had no trouble
with Lou Nova's Cosmic
Punch and Dynamic
Stance.*

would have been worse, Nova said, but he kept his power under tight control. He wouldn't against poor Louis.

University professors were hunted down by sportswriters to comment on Nova's concept of the Dynamic Stance and the Cosmic Punch, and one unnamed academician labeled them "pure poppycock." Did that mean, a persistent reporter inquired, the good professor favored Louis to win? "I do not bet on prize fights," was the frosty reply, but this did not fool boxing fans, who thought the fact that the scientist would not put his money where his mouth was most telling. The press began seeing the coming struggle as one of the irresistible forces against the immovable object—but an immovable object with, apparently, a superhuman Sunday punch.

When the battle was joined in New York's Polo Grounds, a half-million dollars in ticket sales had flowed through the till, an outstanding amount for the era. Nova set himself in his Dynamic Stance at the start, but soon began shifting—north, south, east, or west—off the earth's rotation, in fact just about any way Louis banged him. Then apparently Louis planted himself in the proper position to take the Cosmic Punch as his own. One blow knocked the so-called immovable object reeling, and the next one knocked him clear on his axis, apparently a terrible blow to planetary science.

In a certain sense Nova could feel satisfied with his effort. Not all that many of the Brown Bomber's foes lasted six rounds. Nova had his big payday, and 14 years later made out even better when a sportswriter referred to him as a coward during the Louis fight. Nova promptly sued, calling the charge a lie and certainly beyond the pale of fair comment. He won a $35,000 judgment, proving that cosmic powers were more effective in the courtroom than in the ring.

FOOTBALL

The Greatest Punt-Block Day

Remember that day when a rookie pro footballer blocked three punts in one game? Chances are you don't, and practically nobody else does either. It happened during a game between the Washington Redskins and the Philadelphia Eagles, with Slingin' Sammy Baugh, who besides being the premier passer also handled the punting for the Redskins, a chore at which he boasted the best average in the league. In this game, however, a rookie lineman and former All-American out of the University of Tennessee, Bob Suffridge, drove Baugh daffy. Three times he crashed through the line and blocked Baugh's punts, certainly a one-man record. Yet the incredible accomplishment got virtually no mention in the press around the nation that day, which happened to be December 7, 1941—when the Japanese attacked Pearl Harbor. The newspapers were full of stories of the events that brought the United States into World War II. With all the stunning and tragic news to report, Suffridge's feat, which otherwise would have gotten the tremendous coverage it deserved, ended up with miniscule space or none at all.

It's Just a Game—Almost

Few rivalries in professional football ever matched the crosstown frenzy that infected the Chicago Bears and the Chicago Cardinals. Jimmy Conzelman, a Hall of Famer in the 1920s and coach of the Cardinals in their heyday in the 1940s, viewed the rivalry as a rawmeat affair, and he was deeply affected when the Bears annihilated his team 53–7.

Smiling through the hurt, Jimmy said, "Don't get the idea that being beaten by the Bears 53–7 bothered me a bit. Oh, not in the least. I went home after the game, had a good night's rest and a very hearty breakfast. I said good-bye to the missus and strolled down the hall to the elevator, whistling a light tune. I pushed the elevator button and took in my profile in the hall mirror. I was a picture of elegance in my Cavenaugh hat, tweed sport jacket, and well-shined tan shoes. Then I went back to my apartment and put on my trousers."

The School That Never Was—II

While the Salem Trade School footballers conned Massachusetts high schools (see 1929—The School That Never Was), the Plainfield State Teachers College in New Jersey was a step up both academically and for sheer gall. During the 1941 college season Plainfield Teachers rolled to one victory after another, led by the redoubtable Johnny Chung, the half-Chinese "Celestial Comet" fullback, who boosted his strength at halftime with a special recipe of wild rice. Herbert Allan, writing in the *New York Post*, declared, "John Chung has accounted for 57 of the 98 points scored by his unbeaten and untied team in four starts. If the Jerseyans don't watch out, he may pop up in Chiang Kai-shek's offensive department one of these days." Similarly the *New York Times* and the *New York Herald Tribune* dutifully reported the exploits of Chung and his college as they racked up two more impressive wins. According to press releases from Plainfield Teachers, the school was now a leading contender for the first annual postseason Blackboard Bowl for teaching colleges.

Unfortunately, that would never be for several reasons: There were no Blackboard Bowl, no Plainfield State Teachers, no Johnny Chung. They were all fictitious concoctions by Morris Newburger, a stockbroker at Newburger, Loeb, and Company of Wall Street, and some of his broker cronies. (The right tackle on the team just happened to be one Richard Newburger.) The broker hoaxers spent their time writing joyous press releases and calling sportswriters on Saturday afternoons to report the latest exploits of Chung and Plainfield Teachers. It was a magnificient con that couldn't last, since stockbrokers could no more keep that kind of hoax to themselves than they could keep quiet about a hot stock. A Wall Streeter told a friend who told another friend, and soon *Time* magazine had the story. When stockbroker Newburger heard that *Time* was readying an exposé of his creation, he rushed to the magazine's editorial offices to beg that Plainfield Teachers be allowed to finish out their undefeated season. As a special inducement he even offered *Time* the scores of the remaining game in advance. When *Time* rejected the deal, Newburger decided to put out one last release announcing that Plainfield Teachers had called off the balance of its season, as Johnny Chung and several other players had flunked their exams and could not play football.

Prevent Offense

In a boner as devastating as those in which a player runs toward the wrong end zone, Bobby Yandell of the University of Mississippi made what he regarded as a saving tackle in a game against Mississippi State. He brought down end Ray Poole, who had caught a pass and appeared to have clear sailing for a touchdown. Unfortunately, Yandell had actually tackled his own teammate, under the mistaken belief in the heat of battle that the pass had been intercepted by an opposing player. Yandell's wrongful tackle prevented Mississippi from coming up with the winning touchdown and left Ole Miss on the short end of a 6–0 score.

HOCKEY

Help Wanted

Chicago Blackhawks goaltender Sam LoPresti left the ice talking to himself even though he set an NHL record by stopping 80 shots in a game—that averaged out to a save every 45 seconds. Still the Blackhawks lost to the Boston Bruins, 3–2.

1942 _____

BASEBALL

Slow-Motion Basestealing

Without doubt, catcher Ernie "Schnozz" Lombardi was the slowest player in the major leagues. He was a terrific batter but a lumbering hippo on the base paths. Remarkably, the Schnozz actually stole some bases, averaging out exactly to a half base a year. It often took a miracle to assist him in making it, and the joke was that the Schnozz stole half a base a year, being caught at the halfway mark between first and second. Yet the lumbering Lombardi once actually not only stole second but kept on steaming around the bases until he was safe at home. In a game against the Philadelphia Phillies Lombardi caught everyone by surprise by chugging for second. The unbelieveable sight momentarily froze catcher Bernie Warren, who had never been confronted by such a slow-motion base thief. Rattled, Warren threw the ball way over the second baseman's head into center field, where Ernie Koy had been watching Lombardi's sluglike advance with mouth agape. The distracted Koy let the ball dribble through his legs, and Lombardi steamed—relatively speaking—to third. As the ball continued to roll into deep center, he kept coming all the way home. Slowpoke Lombardi had actually made three bases on an incompetent steal.

FOOTBALL

Only One Stat Counts

In a National Football League oddity the Washington Redskins really mopped up on the New York Giants, taking every statistic in the game. Washington outran and outpassed New York by a wide margin. The only thing that went wrong was the score, which went in favor of the Giants 14–7. New York scored on a 70-yard interception and on a 50-yard touchdown pass. The Redskins piled up 14 first downs in the game and the Giants . . . zero.

1943

BASEBALL

Unscientific Slugging

While pitchers are not expected to be much as hitters, New York Yankee Lefty "Goofy" Gomez clearly abused the privilege and was a fine argument for the American League adopting the designated hitter rule. Gomez hit an anemic .147 during his 13 seasons ending in 1943. At times when he called for a bat, the Yankee batboy would ask, "What are you planning to do with it?"

However, Gomez was never at a loss to explain his slugging strategy. "They throw, I swing. Every once in a while they're throwing where I'm swinging and I get a hit."

One day Goofy shocked everyone in the ballpark, including himself, by banging out a mighty double, and he got a terrific hand from the crowd. A couple of pitches later he got picked off the bag. When he returned to the dugout he was met by irate Manager Joe McCarthy who demanded to know what had happened. "How the hell would I know?" Gomez replied defensively. "I've never been there before."

BOXING

The Punchless Bout

The greatest boxing match ever not fought occurred between Louis Fetters and Carmine Milone in Bristol, England. With the sound of the gong for the first round, Milone bolted from his corner toward his opponent, determined to land a haymaker. The punch didn't connect, but Milone lost his balance, fell, and struck his head against a ring post. He was knocked unconscious and was counted out by the referee, ending a remarkable battle in which neither fighter had landed a single punch.

FOOTBALL

Offside

It isn't always easy to tell who's who on a football team's sidelines, as frequently there are team executives, league officials, and other visitors present. But it came as a total surprise to the Chicago Bears coaches when they looked down the bench and saw sitting there none other than George Preston Marshall, owner of the opposing Washington Redskins. What was he doing there? Coming around just as a sporting gesture to offer greetings, or was he engaged in stealing the Bears' plays? Just then the irate Chicago trainer, who was convinced the club owner was on a spying mission, appeared with several police officers and had him escorted back to his box seat, where he could do no damage, while Chicago rolled to a 41–21 triumph.

HORSE RACING

Therapy

Suffering from ill health, octogenarian Colonel Ed Bradley, famous owner and breeder of Kentucky Derby winners, heeded his doctors' advice about easing up on his strenuous activities. However, he turned them down flat when they tried to get him to stop going to the races. Finally they reached a compromise—the colonel could go to the track but could not place any bets (an interesting concept for a dedicated horseplayer), and a doctor would accompany him to make sure he didn't bet and get too excited.

One day the colonel remarked to the doctor that one of his horses was running and stood a good chance of winning. In fact, Bradley suggested, the physician should put a little something on the horse himself. Not wanting to irritate the old man, the doctor agreed and went off to the $2 window.

When the race started, Bradley's horse shot to the front and maintained a short lead around the turn into the stretch. Caught up in the excitement, the medical man stood up on his seat and screamed for the horse to hold on. It did, by a head. The medical man collapsed in his chair, worn to a frazzle by the excitement. When he regained his composure, he said to Bradley, "You see, Colonel, that's what betting on horses can do to you. I only bet $2 and I feel shot. Just imagine what it could have done to a sick man like you."

Bradley, who had watched the race calmly, nodded. When the doctor started to go cash his ticket, Bradley said, "Doctor, would you mind cashing these hundred-dollar tickets for me? I had a little bet on my horse, too."

1944 _____

BASEBALL

"Take Me Out to Three Ball Games"

A weird three-sided baseball game was played at the Polo Grounds in New York on June 26, 1944, with the New York Giants, New York Yankees, and Brooklyn Dodgers competing against one another. The game was held to aid in the sale of war bonds, but it was definitely considered an experiment toward possible changes in regular-season play. The formula for the game was conceived by Paul A. Smith, a

Columbia University mathematics professor, and the team took turns opposing each other on the field, with one team sitting out every three innings. A crowd of 50,000 spectators turned out for the game(s), which was dominated by the Dodgers. Opposing the Yankees in the first inning, Brooklyn scored a run and then added two more in the next inning against the Giants. The Dodgers scored two more runs in the eighth, and the Yankees picked up a run in the ninth inning against the Giants. The final box score read: Dodgers: 5–9–1; Yankees: 1–4–0; Giants: 0–2–2.

While a good time was had by all, it soon became apparent to the fans that the idea was something strictly out of left field, creating more problems than ever. Strategy went out the window because line-ups could not be set up to allow a team to deal with both a right- and left-handed pitcher, and one team could so botch up against the second that the third team, which might win both their games, might not come out on top. One fan voting thumbs down said, "Just think of the size of the scorecards we'd need!"

HOCKEY

Skating Off to War

During World War II no team in any organized sport was more ravaged by the draft and voluntary enlistments than the New York Rangers. In 1942 New York had finished in first place in their division, but by 1944 the team had lost their best players to the armed services. Indicative of their fate was a loss to the Detroit Red Wings by a score of 15–0, a mark that became the worst loss in National Hockey League history. And that debacle was only the beginning. In the following 25 games the Rangers could not garner even a single victory, losing 21 and tying 4.

1945

FOOTBALL

The Great Draft Loser

George Preston Marshall, the owner of the Washington Redskins, had one of the most successful and profitable franchises in the National Football League—some say despite Marshall's own peculiar habit of inserting himself in team affairs. As a drafter of football talent, Marshall was a disaster, paring his scouting staff to the bone to cut costs and preferring to rely on newspaper and sports publication stories to determine the best college talent available. Thus in 1945 Preston insisted that the Redskins draft All-American Cal Rossi of UCLA. It seemed like a great top pick, to Marshall at least, but oddly no other team seemed to have any interest in Rossi. Marshall later found out why: Rossi still had another year of college eligibility remaining and therefore could not be drafted. Marshall had thrown away his number-one choice. Undeterred, the owner could hardly wait for the following year's draft, and he proceeded to pick Rossi all over again. Once more, no other team exhibited the slightest interest. Again Marshall found out why: Rossi had made it clear to other scouts that he had no interest in a pro-ball career. Once again Marshall had wasted his top pick. And toting up that year's selections done without the advice of seasoned professionals demonstrated what a babe in the draft Marshall was with his whims. Of the 30 picks he masterminded that year, only one even signed with the Redskins.

Goal-Post Boobytrap

It was often said that the worst rules change ever made in professional football was moving up the goal posts to the goal line from the rear of the end zone (see 1932—Shrink That Field). The realignment of the goal posts even cost the Washington Redskins the National Football League championship in 1945. In that game the Redskins had been backed up near their own goal by the Cleveland Rams, and quarterback Sammy Baugh decided to gamble by passing from the end zone. A receiver got open and Baugh let fly, but the pigskin smacked right into the goal post and bounced backward to the ground. It was, to the horror of the Redskins, who were not even aware of the rule, an automatic safety against them, since the little-used rule stated, "When a forward pass from behind the goal line strikes the goal posts or the crossbar ... it is a safety if the pass strikes the ground in the end zone." That meant the difference in the game, as Cleveland eked out a 15–14 victory.

The next year embarrassed league officials altered the rule to state that such a pass would be considered merely incomplete. Of course, the real solution would have been to simply move the goal posts back 10 yards as they were in college football and thus make professional kickers actually have to be as good as the college boys. Incredibly, that change was not made for more than another quarter century.

The Lost Quarter

The prize for the worst quarter ever on defense by a professional football team went to the Detroit Lions in 1945 when they let the Green Bay Packers roll up 41 points in a single period. The Lions actually did it again in 1950 when they gave up the same number of points, 41, in the third quarter against the Rams.

Short Respite

After losing 29 National Football League games in a row, the Chicago Cardinals finally won their first game since 1942, beating their across-town rival Bears 16–7. A new day dawning? Not quite. The Cardinals promptly reverted to their usual inept form and went on a losing tear for the remaining six games of the season.

HORSE RACING

Second Chance

Never Mind II had the dubious distinction of establishing the slowest winning time in a steeplechase. During the 2-mile race the horse refused the fourth jump and the disgusted jockey gave up and headed for the paddock. When horse and rider got there, the jockey was informed that all the other horses in the race had either fallen or been disqualified. Never Mind's rider reversed course and returned to the track. This time the horse took all the jumps, if slowly and gingerly, and went on to finish—in 11 minutes, 28 seconds. The normal time for such a race was around the 4-minute mark.

1946 _____

BASEBALL

Mystery Heckler

Umpire Red Jones was having a rough time with the Chicago White Sox bench in a game at Boston's Fenway Park, after ruling that White

Sox pitcher Joe Haynes had thrown at Ted Williams' head. This produced a series of obscene insults out of the Chicago dugout, and finally Jones wheeled around and thumbed Ralph Hodgin out of the game as apparently the most obnoxious heckler. The abuse continued and it was clear that Jones had nailed the wrong man. So he heaved three more players but still the same abuse continued. Jones thumbed out another man and the vicious heckling went on unabated. Finally, the exasperated umpire cleared the bench of all the remaining coaches and players still in the dugout (nine more in all, leaving the Sox down to the nine players then in the field and a couple more in the bullpen). After the bench was cleared a voice much like the mystery heckler sounded again, but it was never determined whether it had been a spectator in the box seats all along. More likely, some fan had picked

Unable to figure out who was riding him from the Chicago White Sox dugout, Umpire Red Jones thumbed 14 Chicagoans from the bench in one inning, an all-time record.

up the chant just to continue to drive Jones off the deep end. In any event, no one on the White Sox team ever 'fessed up to being the mystery heckler. Jones' 14 ejections in a single inning stand as a record, as well as clear evidence that right or wrong, the umpire is always right.

Now Hear Diz

If Dizzy Dean was known as a zany while playing the game, he carried on that wild tradition later as a baseball broadcaster, with his own brand of dizzy slanguage. For the first time radio listeners and later television viewers learned that in a game runners could be "confidentially tagging up on their respectable bases." (Translation: The runners confidently tagged their respective bases.) Or there was this classic Dean narration:

> Mantle hits a long one. The center fielder's comin' over. The right fielder says, "I got it." They make the catch. There's a throw to the plate. They cut it off. The third baseman's got the ball. Look like they got the runner hung up like a suit of underwear. He throwed back to second. They got him. Look at the way he tried to skitter past. There's a throw. Now, what are they going to call it? He's safe, and the Yankees are ahead now 4 to 2.

If that looks unintelligible in print, it worked marvelously on television with the camera zeroing in on the action that Dean was describing—and quite accurately. It was simple, as long as there were pictures to enhance Dean's commentary. There had been a long fly with the bases loaded on which the man on third scored, the man on second was trapped in a rundown, and the man on first advanced to second. Really plain to see.

Dean in a word was made for television broadcasting. As he said himself, "I'm through talking about things folks ain't seeing." Thus, Dean's narratives added a brilliant element and insight no nonplayer could grasp. Dean was not so much describing the game as *playing* it. He fit his language to the player's own imagery. As he said of a pitcher noted both for a sizzling fastball and lack of control: "Ain't no walkin' up to the plate light-footed against him." And for perfect explanation on why a batter will sometimes let a perfect strike go by: "See it all the time—he's lookin' for a curve and you throwed him a fastball and you catched him frozen and he can't pull the trigger." Similarly, Dean's viewers got payloads of interpretation of various situations, such as "Antonelli didn't have a thing on that last pitch," or "The bases is loaded like a squirrel gun. I bet that pitcher wishes he had a squirrel gun. Don't look to me like he got much else."

Dean made CBS Television's "Game of the Week" a brilliant success, with fans crying for more of his comments and certainly heeding his advice, "Don't fail to miss next week's game," especially not in those cases were there were some pregame ceremonies in which "The boys'll be introduced out there on the flagpole."

Not that Diz didn't have his detractors. In 1946 a group of Missouri schoolteachers protested to the Federal Communications Commission that his radio broadcasts were "replete with errors in grammar and syntax" and were having "a bad effect on the pupils." Coming to Dean's defense was Norman Cousins of the *Saturday Review of Literature*, who saw Dizzy as an individualist and "an American original" whose unique style should not be tampered with.

Many newspaper editorials attacked the teachers for their "smugness," and in the end Dean stayed on the job. Diz himself commented: "I see where some of those teachers is sayin' I'm butcherin' up the language a little. Just remember . . . when me and Paul was pickin' cotton in Arkansas, we didn't have no chance to go to school much. . . . Learn them kids good English, and I'll learn 'em which is a ball and strike."

Diz cleaned up his act a bit, but still a runner would "slud in safe at third" and a batter "flowed out to right." And he could be aggrieved when he felt someone thought his knowledge limited. Such was the case when a British woman journalist interviewing him became exasperated with his fracturing of the language. "Mr. Dean," she said, "don't you know the King's English?" Diz blinked at that one and replied, "Sure I do, and so's the Queen."

For some three decades, almost right up to his death in 1973, Dean was the authentic voice of baseball.

BOXING

Quick Kill

The quickest knockout in boxing history was scored by Al Couture over Ralph Walton at Lewiston, ME. At the bell Walton was still adjusting his mouthpiece in his corner, when Couture put him down with a powerhouse right. The official time was 10.5 seconds (including the 10-second count), which meant, some mathematically inclined observers concluded, that Couture was more than halfway across the ring with the opening gong. However, Couture's 10.5-second kayo does *not* qualify as anywhere near to being the shortest fight on record. (See 1947—"Stop the Fight!")

FOOTBALL

Elementary, Leahy

Shocked when his quarterback, Johnny Lujack, threw three interceptions to Army's Arnold Tucker, Notre Dame Coach Frank Leahy wanted to know how that could happen. Lujack's explanation was rather elementary: "Coach, he was the only man open."

1947

BASEBALL

Forever Larcenous

Ty Cobb has long been regarded as not only just about the most competitive but also the most devious player for getting on base. He bullied umpires into giving him close calls on balls and strikes, and he was an artist at feigning being hit by a pitch. Even after his retirement in 1928, Cobb never lost his get-on-base killer instinct.

Cobb appeared in an old-timers game at Yankee Stadium in 1947 and expressed worry about his ability to swing a bat. He informed rival catcher Benny Bengough that he hadn't had a bat in his hands the past 19 years. "I'm way out of practice and I sure don't want to hit you when I swing," he told the catcher. "Better move back a bit so you don't get hurt."

Bengough gratefully obliged, and the 60-year-old Cobb proceeded to lay down a bunt on the first pitch and race to first base while the red-faced Bengough huffed and puffed and cursed as he was still trying to get to the ball.

The Meek Shall Inherit . . .

It is a given in the war between pitchers and batters that when a few sluggers knock the ball out of the park, the next hitter, even if he's a cream puff, will have to pay. It was Buddy Blattner's misfortune to

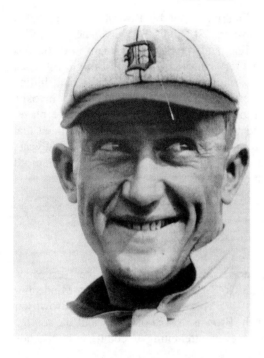

The legendary Ty Cobb only knew how to play to win, and he would "cheat" even in an old-timer's game.

bat far down in the lineup of the '47 Giants, a team that set a record for team homers at 221. This made Buddy fair game for irate pitchers. In one game sluggers Willard Marshall, Sid Gordon, Johnny Mize, and Walker Cooper smacked out four home runs on a total of five pitches.

That brought poor Buddy to the plate, and he was going to have to pay for all his team's slugging transgressions. On the first pitch, a near headbanger, Blattner had to dive into the dirt. He got up and promptly had to eat more dirt on the next pitch. Finally, after a three-ball count, Blattner got a pitch he could hit, and he seized the happy opportunity to make a routine out.

Blattner returned to the dugout and plopped himself thankfully on the bench next to big Walker Cooper. With a straight face, Coop offered a time-honored baseball observation, "I'll say one thing, Blattner—they really respect you."

Foul-Ball Triple

It was the shortest triple ever hit, never going more than two-thirds of the distance toward third base—and foul all the way to boot. The less-than-mighty blast was a dribbler hit by Boston Red Sox batter Jake Jones in a game against the St. Louis Browns. The ball rolled well outside the third-base line, and went no more than 50 or 60 feet in all, but St. Louis pitcher Fred Sanford was afraid it might roll back into fair territory for a hit, so he flipped his glove at the ball, hitting it and stopping it in foul territory. The umpire immediately invoked the rule of the day, which gave a batter a triple if a defensive player tossed his glove at a batted ball. Pitcher Sanford later explained that he thought the rule applied only to fair balls. And in fact a few years later the rule was changed in exactly that manner, but that did Sanford no good, and Jones was credited with an infield triple.

BOXING

"Stop the Fight!"

The shortest boxing match on record did not even last the 10 seconds required for a knockout. At a Golden Gloves tournament in Minneapolis, MN, on November 4, 1947, Mike Collins decked Pat Brownson with an awesome first punch. Brownson was out cold and the referee stopped the contest without even attempting a count, four seconds after the opening gong.

FOOTBALL

Brilliant Interference

In a college game between Washington & Lee and Richmond, W&L halfback Brian Bell took a kickoff and raced down the sideline, picking up a lone blocker. As Bell reached his own 40-yard line, two Richmond tacklers closed in on him. Hoping to catch a dramatic action photo, a sideline photographer focused his camera and shot off a flashbulb. The blinding light stunned the two tacklers and both tackled the blocker instead of the ball carrier. Bell sped away from the action and galloped another 60 yards for the touchdown. After the game the grateful W&L footballers awarded a monogram to the photographer, dubbing him the "star" of the game for making the Richmond players see stars.

1948

BOXING

The Real Longest Count

While the historic Gene Tunney-Jack Dempsey heavyweight championship fight is remembered for the "long count" that allowed Tunney a 14-to-16-second respite and enabled him to get off the canvas and defeat the Manassa Mauler, it is not the longest count ever. In 1948, Marcel Cerdan downed opponent Lavern Roach with a dynamite punch that was so hard it caused Cerdan to topple over as well. Confused, the referee and the timekeeper could not decide whether to proceed with the count against both fighters simultaneously or to rule that they had fallen. Meanwhile, Cerdan bounced to his feet while Roach still remained dazed. Now the referee started his official count, and Roach managed to rise before the 10-count. Actually Roach had been down for more than 30 seconds. Cerdan put Roach away for good in the eighth round with another powerhouse blow, one that did not put the Frenchman down as well.

FOOTBALL

The Play That Fooled Too Many

It was the best bit of quarterback "magic" that star footballer Eddie LeBaron pulled during his college career, so well-executed that it brought only grief for his College of the Pacific team. In a game against San Jose State, LeBaron spun around twice and handed off the pigskin to a running back, who slammed into the line of scrimmage and went down under a swarm of tacklers. The referee blew the whistle, thinking the play was over—as did all the San Jose players as well as virtually everyone in the stands. Actually LeBaron still had the ball, and while the players were still unpiling at the line, the quarterback lobbed an easy pass to a receiver for a touchdown.

The officials were faced with an excruciating dilemma. LeBaron had fooled them, and the whistle had blown, which meant the play was dead. But LeBaron had faked so well that it seemed ridiculous to penalize him for brilliant execution. After a long conference, the officials ruled they had no alternative but to call back the ball. The whistle was ruled supreme, and that meant the ball had been dead. Simply put, LeBaron could not get away with fooling the officials.

Chicago Bears tackle George Connor needed almost half his rookie season to figure out why opposing linemen hauled off and socked him every time he entered the game subbing for Fred Davis.

Making the decision all the more bitter was the fact that Pacific lost what would have been the tying touchdown and went down to defeat 14–7, for their only loss of the year.

Punching Bag Connor

It took Chicago Bears rookie George Connor almost half a season to finally figure out why opposing linemen kept punching him in the face when he was sent into the game to sub for rough-and-mean Fred Davis. At the conclusion of a play involving some vicious line action, Davis would raise his arm to indicate he wanted to be relieved for a spell. An enthusiastic Connor would romp onto the field and move into a three-point position. With the snap of the ball, Connor would face what he thought to be typical indoctrination for pro rookies as the opposing lineman would haul off and punch him in the mouth. This happened game after game until Connor started watching Davis' play closely. He spotted Davis punching out his opponent and then holding up his hand and trotting off the field.

Connor at last realized that Davis was getting himself out of harm's way and letting the rookie face the retribution, as opposing players apparently never even noticed the switch of foes and with blood in their eyes were primed for payback action. Connor solved his dilemma by announcing loudly each time that he was just coming into the game. The opposing players no longer used him for a punching bag but waited for Davis to return to the field.

TRACK AND FIELD

Let's Go to the Instant Replay

In the 1948 Olympics held in London, the United States was highly favored to take the gold in the Men's 400-Meter Relay, with runners Harrison Dillard, Mel Patton, Barney Ewell, and Lorenzo Wright. The Americans got off to a fast start, and after 200 meters they held a slight lead over the British. Then the later runners, Dillard and Patton, really opened up the race and they pushed the final margin to 6 meters. The Americans were jubilant, but then two British judges declared the U.S. runners had been guilty of an infraction, insisting that after the first leg of the race Ewell had passed the baton to Wright beyond the legal passing zone. The Americans were disqualified. The medal ceremonies were held and the gold medals awarded to the British runners-up.

American Olympics officials vigorously protested the verdict, and the British press denounced the Americans as bad sports. Luckily, the 1948 Olympics was the first to have the events officially filmed, and a Jury of Appeal was able to view the films of the race three days later. The film showed two white lines running across the track, one of which marked the 100-meter leg and the other the end of the 110-meter legal passing zone. The judges had simply looked at the wrong line. To the chagrin of the British press, which had continued to rail against the United States, the gold medals were stripped from the British and handed over to the Americans. It was the first time "instant replay" had been consulted in this fashion, and one British publication nevertheless bemoaned this use of "mechanical means" to triumph over human judges.

1949

BASEBALL

Self-Evaluation

Chuck Connors, who would later achieve fame as "The Rifleman" on television as well as many other acting roles, started out as a first-baseman hopeful. He made it to the majors in 1949 with the Brooklyn Dodgers but, alas, had only one at-bat—and promptly grounded into a double play. Pegged out at first, Connors just kept right on running toward the Dodger clubhouse. "Hey, where are you heading?" first-base Coach Jake Pitler yelled after him. Without breaking stride, Connors called back over his shoulder: "To Montreal." Connor's self-evaluation proved on target, as the Dodgers sent him down to the Montreal farm club. Connors made another stab at the big leagues in 1951 with the Chicago Cubs but managed to hit only .239 in 201 at-bats in 66 games. This time Connors kept right on going—to Hollywood and a more satisfactory career.

BASKETBALL

The Foul War

"It wasn't so much a basketball game as an act of war by both sides," one writer summed up the NBA game between the Syracuse Nationals and the Anderson Packers. The starting fives of both teams fouled out in a game marred by a league record of 122 fouls. The Packers won the elbow-punch-kick-and-trip competition with 66 fouls versus 56 for the Nationals. However, the good guys—relatively speaking—won the point score 125–123.

FOOTBALL

Hardest Extra Point Ever Made

No, extra points are not automatic. In the Army–Fordham game Cadet kicker Jack Mackmull did kick an easy extra point after an Army touchdown. But a roughness penalty moved the ball back to the 17-yard line, from where the calm Mackmull split the uprights a second time. However, Army was again hit with a 15-yard penalty, and Mackmull was forced to try from the 39-yard line, a distance of 49 yards to the uprights. The kick sailed wide, but this time a Fordham player drew a 15-yard penalty, which moved the line of scrimmage back to the 17-yard line. Mackmull kicked again, and missed. But Fordham was offside on the play, and the line of scrimmage shifted to the 12-yard line. The holder positioned the ball on the 18, and Mackmull kicked for the fifth time. It was good. Mackmull looked around apprehensively for any handkerchieves on the ground. There were none; the kick counted, although it was a lot of labor for one point.

Early 12th Man

Five years before Tommy Lewis made his infamous off-the-bench tackle (see 1954—The 12th Man), Bob Smith pulled the same stunt— but got away with it, at least for a time. With the final seconds ticking down in a game between Washington & Lee and Virgina, W & L substitute tackle Smith was dejectedly moving down the sideline for the dressing room when Virginia's Ed Bessell took a pass and headed for pay dirt. Smith had had quite enough of that, and he bolted onto the field and brought Bessell down just inches from the goal line. Bessell, surprised by the tackle, fumbled the ball forward across the goal line, and luckily one of his teammates fell on it for a touchdown. Virginia won the game 17–7 with no one aware that Smith had pulled a 12th-man caper until two days after the contest, when the teams analyzed the game films. Since Smith's play did not affect the final outcome of the game, the errant tackle is not as well known as Tommy Lewis', but his was just as classic a boner.

GOLF

Hole-in-One Brew

In the British Open, Harry Bradshaw's golf drive went right into a beer bottle, breaking off the neck and shoulder. Rather than accept a penalty, Bradshaw teed off on the bottle and smashed it with his club, sending the ball a respectable 30 feet.

HORSE RACING

Three-Quarters Goof

In the 1949 Pimlico Cup masterful jockey Eddie Arcaro, riding Blue Hills, finished up well ahead at the end of one and a half miles. He raised his hand in triumph as his mount crossed the finish line. Unfortunately, the race was two and a half miles. Said Arcaro, "I didn't know that it wasn't the finish until I started to pull up and the other horses went by me. Then Jimmy Lynch, who rode Bayeux, hollered, 'We have to go around again, buddy.' "

Arcaro dug into his mount—clearly the best horse in the race—but could only get Blue Hills up to second, behind Pilaster.

1950 ⸻⸻⸻⸻⸻⸻⸻⸻⸻⸻⸻⸻⸻⸻

BASEBALL

Faithful Fan

In 1950 the Brooklyn Dodgers hit upon the idea of the Knot Hole Gang television program involving young ballplayers. Three youngsters were allowed to perform wearing baseball gear, and the one picked as best by a Dodger player judge could come back to talk to his favorite Dodger. Reserve outfielder Cal Abrams seldom was picked for the chore, which paid $50—not an inconsiderable sum in those days of low salaries—because players like Duke Snider, Carl Furillo, and Roy Campanella had greater appeal for the TV audience. Once when Abrams got lucky, he worked out a scheme to earn himself a return appearance the next day for another $50. Years later he still remembered, with some pain, what happened:

> I got hold of this one kid, and I said, "Look, I'm going to pick you as the best fielder, and in turn I want you to say that you want to talk to me in the dugout." That way, I would get an extra $50. So he said, "All right." And so I was throwing the ball to the three kids, and Happy Felton says, "Cal, who do you think is going to make it?" I said, "Number 3." And the kid who I had made the deal with comes over, and Happy says, "Congratulations, here's an autographed ball and a Baby Ruth candy bar. Now who do you want to talk to in the dugout?" I'm waiting out there, and the kid says "Carl Furillo." I almost died.

Have Bat, Will Travel

Pittsburgh first baseman Dale Coogan became the only man in the major leagues ever to hit a home run and be back in the minors before the game was completed. Coogan hit his homer on June 24 in a game against the Brooklyn Dodgers at Ebbets Field. The game was halted by curfew in the eighth inning with the Dodgers leading 19–12. It was completed August 1, with the Dodgers winning 21–12. That same night Coogan, having been returned to the minors, was playing for Indianapolis of the American Association.

Superbobble—II

It can be argued either way whether Tommy Glaviano's errors were actually worse or not quite as bad as the four committed by Mike Grady on one play (see 1895—Superbobble). Glaviano, the third base-man for the St. Louis Cardinals, made three errors on three consecutive plays in the ninth inning against the Brooklyn Dodgers at Ebbets Field. Earlier in the contest the Cardinals were ahead 8–0, but the Dodgers scored four times in the bottom of the eighth. They brought in one run in the ninth and had the bases full when Glaviano's nightmare string occurred. Roy Campanella hit a grounder to Glaviano, who fielded it cleanly but threw wide to second for an attempted force play. This made the score 8–6 with the bases still loaded. Eddie Miksis smacked a grounder to Glaviano, who pegged to the plate to force the runner from third, but once again his throw went wide. Score: 8–7 and the bases still loaded. Then Pee Wee Reese followed with a grounder that skipped right through the hapless Glaviano's legs, per-mitting both the tying and winning runs to come home.

Independent Arbitration

In an American Association playoff game in Columbus, OH, Bill Ayres drilled a ball into the left-field bleachers, but because of the background of white shirts Umpire Bill Jackowski could not tell if it had gone over on the fly for a home run or on the bounce for a ground-rule double. Jackowski conferred with his fellow umpires, but they had been out of position and unable to follow the flight of the ball. The Columbus fans were most eager to help and screamed it was a double. Naturally both teams wanted a ruling in their favor. Then Minneapolis Manager Tommy Heath came up with a solution. "Why not ask Larry Miggins," he suggested. Miggins was the left fielder for Columbus. While it might seem odd for Manager Heath to accept the word of an opposition player, Miggins was known throughout the league as a stickler for honesty. "If there's anybody in the ballpark who will tell the truth, he's the man."

So an impromptu procession of the umpire, managers, and players from both teams headed out to left field. Miggins knew exactly what was coming, and that he was going to be put on the spot, so he tried to retreat to center field. The parade caught up to him, and Umpire Jackowski asked the burning question. Miggins looked aggrieved. "Do I have to answer?" he asked.

"No," Jackowski replied, "but I wish you would. I'll take your word for it."

Miggins looked genuinely pained as he gazed at his teammates. "I'm sorry, fellows," he practically whispered, "but it was a home run."

As it turned out, Miggins' honesty didn't cost his team the game, and visiting Minneapolis romped to an easy win. Columbus recovered from the loss and went on to take the playoff and then the Little World Series as well. In their own fashion even the Columbus fans forgave Miggins' sense of fair play. After about a week they stopped booing him.

BASKETBALL

The Dullest Game Ever Played

Wonder how the 24-second rule started in the National Basketball Association? It followed the infamous "sleeper" game between the Minneapolis Lakers and Fort Wayne Pistons in Minneapolis. Realizing they were facing George Mikan, one of the most dominating centers ever to play the game, the Pistons decided to start "freezing" the ball from the opening tip. Their slow-down game resulted in the Pistons leading 8–7 at the end of the first period. Fort Wayne kept up the freeze in the second period despite a crescendo of boos from the crowd. At the half the Lakers led 13–11. In the third period the Pistons tallied five points to the Lakers' four so that the home team led by one point, 17–16.

The fourth period proved to be the greatest monstrosity so that with just 9 seconds left each team had managed to tally only one point. Then the Pacers' Larry Foust drove in on the basket and put Fort

Wayne up by one point. A last-second shot by Slater Martin of the Lakers went awry and Fort Wayne triumphed 19–18.

The game was "hailed" as the dullest ever in the NBA. Among the dreadful records set were fewest points scored in a quarter, in a half, and in a game. Also the fewest shots by both teams. In the uproar that followed, NBA President Maurice Podoloff announced, "It'll never happen again!" Shortly thereafter, the 24-second clock was adopted, requiring the offense to shoot and at least hit the rim of the basket within 24 seconds or lose possession of the ball.

HOCKEY

The No-Goalie Gamble

With a team behind late in a game, it was quite common for a hockey coach to pull his goalie from the net to get an extra forward on the ice to try for a late score. But in a game between New Westminster and Vancouver in the Pacific Coast Hockey League, the local fans started booing when Coach Babe Pratt of New Westminster did it, regarding Pratt as nuts for a number of reasons. First of all, there were 14 minutes left on the clock, and it was silly to think a team could leave their own net unguarded for that long without being scored upon. Then too the score was 6–2, so New Westminster had to make up four goals, which seemed impossible. But when New Westminster scored a goal the fans cheered. Pratt did let his goalie return to the net when Vancouver had possession of the puck but yanked him as soon as his team got the puck or at least the action switched to the far end of the rink. Then New Westminster scored again . . . and again. With the score 6–5 the New Westminster fans set up a constant din, urging their team on. Incredibly, the Westies then tied the game. Coach Pratt quickly reinstated his goalie to protect the tie. As insane as his strategy had been, it had worked for one of the greatest comebacks ever on ice, with the game ending with the score knotted.

1951

BASEBALL

The "Ayes" Have It

Madcap owner Bill Veeck pulled many offbeat promotions to goose
up attendance at his ballpark, and one of the most popular with the
fans was his "Grandstand Manager's Day" when he owned the St.
Louis Browns. About 550 fans behind the dugout were given "Yes"
placards and a like number "No" placards. Whenever the manager
had a key decision to make in the game against the Philadelphia
Athletics, such as walking a batter, or bunting or bringing the infield
in, he turned to the crowd for a yes or no vote on what to do. The
majority wish was carried out, and it must be said the fans did a major
league job.

The first decision the grandstand managers were called upon to
make was to approve the opening lineup. They didn't, voting to bench
catcher Matt Batts and first baseman Ben Taylor, installing Sherm
Lollar and Hank Arft in their positions. Both proved shrewd moves, as
Lollar came through with three hits and two runs batted in, including a
game-winning homer. Arft joined in with two RBIs. In the first inning,
after St. Louis pitcher Ned Garver gave up five hits to the first six
batters, the fans were asked, "Shall we warm up a new pitcher?"
Demonstrating they had ice water in their veins, the fans voted no. It
was another brilliant decision, as Garver settled down after that and
allowed only two more hits the rest of the game as the Browns won
5–3. A little-known fact was that the great Connie Mack attended the
game and held up a "Yes" sign on a number of occasions.

Although the experiment was an unqualified success in that it did
not prove time-consuming (the game ran only 2 hours, 11 minutes),
Veeck did not attempt an encore, realizing that the fans in the bleachers, left out of the decision-making process, would soon revolt at the
elitism of asking only the box-seat fans for a decision. And if he had
tried it on a regular basis, Veeck also knew 16 major league managers,
who could stand for one game as a lark, would also be in revolt.

Smallest Strike Zone

Some called it baseball maverick Bill Veeck's grandest promotional
stunt and others his worst, one that held the national pastime up to
ridicule. On August 19, 1951, Veeck introduced player ⅛ to the St.

*Maverick baseball owner Bill Veeck's maddest promotion was signing a 3'7"
midget as a pinch-hitter. The diminutive player walked—and was promptly
barred thereafter from major league ball.*

Louis Browns lineup. He was 26-year-old Edward Gaedel, but his
age was of no consequence. What counted was his height—3 feet, 7
inches—and even more importantly that as a batter he offered a pitcher
a strike zone of a mere 1.5 feet. Veeck had checked baseball's official
rules carefully and found there was no stipulation on how tall or short
a player had to be for play eligibility. Veeck found midget Gaedel in
show biz, and he and his confederates trained him on the fundamentals
of the game, of which he knew little. Veeck had his scorecards printed
up for a doubleheader against the Detroit Tigers at St. Louis' Sportsman's Park, and listed in it "⅛ Gaedel." No one paid attention to
that. Whoever this Gaedel kid was, they figured, it was too bad his
debut in the majors was marred by a typographical error in the
program.

Veeck scheduled Gaedel to make his debut in the second game of
the doubleheader. Before the home half of the first inning began, the
public address announcer informed the assembled 20,299 fans: "For
the Browns, number one-eighth, Eddie Gaedell, batting for Saucier."

There was a mighty roar when this anatomical bomb, this brownie for the Browns, strode to the plate, waving three bats all looking like no more than an orchestra conductor's baton. Umpire Ed Hurley immediately called time and summoned Browns Manager Zack Taylor out of the dugout. Taylor came, fully armed with Gaedel's newly signed official American League contract. Hurley looked at the contract and finally nodded. Until then, Tigers pitcher Bob Cain on the mound was roaring with laughter as much as anyone. He thought it was all a Bill Veeck gag going nowhere. Now that he discovered he was really going to have to pitch to Gaedel, he turned grim. How do you pitch to a pixie? Cain's batterymate Bob Swift came to the mound to discuss what to do while Gaedel waved his mini-bat menacingly. "Let's go," he squeaked. "Throw it in there, fat, and I'll moider it." Swift looked back at Gaedel and finally imparted his catching wisdom to pitcher Cain. "Keep it low," he instructed. Cain tried to do so, but he was so rattled he missed the mini-strike zone four times, each of his pitches moving higher and higher, and Gaedel triumphantly threw aside his tiny bat and strutted to first base.

Immediately Jim Delsing was sent in to run for the tiniest batsman in major league history. Gaedel, his cap raised, strutted off the field to thunderous applause. The much-suffering fans felt their hapless Browns now had the ideal leadoff man, a player who would always start the game with a man on first. Alas, it was not to be. The next day Veeck was forced to release Gaedel after American League President Will Harridge refused to approve his contract, saying it was not in the best interests of baseball to permit midgets to play major league ball. Gaedel said he was heartbroken. "Now that someone has finally taken a step to help us short guys, Harridge is ruining my baseball career."

Veeck got Gaedel a number of gag appearances later but none in an actual baseball game. In 1961 Gaedel was mugged in Chicago and later died of his injuries. Only one baseball person attended his funeral, pitcher Bob Cain, the man who couldn't find Gaedel's tiny strike zone in his one and only big league at bat.

FOOTBALL

Winning the "Courtesy Bowl"

Long before Vince Lombardi, Michigan Coach Fielding Yost said it in 1905: "Winning is not everything. It is the only thing." Nevertheless, from time to time college football has tried to restore civility to the game. During a contest between Haverford and Swarthmore, the fans and teams were graded according to appearance, respect for authority, competitive spirit, and mental poise under pressure. The idea sprang from the frequent complaints of rowdyism at football games, and the system was an effort to put more emphasis on good sportsmanship and self-control. The panel of judges were two members of the Philadelphia Northeast Junior Chamber of Commerce as well as the regular game officials who judged the actions of both the players and the fans. When at one point the Haverford fans loudly criticized the officials on a close call, they drew penalties from the judges. It probably cost the team the "Courtesy Bowl," since in the final tally of the complicated scoring system, Swarthmore came out on top 45–43. Incidentally, Swarthmore also won the game 19–7, meaning that good guys can finish first.

Later the same year the same experiment was tried in a contest between the University of Maryland and West Virginia. Both sides proved models of good behavior. The Terp fans got 45 points for "alertness and perfection," and West Virginia got 45 points for emphasizing "character and the will to compete." That might seem to indicate a tie on the field to be in order, but actually Maryland romped 54–7, proving apparently in a perfect world some good guys will still have to finish last.

1952

BASEBALL

The Longest Half Inning

For a time in a game between the Cincinnati Reds and the Brooklyn Dodgers it appeared that the Dodgers' half of the first inning was never going to end. The action started off tamely enough as leadoff batter Billy Cox grounded out for the first out. Sadly for Cincinnati and the four pitchers the team had to use, Cox was followed by 19 batters who got on base. Cox in fact batted three times (he got a single on his next trip and was hit by a pitch after that). Only one of the 19 was out later when Andy Pafko was caught at third in a double steal. Fans using scorecards needed three of them to properly record the action, which went on for an entire hour—the exact playing time of a football game. Brooklyn sent 21 batters to the plate, and they produced 10 hits and seven walks while two others were hit by pitched balls. The Dodgers scored 15 runs and left three men on base by the time Duke Snider struck out to mercifully retire the side.

Needless to say statisticians found records tumbling all around. Among them: most runs scored in one inning—15; most runs scored in the first inning—15; most runs scored with two outs—12; most batters in one inning—21.

The *New York Times* also declared one probable record that was not found in the official books, that of most batters to reach base safely in consecutive order—19. The *Times* could find no instance coming close to that one and no experts or baseball buffs ever came forth with any.

Who's Ted Williams?

One of the most boneheaded instances of baserunning occurred in the bottom of the ninth inning in a game between the Washington Senators and the Boston Red Sox at Fenway Park. The Bosox were trailing 1–0 but had the bases loaded with only one out—and Ted Williams coming to bat. It was an ideal situation for Boston, with their fate to be determined by one of the sport's greatest hitters. The base runners simply had to hold their positions while remaining alert and let Williams' dynamic bat decide the game. On the very first pitch to Williams, Washington catcher Mickey Grasso threw to third base and picked off Walt Dropo. It was a tremendous skull by Dropo, who really had no place to go since it was absolutely insane for him to try stealing home with Williams at bat. If the Boston fans were limp after that play, it was nothing compared to what happened on the very next pitch. Grasso pegged to first base and got Billy Goodman (who definitely had no place to go with a runner on second). Three out—and the dazed Ted Williams was still standing in the batter's box.

Help Wanted

Pittsburgh Pirate first baseman George "Catfish" Metkovich, never accused of being a Gold Glover, was having a nightmare game against the Brooklyn Dodgers with line drives whipping past his head and through his legs with embarrassing regularity. Finally a sizzling grounder ricocheted off Metkovich's shins and bounded into right field. Desperately, Catfish turned to Umpire Augie Donatelli and wailed, "For Cripes sake, Augie, don't just stand there. Get a glove and help me out!"

Mistaken Identity

There are certain players with whom certain umpires have a running war. Umpire Tom Gorman found that Chris Van Cuyk of the Brooklyn Dodgers was the bane of his existence, a bench jockey who never let up on him. One day during a Dodger–Giant game at Ebbets Field, Gorman was getting rough treatment from the Dodger bench. Finally he had enough and marched over to the Dodger dugout and yelled: "All right, Van Cuyk, get out! You're through." Gorman turned red when no one on the Dodger bench stirred. "Come on, get going! Van Cuyk, you're through." Still there was no movement in the dugout, only silence. This time, Gorman thought, Van Cuyk was going too far.

The enraged umpire turned his attention to Manager Charlie Dressen. "You better get that Van Cuyk out of here!" he roared.

"If you want to run Van Cuyk," Dressen replied, "you'd better go to St. Paul, because that's where I sent him yesterday."

BASKETBALL

If It's a Foul, It Must Be Syracuse

The old Syracuse Nationals of the National Basketball Association were notorious for their foul play. In one game in 1952 the Nationals outdid themselves in a game against the Baltimore Bullets by committing a team high of 60 fouls. In the game, Syracuse also set an NBA record for having *eight* players foul out of the game. Since that left the Nationals unable to put five men on the court, the referees permitted the disqualified players back in the game. On any further fouls, however, the Bullets not only got the free throws they were entitled to but technical foul shots as well. As a result, the Nationals came out on the wrong end of a 97–91 score.

Simply Put

It was most un–Ivy League. Harvard University fans took to always booing the visiting teams when they scored, and lacing into the refs whenever a call went against the Crimson. After several games followed this unseemly pattern, the school administration, the faculty, and the student newspaper launched a campaign to get the students to behave in the fine Harvard tradition. At the next game it was apparent that the official pleas were going nowhere as the raucous catcalling continued. Finally at halftime an irate university official seized the public address microphone and boomed out: "Everyone please cease and desist from orally castigating the officials and from making uncomplimentary and derogatory innuendos concerning the representatives of the opposition."

Apparently the official was now speaking the students' language, and the jeering ceased.

BOXING

When the Referee Threw in the Towel

It was a grueling battle for the light heavyweight championship between Joey Maxim and Sugar Ray Robinson, compounded by a brutally muggy 104-degree night temperature in New York City, and it seemed impossible that the men in the ring could go 15 strength-sapping rounds. They didn't. But the man who gave out first was a surprise; it was neither Maxim nor Sugar Ray. It was Ruby Goldstein, the referee, who sat down at the end of the 10th round and was unable to regain his feet. The fight went on with a substitute referee, but that didn't mean the two fighters could go the limit. The great Sugar Ray Robinson was too exhausted to come out for the 14th round, the only time in his entire boxing career that Sugar Ray wasn't around at the end of a bout. Maxim, the only man of the original trio left in the ring, maintained his crown.

1953

BASEBALL

Bustin' Loose

Bill Veeck, the madcap baseball owner, was a total believer in a team having to be loose to win consistently. When his '53 St. Louis Browns were, as usual, in the doldrums and riding an eight-game losing streak, Veeck rented the Aviation Room at Cleveland's Carter Hotel for a get-loose party for his minions. There was piano playing, and drink, and food, and drink, and songs, and drink, and laughter, and drink, and reminiscences, and drink. After midnight everyone was feeling that it was more like having won the World Series than being mired in a sad losing streak. Champagne was opened and squirted and poured on everyone. Pictures on the walls and furniture were wrecked and a good time was had by all, especially Bill Veeck, who had to pick up a $1,850 tab.

But the Browns were good and loose, and the next day they went out and met the Cleveland Indians—and lost their ninth straight.

BASKETBALL

The Worst Long Basket Ever Made

There was no other way to describe it: It was a terrible shot. Standing out of bounds 91 feet away from the basket, Adam Coffman of Greensburg (PA) High put up the ball against Farrell High and watched goggle-eyed himself as it went into the basket. Even the crowd realized Coffman had not really made a super shot, that it had been downright dreadful. Reason: Coffman had not been trying for the basket, but was simply making a long pass downcourt. His aim was so errant that it went in the basket instead.

1954

BASKETBALL

Rupp's Rule

Adolph Rupp, the longtime autocratic coach of basketball at the University of Kentucky, had one guiding rule: Never let up in a game—play to win, pour it on, run up the score. Or as "Ole Adolph," as he was popularly known in Kentucky, put it, "The hell with how you played the game. They still keep score, don't they?" With that sort of attitude, nothing else counted, certainly not political pull. With Rupp, only perfection mattered, not personalities. Don Chandler, the son of Governor A. B. (Happy) Chandler, once recollected about trying to get a playing favor from Rupp:

> I made Adolph's varsity in 1954 and he had me a good seat on the bench. Well, we had to go to Knoxville to play Tennessee and a lot of my friends from prep school were going to be at the game. So I told Coach Rupp, "I'm

Kentucky Coach Adolph Rupp's guiding rule: "The hell with how you played the game. They still keep score, don't they?"

in a bit of a predicament. I told my friends I was the coming star of the team here, and now they're all going to be watching me. I'd appreciate it lots if you'd use me in the game first chance you get. We ought to beat them easy, anyway."

He never said a word to me. That meant he was going to do it, I thought. Well, in the middle of the first half, Cliff Hagan, he was our big star then, got into a mixup and he hit his head on the floor and he was laid out cold. I hear Rupp yelling, "Chandler!" and I jump up. I rip off my warm-up jacket and I run over to Rupp. "Who'm I guarding?" I yell at him.

"Guard, hell," he yells. "Go out there and help the trainer carry Hagan off the floor."

Actually, the governor's son did get in the game, which was well in hand from the opening tip. But it was at bench-clearing time, which meant in the last few seconds of the game, under the Rupp rules.

FOOTBALL

The 12th Man

In the 1954 Cotton Bowl in Dallas, halfback Dicky Moegle of Rice broke into the clear along the sidelines and headed for a sure 95-yard touchdown against Alabama. As Moegle raced past the Crimson Tide bench, it was clear to Alabama fullback Tommy Lewis that he was the only one who could stop him. And stop him he did with a flying tackle. Unfortunately, Lewis was not in the game at the time and had charged off the Crimson Tide bench. The 75,000 fans in the stands sat in stunned silence, and Lewis, now horrified at his whacky misdeed, crawled off the field, taking refuge on the 'Bama bench and cursing himself.

Officials did not hesitate to rule that Moegle would have scored, and the referee picked up the ball himself and marched the ball the rest of the way to the Alabama goal and, raising his arms, indicated a touchdown.

About all Lewis could say afterward about his competitive faux pas was, "I guess I'm too full of Alabama."

Ironically, Lewis later became a high school coach and watched in slack-jawed horror when one of his own players made a similar off-the-bench tackle. At the time, with only a minute to play in the game, Lewis' team was leading 12–7, but the award of a touchdown to the opposition turned victory into defeat, 13–12.

1955

BASKETBALL

Longest Game

The longest basketball game in major college history was played between Purdue and Minnesota. At the end of regulation time the score stood at 57-all. Since at the time there was no time limit in which a team was forced to shoot, the two teams went into a stalling game, trying to control the ball for one final shot that would win the contest. After four overtimes the score still stood 57-all as neither team managed to sink their final tries. Then in the fifth overtime the teams went on a scoring "rampage," each making 2 points. Finally, in the sixth overtime, after much booing from the crowd, the teams stopped their stalling tactics and went for points. Minnesota scored 10, versus 7 for Purdue, giving them the victory 69–66—at long last.

Wrong-Way Riegels of the Court

In a basketball equivalent of Roy Riegels' wrong-way run in the 1929 Rose Bowl (see 1929—Wrong-Way Riegels), Billy Ward of Queen of Peace High in North Arlington, NJ, made a quick layup in a game with Holy Trinity High—unfortunately in Holy Trinity's basket. Actually, Ward had somewhat of an alibi as the referees committed an error by lining up the centers the wrong way on a jump ball. Because of the confusion, Ward, playing forward, got the tap and went in the direction he normally should have from that position on the floor.

His ears burning from that miscue, Ward was eager to make amends. A teammate tried to inbound the ball after Billy's horrible mistake but found no one to pass to. Ward hurried back to help out and took the pass. The rest was pure instinct as he immediately went to the nearest basket—and once again, for the second time in two seconds, laid the ball in the opposition's goal. Queen of Peace's coach sat Ward down to prevent more embarrassment for the chagrined player—and to prevent any more wrongful baskets. Queen of Peace lost the game, 68–61.

Billy Ward lived down his miscues, and the following year was captain of the team. When Queen of Peace went to Holy Trinity that season, he got a standing ovation from the hometown fans.

FOOTBALL

Devoted Crowd

Despite high winds and a temperature of 0 degrees Fahrenheit, the November 12 football game between San Jose State and Washington State College was played as scheduled at Pullman, WA. Total paid attendance: 1.

1956 _____

TENNIS

Perfection

Competing in the 1956 World Table Tennis Championships, England's Richard Bergmann complained that the ball in use was not really round and was too soft. He held up the match for half an hour, examining 192 balls before coming up with one that he approved.

1957 _____

BASEBALL

Instinct or Larceny?

Cincinnati third baseman Don Hoak insisted it had just been a goof, but whether it was or was not, it still brought about a change in baseball rules. Hoak was a runner on second with another Red on first base when the batter slapped a ball between second and third. Hoak, off the base, reverted to his infielder's role and fielded the grounder. This of course meant that he was out, having been hit by a batted ball, but it also broke up what seemed to be a sure double play. Hoak insisted to the press that he had acted on sheer impulse, merely forgetting who he was or at least what he was doing at the moment. Baseball officials weren't so sure of that, but, impulsive act or larcenous baseball, they altered the rules so that thereafter both the hit runner and the batter would be out on such a play.

HORSE RACING

The "Bad Dream Derby"

A few days before the 63rd running of the Kentucky Derby, Texas oilman Ralph Lowe, the owner of Gallant Man, had a dream that his horse had lost the Derby because the jockey misjudged the finish line. Considering the fact that the Derby was a high-anxiety time for many horsemen, it was a rather understandable dream. In any event, Lowe mentioned the dream to Gallant Man's trainer, Johnny Nerud, and Nerud later repeated it to Willie Shoemaker, the 25-year-old jockey and legend in the making as the top rider of all time. Actually, "Shoe"

Jockey Willie Shoemaker stood up briefly on Gallant Man (on the outside) *when he thought the 16th pole was the finish line, permitting Bill Hartack on Iron Liege to come back and win the Derby.*

was not the horse's regular rider but got the mount after jockey Johnny Choquette was suspended for that week for rough riding. Nerud immediately sought out Shoemaker, who had won the "Run for the Roses" in 1955 on Swaps. Nerud brought Shoemaker and Lowe together for dinner in Louisville and Lowe repeated his dream—actually, it was more of a nightmare. In the dream, Lowe said, Gallant Man had the lead down the stretch when suddenly his jockey mistook the 16th pole for the finish and stood up in his irons, so that Gallant Man lost the race. By Derby Day the three men had shrugged off the dream. In a prerace story *Sports Illustrated* prophetically observed, "The one who will win it is the one who can best take advantage of breaks, mistakes, and racing luck. One mistake will be fatal. One break could be decisive."

On the break from the starting gate Federal Hill shot to an early lead, with Iron Liege, ridden by Bill Hartack, settled in second, and Bold Ruler, the huge favorite with Eddie Arcaro aboard, tucked in third. Gallant Man was seventh, as Shoemaker hugged the rail, biding his time. After a mile, Federal Hill still was in front, but tiring, and Iron Liege closed in. Round Table and Bold Ruler closed somewhat but could not withstand the fast rush of Gallant Man. Federal Hill gave way and Shoemaker brought his mount even with Iron Liege. The two horses drove down the stretch, with Round Table and Bold Ruler now third and fourth but not in real contention. It was strictly a two-horse race.

The horses were stride for stride and then Gallant Man took a very slight lead. Hartack, on the inside with Iron Liege, whipped his mount left-handed, trying to keep up with Gallant Man. Still Gallant Man inched slightly farther in front. Gallant Man was not a horse to fade, and as they approached the 16th pole it seemed certain the finish would be Gallant Man followed by Iron Liege. Then it happened. To the astonishment of those who saw it (and not everyone had the acumen to spot it), Shoemaker stood up in the irons "for all the world as though the race was over," one writer stated. It was only the briefest instant, but it was enough to turn horse owner Lowe's nightmare to awesome reality. Shoemaker recovered and got Gallant Man back on stride but not in time. Gallant Man lost by a nose.

A crestfallen Shoemaker fled the jockey's room to avoid the media, and later the stewards suspended him for 15 days "for gross carelessness in misjudging the point of finish." To their credit Lowe and Nerud stood by Shoemaker, and the former even bought him a new Chrysler to soothe the jockey's bitter disappointment. With Shoemaker barred from the Preakness, Lowe decided not to run Gallant Man but to wait for the Belmont Stakes, in which the horse and Shoemaker waltzed to victory by eight lengths.

The result haunted Shoemaker all the more since, but for his boner (perhaps the most costly in all sports history), Gallant Man might well have been a Triple Crown winner. Recollecting the "bad dream Derby" 33 years later for *Sports Illustrated*, Shoemaker said:

At Churchill Downs, you realize, the finish line is a 16th of a mile closer to the first turn than at most tracks. I hadn't ridden there in a year, and I just forgot about that. I pulled up where most finish lines are. Oh yes, and there *is* that dream. It's possible, I guess, that it was somewhere there in my subconscious. I don't know. But it's a fact that something good generally comes out of these things. I know it was a character builder for me. It taught me humility. And that's not a bad lesson for anyone.

1958

FOOTBALL

Shortchanged

A successful coach wherever he went, Bear Bryant reached the zenith of his career in 1958, when he came back to his alma mater, the University of Alabama, where he remained until retiring in 1982. In 1961 he achieved his first No. 1 ranking nationally and never thereafter had a losing season. His national ranking created quite a protocol problem since the university thought it appropriate that the president's salary should be higher than that of the football coach, something many rabid alumni groups would have a hard time comprehending. The problem was solved for two years when Bryant was paid $99,999.99 while the college head got $100,000 annually. Eventually Alabama gave up the ghost and raised Bryant to $120,000.

SWIMMING AND DIVING

There's No Free Swim

Robert F. Legge, a 53-year-old U.S. Navy doctor, swam the length of the Panama Canal, covering the 28.5 miles in 21 hours, 54 minutes. At various times he had to contend with an iguana and a boa constrictor, but his major difficulty was dealing with the swells caused by shipping, which at times slowed his forward progress enormously. When he arrived at Balboa, the swimmer was greeted by the cheers of a large crowd of admirers—and a toll collector who figured out his toll to be 72 cents.

1959

BASEBALL

The Grand Toothache

Walt Alston served 23 years as manager of the Brooklyn–Los Angeles Dodgers, but almost lost his job way back in 1959, only to be saved by a toothache and a long, painful session with a dentist. Alston had taken over the Dodgers in 1954 and led Brooklyn to a strong second-place finish, then won the pennant the next two years and came in third in 1957, the Dodgers' last year in Brooklyn. The next year in Los Angeles was a disaster, as the Dodgers stumbled to a 71–83 record and a seventh-place finish just two games out of the cellar. There were a number of explanations for this fall, including the tragic loss of catcher Roy Campanella and the difficulties the Dodgers' batters had adjusting to the odd dimensions of the Coliseum. Short-fused L.A. fans called all season for Alston's scalp, but owner Walter O'Malley gave him a strong vote of confidence. However, it was clear that 1959 was a must year for Alston. Unfortunately, the Dodgers got off to a miserable start, and finally O'Malley and his assistant Buzzy Bavasi determined that Alston would have to go, to be replaced as manager by Pee Wee Reese. Before a night game it was decided that Alston would be notified he was out as the field manager. But the Dodgers were unable to locate Alston all day. When he showed up at the Coliseum shortly before game time, he explained he had had a vicious toothache and had had a long ordeal at the dentist's office. With Mrs. Alston already present in a box seat, management decided to give Alston a day's grace considering the torment he'd undergone. The Dodgers won the game.

O'Malley and Bavasi consulted and decided to let matters ride for another game or two, even though the press release announcing the managerial changes had already been prepared. The Dodgers won the next two games—and they kept on winning as though they had entirely forgotten how to do anything else. Slowly the Dodgers gained on the two leaders, San Francisco and Milwaukee, and by July it was a three-team race. L.A. went ahead and won the pennant, a remarkable turnaround for a team that had finished next to last the previous year. Not only that, but they took the World Series over the Chicago White Sox, four games to two. Walt Alston never did get his notice. He remained the manager of the Dodgers all the way until near the end of the 1976 season. During his tenure, Alston led the Dodgers to seven pennants and four World Series crowns. He was inducted into the Baseball Hall of Fame in 1983, a year before his death. Did he ever know he was almost dumped back in 1959? If he did, he never said so. Probably not even his dentist knew for sure.

Nobody's Perfect

It was the first time in major league baseball that a pitcher hurled a perfect game beyond nine innings and then went on to lose, in one of the wackiest conclusions ever. Harvey Haddix of the Pittsburgh

Pirates pitched 12 perfect innings against the Milwaukee Braves and then lost the game in the 13th inning when a batter smashed a home run against him with two men on base for a final score, incredibly, of 1–0. It was a case in the end of nobody being perfect.

Haddix had put the Braves down like clockwork for 12 innings but got no scoring support from the Pirates despite their 12 hits off Milwaukee southpaw Lew Burdette, so that the game still stood 0–0.

Everything came unglued in the bottom of the 13th when Felix Mantilla hit a grounder to third but was safe on Don Hoak's errant throw to first. That broke up the perfect game but left Haddix's no-hitter still alive. Eddie Mathews sacrificed Mantilla to second. Hank Aaron, the league's leading batter, was walked intentionally. That brought up Joe Adcock, who unloaded a home run over the right-center-field fence. However, Adcock's baserunning boneheadedness could have turned him into the goat if the Pirates managed to score if they had another turn at bat, but they did not.

When Adcock unleashed his drive, Aaron on first was not sure whether it had cleared the fence and assumed it had dropped just short. He ran to second, touched the bag, realizing correctly that Matilla had scored from second with the winning run. Meanwhile, Adcock, in his excitement at blasting the home run, joyously rounded the bases, passing second base, and was declared out before he got to third for illegally passing Aaron. Adcock was credited with a double and driving in the winning run, but lost his home run, so that later all he was left with was the bragging rights to breaking up a no-hit game with the homer that never was.

Nightmare Inning

The nightmare that was the top of the seventh inning that day in Kansas City is perhaps told best by the line score: 11 runs, 1 hit, 3 errors (and 10 bases on balls plus a hit batsman). The Kansas City Athletics were hosting the Chicago White Sox when excruciating pitching worthy of a Class D baseball team turned a close contest into a shameful rout. The Sox were ahead 8–6 when a hit and three errors got Chicago two more runs with a runner on third base. A's pitcher Tom Gorman proceeded to walk the next two batters—unintentionally— and delivered two balls to the next batter. Kansas City Manager Harry Craft yanked Gorman and brought in Mark Freeman in relief. Things did not get better. Freeman served up two more balls to walk the batter and force in the third run of the inning. Another walk—and another run. Then there was a force-out at the plate, so at least there was one out. Then Freeman walked in another run.

Out went Freeman and in came George Brunetto to take over the pitching, if it could be called that. There came a walk (and a run), another walk (and a run), a hit batter (and a run), a strikeout (of the pitcher), a walk (and a run), another walk (and another run). That meant 11 runs had scored. Then finally there was a ground-out to end the inning—45 minutes of pure torture for the A's pitchers and manager and the suffering Kansas City fans. For the hardy few who remained to the bitter end, the final score was 20–6, White Sox.

Asleep at the Plate

Baseball umpiring is a pressure-cooker situation that few fans appreciate. The umpire has to keep his mind on several things at once. When he loses track, madness can result. In a game between the St. Louis Cardinals and the Chicago Cubs at Wrigley Field, the Cardinals' Stan Musial had a three-and-one count on him when pitcher Bob Anderson delivered a ball that got by catcher Sammy Taylor and headed for the backstop. Umpire Vic Delmore called ball four and Musial trotted toward first. The Cub battery started arguing with the umpire that the ball had been foul tipped and should have been a strike. While they were arguing, Musial, realizing the ball was still in play, raced for second. Unlike the Cub pitcher and catcher, third baseman Alvin Dark was alert to the situation and retrieved the ball behind the plate and pegged to second to try to get Musial. At the same time, Umpire Delmore, still arguing with Anderson and Taylor, unthinkingly took a new ball from his pocket and handed it to the catcher. Pitcher Anderson, suddenly aware that Musial was running, grabbed the ball from his catcher and threw to second. As a result, Musial and two balls arrived at the bag at about the same time. Shortstop Ernie Banks caught Dark's throw while Anderson's ball sailed over second into center field. Musial had not seen two balls coming to second and assumed the game ball had gone to center field and started for third, only to run right into Banks, who tagged him out. After a lengthy conference and argument with the rival managers, the umpires ruled Musial was out because he was tagged by the ball that had been in play.

In the end, Umpire Delmore got rougher treatment than Musial. Because he had been asleep at the plate and put a ball in play that he should not have, he was canned from his job at the end of the season.

1960

BASEBALL

Run for Cover

No pitcher in baseball terrorized opposing batters more than Steve Dalkowski. Hurling in the Class C California League for the Stockton Ports, he had a blazing fastball that put down 665 batters. These, however, were not strikeout victims, but *struck* victims—hit by a pitched ball—which explained why batters trembled in fear when facing Dalkowski. In addition to hitting 665 batters, he also walked 726, and threw six wild pitches in a row. Dalkowski's pitches broke one batter's arm and tore off another's ear lobe. And some say this was not actually his fiercest season. Over a fear-ridden four-year career, he once pitched a one-hitter against the Aberdeen, SD, club and still lost the game 9–8. Another time, between walks and hit batsmen, Dalkowski struck out 24 batters and still had to be taken out in the ninth inning with his team behind.

SOCCER

Whistle Blower

In a scoreless game in Rome between France and Belgium, the Belgian players suddenly stopped dead in their tracks when they thought the umpire had whistled the action to a halt. However, the whistle had been sounded by a super-lunged Italian traffic officer outside the stadium, trying to halt a reckless driver. The French team did not follow suit and kept on playing, netting the ball for the winning point. Despite an angry protest by Belgium, the goal stood.

1961

BASEBALL

On the Other Hand

The ability to find chinks in good hitters' armor is often exaggerated by pitchers. If a good batter knows what he is being served up, he can usually make an adjustment in his swing to be ready for it. Still, for want of anything better to do, managers and pitching coaches make book on opposing hitters. Sometimes they are blessed with what they consider a bonanza when they pick up a player from a rival team. Manager Bill Rigney of the Los Angeles Angels was thrilled having hurler Eli Grba on his staff when they faced the New York Yankees. Dutifully Grba went over the Yankee hitters, pointing out their weaknesses as he remembered them. In a bull session with Rigney and the rest of the moundsmen, Grba said of switch-hitting Mickey Mantle: "When Mantle bats right-handed, throw him high; when he bats left-handed, pitch him low." In the game the Angels' pitchers followed instructions. Mantle batted left-handed, and promptly homered over the right-field wall. Later in the game Mantle came up right-handed and blasted a shot over the left-field wall.

By this time, Grba was sitting on the bench about as far away from Manager Rigney as he could get. Seeing Rigney's icy stare, Grba offered an alibi of sorts: "Or was it the other way around?"

Stand-In

Knowing that his Chicago White Sox could use all the help they could get to fill Comiskey Park on opening day, the promotion-minded owner Bill Veeck invited John F. Kennedy to throw out the first ball. Kennedy did so, but he turned out to be a White Sox fan from suburban Oak Lawn who happened to be named John F. Kennedy—not the president of the United States.

FOOTBALL

The 12th Man

On the final play of the game between the Boston Patriots and the Dallas Texans, the Pats had a lead of 28–21 when Dallas quarterback Cotton Davidson tossed a ball into the end zone, hoping one of his receivers could catch it for the tying touchdown. There was a congregation of players in the end zone, and a defender batted the ball down as time expired. Unfortunately, the "defender" didn't happen to be any of the Boston players. It turned out that a Boston fan had wormed his way onto the field, jumped into the end zone, and foiled the pass for his favorite team—and ran off before any of the officials spotted him. The play stood and the game was over.

1962

AUTO RACING

One-Mile-an-Hour Speedster

In the first Daytona Continental, Dan Gurney, driving a Lotus, looked like a lead-pipe cinch to win as he entered the final lap holding a huge lead over the second-place Ferrari. However, when Gurney's Lotus approached the finish, the engine suddenly died. Gurney jumped out of his car and rushed to the officials to check his time, then hopped back into his car and tried to start the engine. The engine roared and sputtered and died again after Gurney had gone only a few inches. Gurney repeated the process, keeping the car in gear, and it kept inching forward. He was coaxing the Lotus on by using the ignition starter. The best Gurney could do at any time was move his car a scant foot or two while the Ferrari zoomed forward at 180 miles an hour. Gurney's Lotus crossed the finish line the winner moments before the Ferrari streaked by it—too late.

BASEBALL

Footloose

If any one ballplayer typified the dreadful New York Mets in their maiden year, it would be first baseman "Marvelous" Marv Throneberry, who seemed always to do the wrong thing at the right time. Once, uncharacteristically, he unleashed a solid triple in a game against the Chicago Cubs, but he was called out for failing to touch first base—or second base for that matter. When the next batter, Charlie Neal, hit a home run, Manager Casey Stengel prudently made him circle the bases twice to make certain he touched them all.

Such ineptitude made Throneberry the idol of the Mets fans, who were just thrilled to have two major league (if it could be called that) baseball teams back in the city. Fans sported tee-shirts saying, "VRAM" on them—"MARV" spelled backward. Throneberry was so popular, an appreciation party was held for him in an Italian restaurant. Marvelous Marv got there late, couldn't find a seat, and went across the street to a diner to eat.

Majority Rule

During Maury Wills' record-setting year in which he stole 104 bases, the charge was sometimes made by opposing players and fans that umpires were giving the fleet-footed Dodger the close calls. It was not true. The umpires called them the way they saw them, but at times they did march to their own drummer. In a game against the Giants in Candlestick Park, San Francisco was doing a poor job of curbing the speedy Wills. One steal play was particularly close. Umpire Dusty Bogess gave the thumb-up motion to indicate Wills was out, but at the same time he called, "You're safe."

Standing on the bag, Wills said, "Dusty, am I out or safe? Your thumb signaled out, but I heard your voice say safe. Which is it?"

Bogess was in no quandary whatsoever. He said, "Maury, only you and these two Giants," pointing at Chuck Hiller and José Pagan, "heard me call you safe, but 40,000 Giant fans saw me call you out. So, Maury, you're out!"

Bogess was not the first umpire to enunciate this particular solution to such an embarrassing dilemma.

And no appeal.

Go, Mr. Howard

One of the biggest dangers in baserunning is that a player will miss a steal sign, a result that can wipe out a great scoring opportunity and cost the game. As a double safeguard, Manager Walter Alston of the Los Angeles Dodgers set up a system in a game against the New York Mets whereby his signal for a steal was to be backed up by another signal to the base runner by the first-base coach. According to Alston's instructions, to make sure the runner was aware of the sign, first-base Coach Pete Reiser was to call the runner's last name when the steal was on.

With the count 3 and 2 on the hitter, Alston wanted base runner Frank Howard to go with the pitch. Dutifully Reiser, for whom Howard had played at Green Bay, WI, and Victoria, TX, called out: "Be careful now, Howard ... heads up, Howard ... one out, Howard." The batter fouled off the next pitch, but Howard remained anchored to the base. Before the next pitch, Reiser ran through the verbal steal signals again. Again a foul ball—but again Howard remained as firm as a rock. Exasperated, Reiser again repeated his "Howard" calls, until Frank Howard turned to him with a look of genuine pain on his face, and said, "Come on now, Pete, you know me too well to call me by my last name."

Only once that desperate Reiser reverted to an old steal signal did Howard's face light up, and he lumbered off on the next pitch.

Playing Ump

A war of nerves dominates the confrontation of pitcher and batter, in which any trick that does not break the rules (a slight bending is another matter) is permissible. During a game against the Boston Red Sox with the bases loaded, Cleveland's Tito Francona yelled out to hurler Earl Wilson, "Hold it, Earl! Hold it!" Forgetting a cardinal rule of baseball that only an umpire can call time, Wilson stopped his delivery, almost tumbling from the mound. The chagrined pitcher looked on red-faced as the umpire ordered the runners to advance because of what turned out to be Wilson's game-losing balk.

Hot Streak

Infielder and future major league Manager Don Zimmer started the season with the inept New York Mets in their maiden year and got three hits in his first 12 at-bats, an impressive average for the hapless expansion team. But then he went hitless in his next 34 times up. Finally, he came through with a double, and within 48 hours he was traded. The standard wisdom in the grandstand by the already suffering Mets fans was that the club management had been very shrewd in its dealings—trading Zimmer when he was hot.

TRACK AND FIELD

Congratulations

John Uelses became the first pole vaulter in history to clear 16 feet, at a track and field meet in New York's Madison Square Garden, and immediately fans charged to offer congratulations. Sadly, in the process the bar was knocked off, and officials disallowed the jump. Happily, the following day Uelses cleared 16' ¾" to establish the world record in a meet in Boston. This time fans cautiously remained in their seats.

1963

BASEBALL

The Backward Home Run

On June 23, Jimmy Piersall, then with the New York Mets and noted for his bizarre behavior, celebrated hitting his 100th major league home run against the Philadelphia Phillies by running the bases backward. It was not a performance that pleased league officials, who promptly issued a new rule requiring base runners to face the bases. The home run was Piersall's first and last in the National League, as shortly thereafter he was released by the Mets. Manager Casey Stengel declared, "There's only room for one clown on this team."

1964

AUTO RACING

Booster

During the Nassau Speed Week, a Grand Prix for Volkswagens, A. J. Foyt and Dan Gurney concocted an outrageous winning strategy. As the 100-mile race started, Gurney came up behind Foyt in his high-powered VW and kept pushing Foyt at high speed so that within a short time the pair of bugs outdistanced the rest of the field, with Foyt still in front. With just a quarter mile to go, Gurney passed Foyt and zoomed past the checkered flag in first with Foyt second. Gurney immediately was disqualified since his powerfully built car did not meet specification as a regulation production VW. That simply meant that Foyt was placed first and collected the prize money. The two drivers could laugh all the way to the bank, especially since Foyt's VW was absolutely the slowest entry in the race.

Slow Stop

During a run on the Bonneville, UT, salt flats, Craig Breedlove's jet-powered car went out of control. The skid marks measured more than 5 miles.

BASEBALL

Look Ma, No Hits

Hurling for the Houston Colts against the Cincinnati Reds, Ken Johnson gained the dubious distinction of becoming the only pitcher in the majors to lose a nine-inning complete-game no hitter. In the ninth inning Cincinnati's Pete Rose laid down a bunt and Johnson threw wild to first, which allowed Rose to hustle all the way to second base on the error. After moving to third on a groundout, Rose came across with the only run of the game, on Nellie Fox's error at second base.

FOOTBALL

Riegels Repeat

In a game against the San Francisco 49ers, Minnesota Vikings lineman Jim Marshall "pulled a Riegels" (see 1929—Wrong-Way Riegels). He picked up a 49er fumble on the San Francisco 40-yard line and ran it back 60 yards across the Vikings' goal line. As he threw the pigskin gleefully in the air, Bruce Bosely of the 49ers threw his arms around Marshall and thanked him for the two-point safety he'd just scored for San Francisco.

The misplay was almost a replica of Roy Riegels' boner that cost California the 1929 Rose Bowl against Georgia Tech. Riegels never got off the hook for that monumental error, but Marshall was more fortunate, as his team nevertheless went on to win the game 27–22. Marshall enjoyed great demand as an after-dinner speaker at the conclusion of the season, while Riegels was once again subjected to flashback accounts of his own disastrous run.

GOLF

Across the Country in 386 Days

It was not an idea that Jules Verne thought of, but Floyd Satterlee Rood did. The golf enthusiast came up with the mind-boggling idea to make the entire United States his fairway, by golfing from coast to coast. Rood teed off on his first shot on September 14, 1963, along the Pacific Ocean surf and continued his game along a course that would run 3,397.7 miles. He took 114,737 strokes—which had to be

considered par—by the time he finished up at the Atlantic Ocean on
October 3, 1964. He lost 3,511 golf balls along the way.

OLYMPICS

Apology

In the 1964 Tokyo Olympics, Japan's top marathoner, Kokichi Tsuburaya, considered to have a real shot at the gold, entered the stadium in
second place, followed by 10 meters by Basil Heatley of Great Britain.
Despite being cheered on by the local spectators, Tsuburaya, running
in only his fourth marathon, tired badly and Heatley passed him on
the final turn. Still, Tsuburaya's third-place finish was the first medal
Japan had earned in track and field in 28 years, and he was regarded
as a national hero. A member of the Training School of the Japanese
Ground Self-Defense Force, he was ordered to resume training immediately for the 1968 Olympics and to stop seeing his fiancée. However,
Tsuburaya never recovered from what he regarded as his failure for
his country's honor, and he worried that he would never regain his
full running strength. He committed hara-kiri, apologizing to his country and noting, ''Cannot run anymore.''

1965 _____

BASEBALL

No-Hitters and No Support

Jim Maloney of the Cincinnati Reds twice pitched regular-game no-
hitters in the same season, but was stymied when his teammates were
unable to generate any runs themselves during the first nine innings.
In the first game, at Crosley Field against the New York Mets, Maloney pitched a perfect 10th inning as well, but in the 11th, weak-hitting
Johnny Lewis—whom Maloney had struck out three times previously—blasted a 2–1 pitch against the barrier in center field for a
game-winning ground-rule home run.

Later in the season, Maloney went through another nine-inning no-
hit stint against the Chicago Cubs, but it appeared to be, to use the
words of Yogi Berra, ''déjà vu all over again,'' as the Reds' bats
were silent and produced no runs. However, Cincinnati finally pushed

over a run in the 10th inning and Maloney at last won himself a no-hit game.

Exercise in Versatility

In one of baseball owner Charley Finley's more inspired promotions, he dreamed up the idea of star shortstop Bert Campaneris of his Kansas City Athletics playing all nine positions in a single baseball game. The fact was that Campaneris was a superior utility man well capable of handling any infield spot. To hype the promotion further, Finley took out a $1 million insurance policy on his star player for the game. Campaneris started off in the first inning at his regular shortstop post. In the second inning he switched to second and in the third inning he was at third base. Then he switched in succeeding innings to play left, center, and right fields.

In right field, Campaneris committed his only error of the game. Mr. Versatility took up first-base chores in the seventh inning. And in the eighth inning he went to the mound, where his performance raised some questions as to whether he could have been a top-flight hurler. Jose Cardenal, who happened to be Campaneris' second cousin, was first up and popped up. But after that Campaneris allowed a run on one hit and two walks. In the ninth inning, Campaneris moved behind the plate for the supreme test. With two men on base, the Angels attempted a double steal, with big Ed Kirkpatrick streaking in from third. Campaneris put the tag on Kirkpatrick, who bowled him over to try to shake the ball loose, but Campaneris held on to it. He also exhibited a catcher's fiery spirt by bouncing up off the ground ready to take on Kirkpatrick for what he regarded as too inspired a collision. Because of a battered shoulder, Campaneris left the game, to the cheers of the Kansas City fans. Oh, yes, if anyone is interested, the game was tied 3–3 after nine innings, and K.C. pulled it out in the 13th.

FOOTBALL

Fifth-Down Stabler

When Kenny Stabler was a sophomore quarterback at Alabama, he pulled the equivalent of referee Red Friesell's monumental boner of allowing Cornell an extra down against Dartmouth (see 1940—"Fifth-Down Friesell"). Although Stabler would become known in his later college days and even more so in the pros as a quick-thinking field general who functioned with precision under pressure, he missed the boat when the highly favored Alabama Crimson Tide took on Tennessee. The way the game developed, it was set up for what would become typical Stabler last-minute heroics as Stabler was inserted in the game because the Tide's star quarterback Steve Sloan had proven ineffective in a 7–7 game.

With a stirring two-minute drill, Stabler brought Alabama to just inside the 10-yard line for a first down and goal to go with just under a minute to play and no Alabama timeouts remaining. On first down, he handed off to his fullback, who gained 2 yards. Then Stabler faded back on what was to be either a pass or pitch-out play but was tackled for a 10-yard loss, setting 'Bama back to the 18-yard line. On third down, Stabler faded to pass, then scrambled and made it all the way to the 4-yard line before being brought down, unfortunately still in bounds so that the clock did not stop. Now there were only 10 seconds left, not enough time for Coach Bear Bryant to send in the field-goal kicker. It was clear that Stabler would have to call an all-or-nothing play for the tie-breaking touchdown.

Stabler brought the team up to the line, took the snap, and inexplicably tossed a quick pass out of bounds! Alabama was forced to give up the ball with just six seconds left in the game without even trying to score. Stabler had been the only person in the stadium who had lost track of the downs. He thought it was only third and that he was stopping the clock so that Alabama could win the game on a fourth-down field goal. The trouble was that a team could not try a field goal on fifth down. A disconsolate Stabler went to the bench, while a jubilant Tennessee team ran out the clock with one final play.

GOLF

Big Blow

The 10th hole at Miracle Hills Golf Club in Omaha, NE, was 444 yards long with a drop-off at the 290-yard mark. Twenty-one-year-old Bob Mittera was a good golfer but had never driven a ball more than 250 yards—but he made a hole-in-one on October 7. Just as Mittera teed off, a 50-mph gust roared along the fairway and lofted the ball over the drop-off. The ball simply kept right on rolling 154 yards straight into the cup for the longest recorded hole-in-one.

HOCKEY

The Rowdie Twins

It is not unusual for two hockey players involved in a fight on the ice both to be hit with penalties. But John Ferguson of Montreal and Gary Bergman of the Detroit Red Wings really mixed it up. On a single play, Ferguson got hit with three penalties for charging, slashing, and high-sticking, and Bergman was socked for two, charging and slashing. Together the ice rowdies racked up five penalties on the one play.

1966

BOXING

Mighty Punch

While still in his teens and well before he went on to become the lightweight champion, Roberto Duran hustled bets on his boxing skills in his native Panama. At a fair, bettors plunked down money that Duran could not put down a certain opponent with one punch. Duran took the action and with a blistering right to the head sent his opponent to the ground. It was a horse! The incident was appropriated by Hollywood in Mel Brooks' comedy *Blazing Saddles*.

1967

FOOTBALL

Mixed Emotions

In a remarkable high-low result, Howard Cosell became the only sportscaster ever to come in "most popular" and "least popular" in the same poll. Cosell indicated on whose side he was: "There never has been one like me before, and there never will be one like me again."

TENNIS

Court Marathon

The scores looked more like the results of football games—26–24, 17–19, 30–28—but they occurred in the doubles match at the U.S. Tennis Open when Robert Wilson and Mark Cox triumphed over Ron Holmburg and Charles Pasarell. The match took 6 hours, 23 minutes.

1968

BOXING

The Final Test

After taking the gold medal at the 1968 Olympics in Mexico City, middleweight Chris Finnegan, a 24-year-old British bricklayer, still faced the inevitable final hurdle, a urine test for drugs. But there was a hang-up. Finnegan declared, ''Now if there's one thing I've never been able to do, it's have a piss while someone's watching me. I can never stand at those long urinals you get in gents' bogs, with all the other blokes having a quick squirt.''

Intensive efforts were made to get Finnegan to produce, as water faucets were turned on, and people whistled and whispered encouragement. Finnegan downed several glasses of water. Nothing. Three or four pints of beer also failed to achieve the necessary results. Finnegan then sat for a television interview and afterward was escorted to a local restaurant for a victory celebration. All the while two Olympic officials were at the ready with the necessary flasks. Finally, at 1:40 A.M. Finnegan jumped to his feet and asked if anyone would care for some urine. The officials trooped into the men's room with the boxer, obtained their sample, and rushed back to the laboratory.

The results were negative, and Finnegan officially earned his gold.

FOOTBALL

Three Downs and Out

In a colossal boner for the National Football League involving six officials, the Los Angeles Rams were robbed of a legitimate chance to win a vital game against the Chicago Bears. The score stood 17–16 when the Rams failed to complete a third-down pass as the clock was

running down. Incredibly the officials—all six were involved—
mistakenly thought it had been a fourth-down attempt, which meant
that they had to turn the ball over to the Bears. Films of the game
later confirmed the fact that it had really been fourth down coming
up for Los Angeles. As a consequence of their mistake, all six officials
were suspended by the league from officiating any more games for
the balance of the season.

GOLF

Golf's Biggest Boner

There never was a boner on the fairway to match what happened to
Argentine golfer Roberto de Vicenzo in the 1968 Masters at Augusta,
GA. Going into the final round, de Vicenzo was tied for seventh place,
two strokes behind the leader, Gary Player. But the South American
came out firing that round. He scored an eagle 2 on the first hole and
then birdied the next two. At the end of the front nine, he had blistered
his way into the lead with a 31, driving most of his competitors out
of contention, all except Bob Goalby, who was competing two holes
back. De Vicenzo kept up the torrid pace, and on 17 he shot a birdie
3 to stand 12 under. But back on 15, Goalby sank an eagle 3. On 18,
de Vicenzo gambled on another birdie but hit the ball over the green
and ended up bogeying the hole. His goof on 18 had gotten de Vicenzo
all bent up, and he was so distracted that he failed to give his card,
kept as was customary by his paired golfer, Tommy Aaron, more than
a cursory glance before signing it.

Meanwhile, Goalby took a bogey of his own on 17 and needed a
par on 18, or so he thought, to bring about a playoff. He made par,
and was happy to come out with a tie. But that was not the case. It
turned out that Aaron had inadvertently written a 4 instead of a 3 for
the 17th hole. De Vicenzo violated a given in golf by signing his card
before adding up and checking all the figures. The card showed that
de Vicenzo had a 66 for the round when he had really played 65. The
rules of golf are rigid on such matters. If a golfer signs a card with
the score less than what he actually shot, he is automatically disqualified. If he signs a card that shows a higher score, he is stuck with it.
That is what happened to de Vicenzo, and Goalby simply backed into
taking the Masters.

If the matter was officially settled, it was not accepted by the public.
Letters of protest poured into Masters officials' offices from all over

the world supporting de Vicenzo. By contrast, Goalby got hate mail. "People actually thought I had kept his card and given him a higher score," Goalby said later. De Vicenzo estimated he got "one million letters and telegrams of sympathy." But as to suggestions that he try to get the results altered by legal action, de Vicenzo refused, insisting rules had to be followed and expressing sympathy for Goalby. De Vicenzo's boner was to result in a huge payoff for him. He got a quarter-million dollars in endorsements and a long contract from Coca-Cola. All in all, de Vicenzo made far more money that he had after winning the British Open in 1967. It was all zany—but profitable.

Puttering Around

How many putts would a pro putter need if a pro putter couldn't putt a 3-foot putt? The answer: a lot. In the 1968 French Open, British pro Brian Barnes needed a little 3-foot putt for par. He blew the shot and then foolishly tried to rake the ball back into the hole—and blew that as well. So he putted again and missed. And putted again and missed. Now losing his cool, Barnes slammed the ball back and forth, even saddling his score with a two-stroke penalty, for once straddling the lie of a putt. Altogether he needed 12 putts to get in the cup, so he ended up with an 11-over-par 15.

HOCKEY

Blowing Their Top

In 1968 the Philadelphia Flyers of the National Hockey League were forced to shift their last seven home games to other cities—Quebec, Toronto, and New York. It was not a matter of drawing poorly at home. They were forced to give up their home rink advantage at the Spectrum because of the condition of the arena's roof. Four times in March the roof had been blown off.

HORSE RACING

Pleading Ignorance

Neither Willie Shoemaker (see 1957—The "Bad Dream Derby") nor Eddie Arcaro (see 1949—Three-Quarter-Race Goof) came up with anything close to the creative excuse offered by Jockey William

McKeever for a similar riding miscue in a major race. In the Preakness at Pimlico, McKeever stood up in the irons at the 16th pole, misjudging it for the finish line, so that his mount, Nodouble, finished fourth (third after the disqualification of another horse). In his own defense after the race, McKeever said, "Well, how should I know where the finish line is? I've never rid here before."

OLYMPICS

Red-Hot Competition

At the 1968 Winter Olympics at Grenoble-alpe d'Huez, France, the East German women's luge competitors behaved rather strangely, always appearing for their runs at the very last moment and disappearing immediately thereafter. In the finals the East Germans finished first, second, and fourth. Because of their odd behavior, their toboggans were inspected, and it was determined after an investigation that they had all illegally heated the runners over an open fire just before their runs. All three finishers were disqualified by the unanimous vote of the Jury of Appeal. The East German Olympic Committee made a silly try at blaming the affair on a "capitalist revanchist plot," but that cut no ice, since it had been the Poles who had first blown the whistle.

TRACK AND FIELD

Successful Flop

At the Mexico City Olympics, high-jumper Dick Fosbury from Oregon State set a new Olympic record of 7' 4½" and won the gold medal. What was unusual—"crazy," according to many of the world's coaches—was that he jumped backward, in what became known as the Fosbury Flop. Fosbury's technique was to race up to the bar at top speed and take off with his left foot. Then, instead of bringing his right foot up and across the bar, the usual procedure, Fosbury pivoted his right leg back and jumped head-first with his back to the bar. While the *New York Times* called it "the first flop that ever was a success," Payton Jordan, the Olympic coach, feared the flop could wipe out a generation of high jumpers. "They'll all have broken necks," he predicted. Fosbury dismissed such worries and predicted his technique would be the flop of the future—and he proved more prophetic than zany. In the 1980 Olympics, 13 of the 16 finalists were doing the Fosbury Flop.

1969

BASEBALL

"Kissing Bandit"

Morganna, the exotic dancer, started her career as "Baseball's Kissing Bandit," racing out on the diamond to kiss ballplayers. Clad in sneakers, shorts, and a very tight sweater, Morganna picked Pete Rose as her first smoochee. In her first dozen tries, Morganna was stopped short of her goal only twice, which by her own standards was a "pretty good batting average, huh?" Her favorite smoochee was George Brett—"He's a great kisser and a fantastic baseball player." Jim Palmer ranked second—"He looks so cute in his undies."

BASKETBALL

The Globetrotters Come Home

In 1969 the Harlem Globetrotters made an appearance in Intermediate School 201 in New York. It was the first time in 42 years and 9,500 games that the Harlem Globetrotters ever played in Harlem.

FOOTBALL

Upsetting Development

The day after their unthinkable win in Super Bowl III (before which Joe Namath made his famous prediction, "We're going to win Sunday. I guarantee you"), the overjoyed New York Jets reeled onto their plane in Miami for a triumphant return to New York. They were greeted at the airport by thousands of fans who yelled for a look at their Super Bowl trophy. The call went out to bring out the trophy, but none was forthcoming. Then the horrendous truth struck home. The team had forgotten it back in Miami. As Frank Ramos, the Jets public relations director, said, "After all the celebrating that went on,

*Exotic dancer
Morganna, a.k.a.
"Baseball's Kissing
Bandit," mashing
George Brett.*

I don't think anybody was in any condition to think about things like who had the trophy. Some of the guys had enough trouble finding the airport.''

TRACK AND FIELD

Go, Gramps, Go

Larry Lewis stormed to a new world's record in the 100-yard dash in 17.8. If that doesn't seem all that fast, the event was for runners in the 100-years-and-up class. Lewis was 101.

1970

BASEBALL

Pay Dispute

It probably happened just one time, and certainly it was not an act repeated in recent years as ballplayer pay exploded to amazing heights. Outfielder Al Kaline was not an outstanding athlete, but he worked hard to hone his skills to become a 22-year veteran very popular with Detroit fans. In 1970 the Tigers management informed Kaline he was getting a raise that would make him the first $100,000-a-year member of the Tigers. "I don't deserve $100,000," Kaline responded, probably thinking back to the likes of superstar Hank Greenberg who got his $100,000 only after he left Detroit for the Pittsburgh Pirates (and well over his prime). "I'll play for the same salary I played for last year." Kaline drove a hard bargain, but he won out.

BASKETBALL

Longest Basket Not in the Record Books

You won't find it in the record books, but it remains the longest scoring shot ever made in college basketball. Steve Myers of Pacific Lutheran University was at the other end of the court and threw up a shot that later was measured at 92' 3½". Wait a minute, how can a basketball shot measure that long? Only if the player is standing out of bounds, which Myers was doing. Therefore, the referee disallowed the basket. However, the fan uproar was so immense that the officials, who had been duly impressed as well, reversed themselves and let the basket count. Actually, the longest legal shot in college ball was made by Marshall University's Bruce Morris in a game against Appalachian State in 1985. Morris, standing just inches from his own baseline, grabbed a loose ball as the first half was ending. He whirled and threw a line drive that touched nothing but net as the buzzer sounded. The shot was measured at 89' 10".

FOOTBALL

Wrong Call

In perhaps one of the worst business decisions concerning sports, Bob Wood, CBS Network president, turned down "Monday Night Football," saying, "Preempt Doris Day? Are you out of your mind?"

1971

BASKETBALL

At Least They Got on the Board

In one of the sorriest of shooting nights, the Wynot (NE) High School Blue-devils were defeated by the Niobrara High Lions 118–4. Actually, Niobrara could have had a shutout since the Blue-devils had failed to make a single field goal, but the victors had let the inept opponents go to the foul line 18 times. Wynot converted only four of them, but at least they averted a goose-egg. And Wynot could take some comfort in doing better than Jonesboro Baptist School in Monticello, AR, had done in a 1931 game when it likewise proved incapable of putting a shot from the floor through the net and only converted a single free throw in a dismal 143–1 loss.

FISHING

Prize Snack

In New Zealand, a fisherman competing in a surf-casting tournament caught a fish he reasoned was too small to win so he simply ate it. He then discovered it was the only fish caught in the entire contest, so his tiny snack had cost him the $250 prize.

FOOTBALL

Helping the Offense

In what on the surface appeared to be a play too improbable for words, Miami was on the University of Florida's 8-yard line with a minute left to play when Miami's John Hornibrook took the pigskin and rushed toward the goal line. As he did so, the entire 11 men on

Florida's defense "slipped" and fell to the ground, making Horni-brook's TD scamper a piece of cake. Not that this was a disaster for Florida, as they were ahead 45–8 at the time. And the Florida fans applauded their team's apparent defensive lapse. It was the last game of the season, and like the Florida players, the fans wanted to see quarterback John Reaves back for one final series so he would have a chance to break Jim Plunkett's career passing mark of 7,547 yards. Reaves came into the game and toppled Plunkett's record with a 15-yard pass to Carlos Alvarez.

Poor Great Defense

Normally it would have been a great defensive play, but it didn't turn out that way. In a game against Northwestern, the Michigan Wolver-ines' Dana Coin attempted a 51-yard field goal. The kick was a line drive that had the distance and was going to clear the crossbar, but Northwestern's Jack Dustin, standing in front of the goal post, timed it beautifully, jumped up, and batted the ball back into the end zone, saving the three points. However, Michigan receiver Bob Rather came storming down under the kick and fell on the ball to give the Wolver-ines a touchdown. Thus, Dustin's brilliant defensive play turned into disaster, ending up costing his team an extra four points.

Disguised as Professionals

On Halloween the Cincinnati Bengals gave perhaps the most inept performance on record by a professional football team when they lost to the Houston Oilers 10–6. The score was hardly indicative of the horrendous performance of the Bengals, whose botched running and passing "attack" resulted in a *minus* 52 yards.

GOLF

The Terrible Agnew

Having been forced to resign the vice-presidency in 1973 and finally accepting a deal permitting a no-contest plea for income tax evasion involving kickbacks, extortion, and bribery over a 10-year period, Spiro Agnew was hardly a credit to his high office. Alas, Agnew's record on the golf course was also lamentable. Teeing off in a golf match in Palm Springs, CA, in 1971, he took a full swing at the ball

and smacked a 66-year-old spectator on the arm. Then the ball bounced
off the man and hit his wife. Agnew's very next shot smashed into
the left ankle of a woman in the crowd, who had to be taken by
ambulance to the hospital. After that Agnew simply skipped the first
hole and moved to the second tee.

1972

BASKETBALL

Where's the Basket?

In a game with the New York Knicks, the Milwaukee Bucks of the
NBA held a commanding 86–68 lead with six minutes to go, and then
made one of the most impossible collapses ever by failing to score in
the last half of the final quarter. New York won 87–86.

FOOTBALL

Two Into One Doesn't Go

It was described as the worst job of tackling in the National Football
League, but there was a logical reason offered by a number of scien-
tists to explain what happened. In a game against the Los Angeles
Rams, Minnesota Vikings' bulky fullback Bill Brown caught a short
pass and immediately Los Angeles lineback Jim Parnell hit him from
one side and defensive back Jim Nettles from the other. Unfortunately
for the two tacklers, they met the fullback at the same split second,
each tackling a very beefy target who was being propped up by the
force of a tackle on the other side. The effect was to turn pass receiver
Brown into a stone wall. The two tacklers slid right off him, and
Brown lumbered downfield for a 76-yard touchdown. The bizarre play
made the difference in the final score as the Vikings won 45–41.

White House Hotline

Preparing for Super Bowl VI against the Dallas Cowboys, Miami
Dolphins Coach Don Shula was interrupted by a late-night telephone
call from President Richard M. Nixon, who was checking in with a
suggested play. Shula's comment afterward was open to more than
one interpretation: "I thought it was some idiot calling at that late

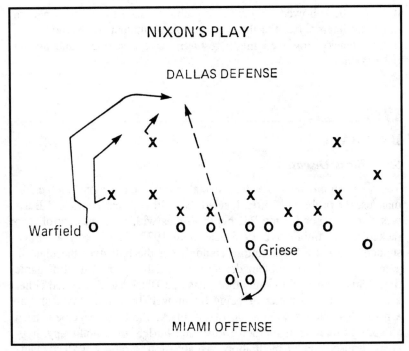

The Nixon play designed for the Miami Dolphins proved to be a bust.

hour." Shula did use the play in the big game, however. Paul Warfield shot downfield in a down-and-in pattern, but Dallas Cowboy linebacker Lee Roy Jordan raced over to help out Mel Renfro, who likewise was not fooled by the play. Quarterback Bob Griese did the only thing he could, wisely overthrew flanker Warfield, and the play ended up a dud.

OLYMPICS

Sex for the Nonamateur

Reversing the generally held beliefs of many athletic coaches, a medical adviser for Great Britain's Olympic team urged the athletes to engage in "about half an hour of sexual activity . . . to maximize the onset, quantity, and quality of sleep" the night before their athletic events. However, that bit of advice was tempered by the caveat that it should be followed only by those athletes accustomed to a pattern of sexual intercourse. For the relative sexual amateur, he warned, "the muscle tension involved might result in severe stiffness and aching the next day."

1973

BASEBALL

Steve Blass Disease

Today when pitchers develop mental block in their hurling performances, the problem is often labeled the "Steve Blass Disease." Blass was a top pitcher for the Pittsburgh Pirates with brilliant control who racked up an impressive 19–8 season in 1972. The next year, Blass suddenly lost it all. He simply couldn't get the ball over the plate in games. He had no problem during practice, but turned wild at game time. This suggested to some therapists that Blass had developed either a fear of killing a batter or being hit himself by a line drive, and as a result his pitches went wide of the mark. Pirate management tried all sorts of treatments on their former star hurler—psychotherapy, hypnosis, transcendental meditation, visualization. Nothing worked. During 1973–1974 Blass won only three more games and was out of baseball. (Sometimes Steve Blass Disease strikes more selectively. In 1985 the New York Yankees signed Ed Whitson to a $4.5-million contract, but he developed a mental block about pitching at Yankee Stadium. When he lost game after game, the Yankees gave up on him and traded him back to San Diego—and Whitson proved to be an effective hurler once again.)

Moist Protest

The most common illegal pitch in baseball is of course the spitball, and the argument is often made that the major league establishment doesn't really want it stopped. In 1973, a vintage year of complaints about the spitter, Bobby Murcer called Commissioner Bowie Kuhn "gutless" for not having umpires crack down on the pitch. And Billy Martin of the Texas Rangers ordered his hurlers to throw spitters wholesale as a protest against Gaylord Perry, the decade's premier spitballer, who was pitching against them. Nothing was done to curb Perry, but officials hit Murcer with a $250 fine and Texas pitcher Jim

Merritt for $1,000 for following his manager's orders. Martin drew a three-day suspension. Commenting on the developments, writer Dan Gutman declared, "In other words, cheating is okay—but bringing it to anyone's attention is illegal."

BASKETBALL

Home Court Advantage

There was a kicker in the astounding record compiled by Rich "Pee Wee" Kirkland, who tore up the semipro competition for the Lewisburg (PA) Hilltoppers. Although he was only 6'2", 27-year-old Pee Wee came up with some truly amazing stats. He averaged 70 points a game, and twice during the 1973–1974 season he scored more than 100 points. True, he was held to his worst performance of the year by the Lithuanian Club of Shamokin, PA, who "limited" him to a puny 47 points. However, Pee Wee got his revenge against the Lithuanians in their next matchup by scoring 62 field goals and 11 free throws for a grand total of 135 points.

Ex–New Yorker Pee Wee was a wonder player and the Hilltoppers a wonder team, averaging over 160 points a game. What then was the catch in Pee Wee Kirkland's performance? Actually there were two items that stacked things in his favor. The Hilltoppers never traveled, instead playing all their games at home. And they were backed up by the most vocally partisan fans that opposing teams ever encountered. But then again, that was the way it had to be for Pee Wee and the Hilltoppers, who all resided at the Federal Penitentiary at Lewisburg, PA.

FOOTBALL

Another Fumble

After the Denver Broncos lost 33–14 to the Chicago Bears, a disconsolate Denver fan shot himself in the head, leaving a note that declared: "I have been a Broncos fan since the Broncos were first organized and I can't take their fumbling anymore." However, the fan proved no more competent than the Denver fumblers and botched his suicide attempt. Police sympathetically kept his name secret.

"The Play"

To this day it is called "the play," typifying Detroit Lions defensive tackle Alex Karras' description of field-goal kickers: "They come in singing their little song. 'I am go-eng to keek a touchdown; I'm go-eng to keek a touchdown.' " "The play" itself occurred in Super Bowl VII between the Miami Dolphins and the Washington Redskins. In the fourth quarter, Miami was leading 14–0 and had a chance to kick a field goal that would effectively put the Redskins out of contention. Garo Yepremian, a little 155-pound soccer-style kicker from Cyprus, came into the game for the three-point try, but the Redskins, typical of their excellent special-team play, poured through the line and blocked the kick. The ball bounced back into Yepremian's hands, but the little kicker had no experience handling the pigskin. Had he fallen to the ground with the ball, the Dolphins would simply have lost possession, but Washington would still have a long way to go. Instead, Yepremian started to run, much like a boy amid giants. Then he appeared to panic and may or may not have attempted a pass. Whatever he was trying to do, he proceeded to fumble the ball, and alert Redskin Mike Bass picked it off in midair and ran half the field for a touchdown. Yepremian had a chance to redeem himself with a saving tackle but missed. Miami still won the game 14–7, but after a fashion, Yepremian had indeed managed to "keek a touchdown"—but for the wrong team.

SOCCER

Job Application

It was as good an offer as England's World Cup soccer team would get. Shariff Abubakar Omar, Kenya's most illustrious witch doctor, volunteered to become a trainer for the team, writing a letter to Sir Alf Ramsey, the British coach: "I am interested in signing a one- or two-year contract with you with a view to improving England's chances of winning the world trophy."

Sir Alf politely informed Dr. Omar that his team would not be able to avail itself of his metaphysical service. It should be noted the English soccer team failed to survive the preliminary rounds of the World Cup play.

1974 _____

BASEBALL

See How They Run

Among the zanier men ever to own a baseball team, Charley Finley was noted for coming up with wild ideas. Among his capers as head of the Kansas City and Oakland A's were having his starting team come onto the field riding mules; designing a "Pennant Porch" at Kansas City's Municipal Stadium by moving in the right-field foul pole and angling the fence so that it was at one point a mere 296 feet from home plate so his sluggers would have as easy a time hitting homers as the New York Yankees did at their home stadium; and having a cartoon-style statue pop out of the ground just behind home plate to supply the umpires with baseballs.

As long as Finley stuck to gimmicks for their publicity value, he caused little harm and they would in short order be killed by the baseball commissioner. Occasionally, however, he would come up with lamebrain strategies that he was sure would revolutionize the game. Wouldn't it be great, he reasoned, if track and field runners could be brought into the game as "designated base runners" or base-stealers supreme. It was a simplistic experiment that flopped for the simple reason that pure speed does not a base stealer make, that what is required is a feel for the game, honed by dedication and long play. Finley brought in speedster Herb Washington to prove his theory. It was an exasperating experience for baseball men. As Oakland Coach Irv Noren recollected, "He got on first once this year [1974] and asked me whether to steal on the second pitch. The only trouble was there was already someone on second."

BASKETBALL

Three and Out

In a particularly inept display of free-throw shooting, Los Angeles Laker center Elmore Smith took three-shots-to-make-two and proceeded to miss all three. While that poor shooting is not too rare an event, Smith's performance was notable in that he threw up three air balls, none of his shots touching either the rim or the backboard!

FOOTBALL

Goose-Egg High

It was said of the Bethel (OH) High School football team that they were rather dismal in the 1970s. And 1974 could stand as a vintage year, as Bethel's opponents racked up 544 points while Bethel failed to score a single point. Final scores were 40–0, 53–0, 92–0, 89–0, 50–0, 56–0, 36–0, 33–0, 46–0, and 49–0. Actually the scores don't tell the full story. The 89–0 game was called after only three minutes in the third quarter, and the 56–0 margin could have been much greater, but the victorious team opted trying for field goals on first down. Still Bethel once almost did march for a touchdown. They reached the 1-yard line but couldn't punch the ball over in four tries.

Sorehead Suit

Outraged by the poor performance of the Philadelphia Eagles during the season and specifically for being "inept, amateurish in effort, and falling below the level of professional football competence expected of a National Football League team," four season-ticket holders filed a breach of contract complaint and demanded a cash refund on their tickets for the remaining games. The Eagles won that case—if little else that year.

GOLF

Longest Shot

Among the competitors in the U.S. National Seniors Open Championship at the Winterwood Golf Course at Las Vegas, Michael Hoke Austin, a 64-year-old Californian, was one of the best drivers in the competition. But even he was amazed at what he did on the fifth hole, a 450-yard, par 4. Austin's tee-shot went all the way to the green, landing just a yard from the hole. And then it just kept rolling past the cup. Austin's blast went 515 yards, the longest tee-shot on record. Overall, it was a heck of a way just to end up with a par 4.

PIGEON RACING

Bringing Up the Rear

Blue Chip, a racing pigeon belonging to Englishman Harold Hart, was released in Rennes, France, and arrived in its loft in Leigh, England, on September 29, 1974—seven years and two months later. Since the distance from Rennes to Leigh is 370 miles, it meant Blue Chip had achieved an average speed of 0.00589 mph, considerably slower than the fastest time recorded for a snail!

TURTLE RACING

Taken for a Ride

Two hundred entries from nine nations showed up for the New World International Turtle Track Commission's 1974 competition, and at first the race appeared to have been a glowing success. But then a highly upset Cutler Jissom, chairman of the NWITTC, was forced to announce that the results had been tainted by fraud. It turned out that the winning tortoise had been surreptitiously mounted on the chassis of a toy car and then mechanically propelled. Chairman Jissom said sadly, "This year turtle racing stood on the verge of being a mass sport. Now attendances are bound to fall off." And one sports observer echoed, "How indeed can you have faith in a race in which a tortoise runs like a rabbit?"

1974–1975 _____

HOCKEY

Comedy on Ice

Generally regarded as the worst National Hockey League to take the ice, the Washington Capitals completed their 80-game season with only 8 wins, 67 losses, and 5 ties. From February 18 to March 26, 1975, they lost 17 straight games. While this was not a record losing streak, the Caps did it the hard way—failing to score a single goal in the process. It can hardly be said they improved much the following season, as they won 11, lost 59, and tied 10.

The team's long-suffering coach, Tom McVie, said, "I'd rather find out that my wife was cheating on me than to have to keep losing like this. At least I could tell my wife to cut it out.''

1975

GOLF

Using a No-Iron

It was to say the least a very respectable score. Joseph Flynn scored an 82 for the 18 holes of the Port Royal Golf Course in Bermuda. It could be said that Joe sported a fine pitching arm—since he did it without golf clubs. He threw the ball the entire way over the 6,000-yard course.

1976

BASEBALL

It's Lonely at Short

On June 26, 1976, Toby Harrah of the Texas Rangers managed to play through an entire doubleheader at shortstop without making any kind of a fielding play, with no assists or putouts, or even touching the ball.

McCarver's Fence-Clearing Single

A home-run trot is a beautiful thing to see—provided it is a home run and the batter doesn't use two left feet running the bases. Perhaps if catcher Tim McCarver of the Philadelphia Phillies had more experience with a home-run trot, he might not have botched the job. With three men on base, McCarver socked a mighty blow to right center in Pittsburgh against the Pirates. Running toward first, McCarver watched to see if the ball cleared the 375-foot barrier. When it did, he lowered his head in a modest victory trot, rounding first and heading for second. They say a home-run trot has a dreamlike quality to it— and certainly McCarver was doing it with a certain sleepy quality. Then as he neared second base, he awoke from his glory dream. The thought finally hit him. Where was Garry Maddox? Maddox had been the runner on first. The trouble was that Maddox was *behind*

McCarver. With proper discipline he had held up to see if the ball was caught, in which case he would have tagged up and moved to second easily after the catch. The ball ended up clearing the wall, and Maddox looked on in astonishment as McCarver passed him. He picked up his pace, trying to get ahead of McCarver, but it was too late. McCarver was automatically out for passing a base runner who should have been in front of him. All three base runners scored, but McCarver was out, credited officially with a single—a fence-clearing one—but thanks to some incredibly bad baserunning, just a single.

BASKETBALL

Foul, Foul, Foul, Foul, Foul

Kevin Doherty of Davidson College established a dubious NCAA record when he entered a game midway in the second quarter. He committed a foul for charging only 2 seconds after he touched the ball and then committed three more infractions in the next 36 seconds. He committed his fifth foul just 5 minutes, 6 seconds after entering the game and was tossed out. No other player ever picked up five fouls so quickly.

Safest Foul in the Game

During the 1976–1977 National Basketball Association season, center Kim Hughes of the New York Nets was clearly the player opposing teams most enjoyed fouling. He made only 19 of 69 free throws he attempted. This works out to a .275 percentage, the lowest ever for a full season by a professional.

Turnabout

In a strange high school basketball game in Spartanburg County, SC, the girls' team from Mabry ran away from their opponents from D. R. Hill in the first half, racking up 26 points to *none*. It looked for all the world that the final result was obvious, but in the second half, Mabry's players lost their shooting completely and failed to make a point. Meanwhile, D. R. Hill got back on track and tallied 28 points, to win the odd game 28–26.

HOCKEY

Split Verdict

Detroit Red Wings hockey star Dan Maloney was arrested on a charge of assault for fighting with a Toronto Maple Leafs player during a game. Brought to trial, Maloney was found not guilty, but the jury added, "While our verdict was based on the evidence and the law . . . we hope these actions to do not continue in the future." In other words, Maloney was not guilty but shouldn't do it again.

1977

BASEBALL

Yogi Was a Mooch

Star pitcher Whitey Ford of the New York Yankees was one of the most successful practitioners of doctoring up a baseball. Whitey was never caught during his playing days and there was no proof against him until he revealed all in a 1977 book and a *New York Times* article titled "Confessions of a Gunkball Artist." Whitey made up a special brew of baby oil, turpentine, and rosin that he secreted in a roll-on deodorant bottle. He applied the stuff to his body and several spots on his uniform shirt so that he had enough for an inning's work.

While Ford got away with it for years, catcher Yogi Berra was less fortunate. Yogi was a clubhouse mooch, almost never buying his own toiletries, instead appropriating everyone else's. One day, Mickey Mantle put Ford's deodorant bottle where it would be a sure invitation to Yogi. Berra used the roll-on.

As Ford recalled, "The next thing we heard was Yogi hollering and bellowing things like, 'Son of a —, what the hell is this stuff?' " Yogi's arms were actually stuck to his sides. The team trainer dissolved most of the gunk with alcohol, but they had to shave his armpits to set him free.

Capping The Good Luck

When southpaw Vida Blue hit the big leagues in 1974, he won 17 games with the Oakland A's and firmly believed he derived good luck

In 1977 pitcher Whitey Ford revealed all about his "gunkball" and how his special brew once ended up "gluing" Yogi Berra's arms to his sides.

from the baseball cap he wore. Vida saved the cap for the next year and won 22 games. There was no stopping Blue from using the cap a third year, and he won 18 games. Naturally Vida came back with the cap again in 1977, but by then it had become a cause célèbre with the umpires. The problem was that the cap was stained, faded, dirty, and by no means odor-free. The umpires told Blue the cap had to go. Vida protested, but he was issued an ultimatum—either the cap goes or he does. Glummly, Blue finally bowed to the demands. His Oakland teammates held a pregame good-luck ceremony on the field in which Blue's treasured cap was consumed in a fire. Without his good-luck cap, Blue went on to lead the American in one category of pitching that year—19 losses.

Born-Again Ballplayers

In the 1970s there was a big movement on major league teams by players who were born-again Christians to have "chapel" before Sunday games. Other baseball people felt the idea did not belong in the dugout or clubhouse and felt the practice demeaned religion as much as playing ball inside a church. One of the most unreconstructed was Baltimore Orioles Manager Earl Weaver. Once in a 1977 game, Weaver watched with sadness and anger as outfielder and born-again Christian Pat Kelly batted with the bases loaded and the count full. Kelly swung and missed a ball that didn't stand a prayer of being called a strike and that would have forced in a run in a close ball game. The next day was Sunday and Kelly ran into the manager just after the team's chapel service. "Skipper," Kelly said, "don't you want to walk with the Lord?"

"I'd rather you walk with the bases loaded," Weaver said sourly.

Kelly remained undeterred in his efforts to bring Weaver into the fold, asking him when was the last time he had dropped to his knees and prayed. Weaver answered, "The last time I sent you up to pinch-hit."

BASKETBALL

Stall-by-Stall

Radio announcer Frank Manson said his play-by-play description of the game between Hillside High and Person High of Roxboro, NC, was the toughest broadcast he'd ever made. Rather than do a play-by-play, Manson was forced to do what could only be called a stall-by-stall broadcast. Before the game, Person High Coach Reid Davis declared he intended to "slow things down" because of the oppositions's overwhelming height advantage. Hillside grabbed the ball after the opening tip and scored. That gave Person the ball, and the team proceeded not merely to slow things down but to paralyze them. They held the ball the entire time, putting up a shot only as time was running out at the end of each quarter. During "play," announcer Manson scrounged for anything to fill the void in the action. "I interviewed the baseball coach, a county commissioner, the county manager, and anyone else who happened to be around." Then he would shift back to the high drama of Person's quarter-ending shots. Person missed every time. The final score was Hillside 2, Person 0.

BOXING

Punchless Kayo

There have been any number of boxing bouts in which "mystery punches" have resulted in controversial kayos, but there is no doubt that Harvey Gartley of Saginaw, MI, went down for the count in a legitimate punchless battle in the regional Golden Gloves tournament. Concentrating on his "dazzling footwork," witnesses of Gartley's bout with Dennis Culette said, "[He] danced himself into exhaustion and fell to the canvas." Gartley was counted out after 47 seconds of the first round. Opponent Culette did throw several punches; they all missed, but at least he managed to remain standing.

FOOTBALL

Punt ... Please

Generally conceded the worst college football team of all time, the California Institute of Technology Beavers lost their first game in 1893 by a score of 60–4. By 1977 the Beavers record stood 107–322 with 16 ties. However, these figures hardly reflect the ineptitude of the team, since for many years other schools insisted on letting Caltech only play their junior varsities. When Caltech actually beat California State University at San Diego, 34–31, the latter institution disconsolately gave up football.

Caltech did have excuses, of course, being an institution that ranked high in the nation for excellence in technology and science and one that never gave out football scholarships. The average IQ of its students was above 140, which was close to the weights of many of its gridders. But at least the school boasted a truly erudite and inspiring cheer:

Secant, cosine, tangent, sine
Logarithm, logarithm,
Hyperbolic sine
3 point 1 4 1 5 1 9
Slipstick, sliderule
TECH, TECH, TECH.

That cheer was silenced in 1977 when Caltech suspended its football program. Heard no more also was its inspirational first-down cheer:

Punt, punt, punt,
Punt, punt, punt,
PUNT, PUNT, PUNT.

Evaluation

After the Tampa Bay Buccaneers lost their 26th straight game, a reporter asked Coach John McKay what he thought about his team's execution. He responded, "I'm in favor of it."

Outthinking the Other Side

During a game between East Carolina University and William & Mary, Jim Johnson, a former East Carolina coach, was on the sideline rooting for his former charges. With East Carolina ahead 17–14 and William & Mary driving for a score, Johnson correctly diagnosed the next play, a bootleg by quarterback Tom Rozantz. Johnson was very upset that East Carolina hadn't figured out the likely play, and he paced the sideline nervously. The quarterback bootlegged the ball and started around his end for the goal line. "I was wondering what I would do if the play came my way," he said later. "Then I was standing near the 5 and here he comes. I had to make a quick decision."

His quick decision sent the 65-year-old Johnson right onto the field to collide with Rozantz. As quarterback Rozantz said later, "It was a good hit. He read the play perfectly and I never saw him coming." Despite the older's man's tackle, the ball carrier's momentum carried him over the goal line. Ex-Coach Johnson was led from the field to the cheers of the crowd relishing his pluck, but he muttered, "I'm getting too old for this."

1978 _____

BASEBALL

Out of Temptation's Way

During the season, Atlanta Braves Manager Billy Cox frequently vowed to limit the appearances of his ace reliever, Gene Garber, but as often as not, the Braves would get in trouble in the late innings, and Cox was forced to call on Garber many more times than he felt he should have. At last, determined to give the pitcher a guaranteed day off and keep himself from temptation, the resourceful manager came up with an unusual ploy of inserting Garber in the lineup in center field. He had no intention of using Garber in the outfield, and as soon as Garber was slated to bat in the first inning, Cox sent Rowland Office in to pinch-hit for the misplaced pitcher. With Garber substituted for, he could no longer appear in the game in relief. Cox happily told Garber to sit on the bench and relax, knowing he had boxed himself in a corner so that he could not change his mind and call on his reliever to pitch.

FOOTBALL

From the Raiders' Dubious Bag of Tricks

With San Diego leading the Oakland Raiders 20–14 in a National Football League game, Oakland drove to the Charger 14-yard line with only 10 seconds left to play. Raider quarterback Kenny Stabler was tackled as he tried to pass, and while falling, he fumbled the ball forward. Raider Pete Banazak got a hand on the ball and batted it farther forward toward tight end Dave Casper, who did the same thing until the ball bounced in the end zone, where Casper pounced on it for a touchdown. Despite complaints by the Chargers, the officials declared Stabler's fumble had not been intentional (which would not have been allowed) and gave the score to Oakland for a 21–20 victory. Later, Stabler confessed that he had fumbled the ball on purpose. And running back Banazak said, "Sure I batted it." And Casper chimed in, "I helped it along, then jumped on it."

The play was clearly a loophole in the rules, and to counter such ploys a new regulation said that on any fourth-down fumble or fumble in the final two minutes of either half, only the player who actually fumbled the ball could recover it and run with it. If any other offensive teammate recovered the fumble, he could not advance it and the ball had to be returned to the spot of the original fumble. The rule removed another dubious play from the Raiders' notorious bag of tricks.

1979 _____

BASKETBALL

Cold Streak

They held a regulation basketball game between two girls' high school teams in Sheldon, IA, but no one scored. Amazingly, after four quarters the score was Sibley High School 0 and Melvin High School 0. They played three overtime periods—and still no one scored. Finally, both teams got "hot" in the fourth overtime, and Melvin won it, 4–2.

FOOTBALL

Take My Tickets ... Please

A very disenchanted Atlanta Falcons ticket holder, related *Atlanta Journal* columnist Ron Hudspeth, tried to give away a pair of tickets for the team's upcoming National Football League game to strangers at a shopping mall. No one would take them. So the fan stuck the tickets under the windshield wiper of his car, hoping someone would heist them while he did some shopping. When he returned to his car, he found the two tickets still there—along with four others.

HOCKEY

Long Shot

Trailing by one point in an NHL game against the New York Islanders, the Colorado Rockies had a one-man advantage because of a penalty and sought to press that advantage by pulling their goalie to get yet another extra forward on the ice. In a storming assault, the Rockies charged at the Islander goal, and one of them cut loose a vicious shot that was stopped by Islander goalie Billy Smith. The puck richocheted off Smith's stick and kept going and going and going and floated into the empty Rockies' goal. Smith thus became the only goalie in the history of the National Hockey League to score while playing goalie.

TENNIS

Way Out

In her first Wimbledon tennis championships, 18-year-old Linda Siegel of the United States was losing to Billie Jean King when she suddenly had much bigger woes to cope with. As she bounded around the court, she realized she had popped out of her halter-neck dress. Linda's match was now worth more than simple sports section coverage, or more precisely uncoverage. Linda made the front pages of most London papers the following day. The normally relatively reserved *Daily Telegraph* declared, "The lawn tennis was not spectacular, but Miss Siegel, needing to make some adjustments, did not learn of the strategic value of a pin." Robert Maxwell's more juicy *Daily Mirror* offered a front-page full-length revealing picture slugged "Win or Bust" and informed the readers: "The 18-year-old Californian, wearing a daringly low-cut outfit, gave a stunning display of her form. The thriller kept all heads turned one way. Then Linda's dress—braless, backless and, as she admitted later, 'a bit reckless'—could take the strain no longer. Linda, clearly was out."

Quite naturally, several tabloids sought to have Linda model nude photos for their publications. Linda preferred sticking to tennis, which normally was much more conservative.

1980 _____

FOOTBALL

What If They Lost?

Is professional football getting too rough? After the Chicago Bears pulled out an overtime win over the Detroit Lions, defensive end Dan Hampton, who hadn't been playing when sudden-death play ended, hopped off the bench whooping and charged across the field to join in his team's celebration. He found himself right in the middle of some wild patting, pounding, and pummeling—and ended up with a broken nose when one of this teammates slammed his face mask into it.

U.S. hockey team celebrating the winning goal—"the shot heard around the world"—in the 1980 Olympics, a feat that also earned Coach Herb Brooks one free beer a day for life.

HOCKEY

Limit, Please

Perhaps the emotional highpoint of any Olympics of the last few decades was the victory of the underdog U.S. hockey team, which took the gold over the favored Russians at the 1990 Lake Placid Winter Games. On their way to their first-place finish, the U.S. skaters defeated the Russians 3–2 in a game that loosed a triumphal reaction throughout the country. Back in their dressing room, the charged-up U.S. skaters sang "God Bless America," although they couldn't remember the words, and Coach Herb Brooks hid his emotions by locking himself in the men's room. "Finally, I snuck out into the hall," he recalled, "and the state troopers were standing there crying."

The same emotional jag showed up at Brooks' favorite watering hole as well. Brooks said, "My bartender said I could have one free beer every day for the rest of my life. I asked if I could bunch them up every so often. He said no."

HORSE RACING

See How They Run Away

Spectacular Bid was one of the most successful colts in racing history, and with 25 victories in 29 starts it was announced that the $200,000-added Woodward Stakes at Belmont would be his final start. Unfortunately, Spectacular Bid so dominated racing at the time that horse after horse originally nominated for the race dropped out, their owners and trainers seeing no possibility of beating this outstanding colt. At race time there were no opponents left for Spectacular Bid and a walkover was ordered, the first in flat racing in 31 years. In a walkover the horse simply has to run the course to be declared the winner. Spectacular Bid, with jockey Willie Shoemaker aboard, romped around the track to the cheers of the spectators, who had but one regret: They could not bet on him. Spectacular Bid collected $73,300, only half of what the purse would have been if the race had been contested. If Spectacular Bid had been a trifle less sensational, he would have raked in much more money for his owners in his final race.

Spectacular Bid under Willie Shoemaker wins by more than daylight, having frightened away all the competition and thus copping a one-horse race in the Woodward Stakes.

1981 _____

SOCCER

Hit Him with the Mike

When Kevin Slaten of the St. Louis Steamers tried to punch a player of the opposing team, he was ejected. However, what made this unusual was that Slaten was not even a Steamers player or member of the coaching staff, but rather the announcer for the team.

1982

BASEBALL

On Second Thought

What happens when a team has second thoughts about a trade? If they are the Toronto Blue Jays they simply get their original player back. In June the Blue Jays shipped outfielder Wayne Nordhagen to the Philadelphia Phillies for outfielder Dick Davis. The same day the Phillies sent Nordhagen to Pittsburgh for outfielder Bill Robinson. Then just a week later the Pirates agreed to send Nordhagen back to Toronto for Davis. Trading score for Toronto: 2 trades, 0 change.

Dietary Deadline

The Pembroke State (NC) University baseball team walked off the field and forfeited a baseball game tied at 8–8 in the ninth inning. The boys had no choice, since the cafeteria was going to close in five minutes.

BASKETBALL

Bench Protest

During a pregame warm-up, second-stringer Gerald Johnson of Oral Roberts University kept taking shots from the midcourt line. One of his coaches chastised him and told him to concentrate on taking ''game position shots.'' Johnson nodded and sat down on the bench and shot the basketball from there.

Slow Losers

By halftime of a game between Baptist Christian College and Delta State Statesmen in Cleveland, MS, the Statesmen roared to a 70–21 lead. It was clear to the Warriors that they were certain losers, and they became more concerned with not letting their opponents go over 160 points, which they thought to be the national record. So instead of trying to score points, Baptist Christian tried a unique method, freezing the ball so that the Statesmen would have less opportunities to score. Just before the Warriors went into their stalling routine, Coach Mel Hankinson of Delta State pulled all his starters for second-stringers as a sporting gesture to hold down the score. Hankinson was nonplussed by a team freezing the ball when they were losing by something near 100 points.

The final score was 155–49, and Baptist Christian achieved its goal of keeping Delta State under 160 points. However, the losers' knowledge of basketball records matched their inept play on the court. They could have tried scoring points to cut their losing margin rather than slowing the game since the national most-points record was actually 210.

CRICKET

Cricket Mad

Englishman Michael Rowley presumably could have scored a point in his favor at his wife's divorce action. As he noted later, "I told her from the beginning cricket would always come first." Mrs. Rowley won dissolution of the marriage on the ground that her mate was "cricket mad."

Rowley might have been able to sway the official decision if he had been able to be present during the court proceedings—but he was unavoidably occupied keeping score for his favorite cricket team, the Worcestershire Marauders.

FOOTBALL

Home Snowplow Advantage

The home field advantage is one thing in football, but the New England Patriots took it a step further in a game played against the visiting Miami Dolphins in the midst of a brutal snowstorm. Given the conditions, neither team was able to put any points on the board. Then the Patriots got the ball close to the Dolphins' goal line and kicker John Smith was sent in to attempt a game-winning field goal from 16 yards out, hardly a guarantee with all the snow. Magically, a snowplow, ordered by New England Coach Ron Meyer, wheeled out on the field and cleared the snow away from the spot where the ball would be placed for Smith's field-goal attempt. Smith came through and the Patriots triumphed 3–0—a tribute not only to the home field advantage but to the home snowplow advantage as well.

Victory March

It was the last play of the game between the University of California and Stanford University. Stanford had forged into the lead 20–19 with just seconds left on the clock, which meant that as soon as the California Bears kickoff return man was tackled, the game was history. California tried a desperation play in which the players came charging up the field tossing laterals from one to another. As the first Bear runner was hit, he got off a successful lateral. The Stanford band, thinking he still had the ball, marched onto the field in a victory salute to their team. Meanwhile, the Bears kept on lateraling—a second, third, fourth, and fifth time, and by then the ball carrier crossed the goal line with the winning touchdown, having not only dodged Stanford's tacklers but its musicians as well. Since whatever interference there was emanated from the Stanford side, officials ruled that the play stood and California had pulled off a bizarre miracle finish.

TRACK AND FIELD

The Mile in 3:31.25—Ho Hum

There have been many runners who have run the mile in less than 4 minutes since Roger Bannister first did it in 1954. But a mile run in 3 minutes, 31.25 seconds? It happened in 1982, and the man who did it was American Steve Scott, competing in a race in Auckland, New Zealand. Not only that, but Mike Hillardt of Australia finished only one second off the winning pace, while Ray Flynn of Ireland came in third only a half second further back. Even the fourth-place finisher, John Walk of New Zealand, ran 3:33.93. The race, however, did not exactly stun the running world. It had been run on Auckland's main street and not on a regular, level mile track. The street sloped down hill, dropping 200 feet in the course of the mile run. Thus, gravity gave Scott and the others a whopping boost.

1983

BASEBALL

Fowl Play

In a game between the New York Yankees and the Toronto Blue Jays in Toronto's Exhibition Stadium, Yankee outfielder Dave Winfield threw a ball that hit and killed a seagull witnessing the game. Winfield was arrested by Toronto police for killing the bird and had to post $500 bond and sign an agreement to stand trial on the Yankees' next visit to the city. Winfield called the killing an accident and said, "It is quite unfortunate that a fowl of Canada is no longer with us." In the end, Ontario officials decided the fatal bird beaning was accidental and dropped charges.

Five years later, the Blue Jays announced they would pay a falconer $100,000 a year to scare away gulls from the new Sky Dome Stadium, which featured a retractable roof. It was expected that gulls from Lake Ontario would invade the Sky Dome as they had Exhibition Stadium. The falcon employed was named Winfield.

Pine-Tar Tantrum

While the controversy about George Brett's illegal bat was one of the high points of this baseball season, a similar but more violent result followed a ruling in an Appalachian League game at Pulaski, VA. Bristol's Mike Ward hit a sharp ninth-inning single, but the umpire ruled his bat had too much pine tar on it. When he was called out, the angry Ward seized the illegal bat and hurled it completely over the grandstand into a grove of trees, unaware that beyond the trees was the stadium parking lot. The bat damaged two cars and smashed the windshield of a third, resulting in $758 in damage, no minor sum out of a minor league salary.

BASKETBALL

After the Ball Game Is Over

It is not at all unusual for a basketball game to be decided on one or two foul shots made after time has expired, but in the 1982–1983 season of the Southwestern Athletic Conference, the Grambling Tigers were allowed eight shots after the game clock had run out. The game between Grambling and the Alabama State Hornets was tied 80-all with 10 seconds remaining, but Bill Hobdy of Grambling was fouled and sank both free throws. The Hornets still had a chance to win or tie but lost the ball to Grambling and fouled Hobdy again just as the buzzer sounded. This call enraged Hornets Coach James Oliver, who rushed onto the court to protest. When he ignored the referee's order to sit down, Coach Oliver was hit with a bench technical. That really set Oliver off, and he so raged that he drew two more bench technicals. Since bench technicals are two-point fouls, Hobdy got eight shots from the line with time expired. He hooped all eight, a record for after-the-game points, giving Grambling a 90–80 victory.

FOOTBALL

Get 'Em a Road Map

After his punt returner ran 54 yards the wrong way for a safety, Al Antak, Camas (WA) High School coach, opined, "We need to start teaching geography a few years earlier."

Making Monkeys of the Experts

In a fit of exasperation a sports columnist for the *Dallas Morning News* who had failed abysmally in his attempts to pick the winners of football games wrote that a monkey in the zoo could probably do better and pick at least half the games right. It was decided that Kanda, a year-old gorilla, should be given a chance at football handicapping. The zookeeper wrote the names of opposing teams on slips of paper and held one in each hand. Whichever hand Kanda slapped was the animal's choice. Kanda's selection produced 10 wins, 3 losses and a tie. That was enough to impress the newspaper, and Kanda was added to the *Morning News'* six-man panel of experts. By the end of the third week, the gorilla had a grand total of 27–14–1, for a winning percentage of .642, while the rest of the panel averaged out to .464. At this point the rest of the panel revolted, objecting to a gorilla making monkeys of them.

In a bizarre penalty situation, Bill Hobdy of Grambling scored eight free throws after time had expired in a game against Alabama State.

GOLF

Clarification

Now a fixture on the professional golf circuit, Karen Permezel hailed from Yackandandah, Australia. Finding the name to be more than they could handle, sportswriters asked for some pinpointing of the town so that it could have an alternate identification. With a perfectly straight

face she happily helped them out: "It's near Mount Murramurrabong."
And where exactly was that? "Not far from Tangambulanga." Most
writers settled on describing her as the golfer from "down under."

1984

BASEBALL

Premature Celebration

It happens almost every game. When the final out of the final inning
is recorded, the ritual calls for the catcher to charge out to the mound
to hug and congratulate his pitcher. That was what Minnesota Twins
catcher Dave Engle did in the top of the ninth in a game with the
Toronto Blue Jays. With men on first and second and Minnesota clinging to a 1–0 lead, reliever Ron Davis got pinch-hitter Rick Leach to
hit a certain double-play ground ball. As the final peg went to first
base, Engle bounded from behind the plate to go out and congratulate
Davis. What he failed to notice was that first baseman Kent Hrbek
muffed the relay so that Leach was safe. Not only that, but base runner
Mitch Webster never stopped running from second base and headed
home. Hrbek retrieved the ball and looked to throw to the plate—but
there was no one there. A red-faced Engle was standing on the mound,
mouth agape. Instead of the game being over as the catcher had
thought, his gaff had permitted the tying run to score. To complete a
perfectly embarrassing game, Toronto pushed over four runs in the
10th inning and won 5–2.

FOOTBALL

For They Are Jolly Good Raiders

Tough "take-no-prisoners" linebacker Ted Hendricks claimed there
was a good side to the bad boys of the Oakland–LA Raiders: "Because
of us there's the no-clothesline rule, the no-spearing rule, the no-
hitting-out-of-bounds rule, the no-fumbling-forward-in-the-last-two-
minutes-of-the-game rule, the no-throwing-helmets rule, and the no-
Stickum rule. So you see, we're not all bad."

HANDBALL

Everybody Got That?

At a news conference after a team handball contest between the United States and West Germany, a reporter asked in German how long and hard the Americans had trained. U.S. coach Javier Garcia Cuesta said in English, "We've been together since January, training five days a week, four or five hours a day." Then the German translator took the microphone and said, "We've been together since January, training five days a week, four or five hours a day." This too was in perfect English.

1985

BASEBALL

Team Loyalty

Attending a New York Yankees game at Yankee Stadium, 34-year-old Joann Barrett felt a sharp sting in her right hand. She had been struck by a bullet. From her position in the stands it was obvious the bullet had to have been fired from inside the stadium, although the culprit was never located. The police also failed to find the bullet at first. Two days after the shooting, Barrett discovered it inside her purse. She was asked if she would keep on attending Yankees games. "I am," she announced with feeling, "a Mets fan now."

GOLF

Follow the Loser

At the French Open, golfers American Kent Kluba and Mexican Raphael Alarcon suffered a special indignity of being among the lesser-known competitors. No one in the gallery cared to troop along with them—and show them where to go. After the pair completed the second hole, they made for what they thought was the next tee. Only after making their drives did they discover they were going for the 13th green. Their detour cost each a two-stroke penalty and sank them deeper down in the standings.

HORSE RACING

Beating a Winning Horse

In an unusual finish-line horse-racing boner, top jockey Jorge Velasquez made an error that cost his mount, Southern Sultan, the Display Handicap at Aqueduct Racetrack. Velasquez had Southern Sultan on the lead and dug into the horse to make sure none of the other mounts could catch him through the stretch. Unfortunately, he had forgotten the race still had another mile to go. By the time he realized his mistake, the jockey could not arouse his mount back into contention, and Southern Sultan finished way up the track.

1986 _____

BASEBALL

Big-Money Distraction

Frustrated Houston Astros Manager Hal Lanier decreed that all television sets were to be removed from the team's clubhouse. Instead of taking infield practice, too many of the players were spending most of the time watching "Wheel of Fortune."

How About a Few More Homers?

On July 6, 1986, Atlanta's Bob Horner came to bat against Montreal's Andy McGaffigan and walloped a home run. In the fourth inning Horner did it again. And in the fifth inning he did it a third time. In the ninth inning Horner faced Expos relief ace Jeff Reardon and hit his fourth homer of the game. Eleven major leaguers had accomplished that feat, but Horner was only one of two batters in history to have such a wasted effort. Unfortunately, three of his blasts had been bases-empty affairs while only the one in the fifth came with two men on. Despite Horner's four four-baggers, the hometown Braves lost 11–8. The last "loser" to match Horner's record was Ed Delahanty of the Philadelphia Phillies, who did it 90 years earlier against Chicago. Despite Delahanty's four home runs and a single, the Phillies came out on the short end of a 9–8 score.

BASKETBALL

The Paper Cup Defeat

In a home game against the University of Texas–El Paso, the University of New Mexico needed to be saved from their hometown fans. With just two seconds left on the clock and New Mexico leading 70–69, TEP's Wayne Campbell went to the free-throw line in a one-and-one opportunity. Just as Campbell fired up his first attempt, a paper cup flew past his line of vision. The throw missed and Campbell should have lost his opportunity at a second shot, guaranteeing New Mexico the victory. However, the referee ruled the throw did not count because of the paper cup. Campbell was allowed a repeat first throw and made the shot. Now entitled to the second free throw, Campbell came through again for a 71–70 win for the visitors. New Mexico had been knocked off by a paper cup.

FOOTBALL

Mooner McMahon

In the early part of his career with the Chicago Bears, quarterback Jim McMahon was notorious for his flaky acts, everything from being a wicked head-butter to violation of official rules about forbidden messages on his headband. At Super Bowl XX, McMahon revealed another side of his character. Having been well bruised up in previous games, McMahon imported his personal acupuncturist to New Orleans during practice week for the big game to relieve his aches and pains. Since he had been suffering mightily in his own backfield, he had a well-needled rear, and he could not resist the temptation of showing it off for the benefit of the press by baring his behind publicly in a full-moon position, gaining fame as the No. 1 Chicago Bare. This and other putative acts upset some New Orleans citizens, and a contingent of them picketed in front of Chicago's hotel with a banner declaring: ''McMahon has no class. He only shows his ass.''

Rating Game

Philadelphia Eagles Coach Buddy Ryan was never known for his graciousness and didn't even pull in his horns when cutting players from the squad. Concerning running back Earnest Jackson, whom he consid-

Quarterback Jim McMahon was long the leading flake of the Chicago Bears, famed for his butch haircuts, wild headbands, head-butting, and mooning for the press.

ered an all-pro pain, he said, "Get him out of here. Trade him for a six-pack. It doesn't have to be cold."

HOCKEY

Action Flick

Tony Blanda put his videocassette recorder to use taping hockey games and then erased all but the fights. He ended up with over 6,000 melees and started lending or trading them with U.S. and Canadian collectors. "It's a hobby, like stamps," he said.

1987

BASEBALL

The Great Potato Pickoff

It was a most inventive twist to the old hidden-ball trick. With the Eastern League's Reading Phillies having the potential winning run on third with two out in the ninth inning, Williamsport catcher Dave Bresnahan called for time, informing the umpire that his glove padding was coming out through a tear. Bresnahan went to the dugout and got not only a new glove but a peeled potato. Before the next pitch, the second-string catcher switched the raw potato to his throwing hand, and after catching the pitch in his glove, he fired the potato past third baseman Oscar Mejia in an apparent pickoff play. Seeing the "ball" zoom into left field, baserunner Rick Landblade raced for home and was shocked when the catcher triumphantly slapped the tag on him. Reading Manager George Culver lodged an immediate protest, and the umpires saw it his way. The runner was declared safe, while Bresnahan was charged with an error and ejected from the game. Later, the sneaky catcher was denounced by Williamsport Manager Orlando Gomez, fined $50, and shortly thereafter given his release. (However, Bresnahan's release was to be expected anyway, since he was hitting a puny .149.)

Oddly, the trick brought Bresnahan more fame than anything he'd done legitimately on the playing field, and the Williamsport club realized it had a folk hero in tow. The club set up a special promotion game, with the admission of $2.75 reduced to $1 if fans also brought a potato. Bresnahan was present to autograph the tubers. (He also took the opportunity to pay his own fine with 50 potatoes.) The following year, Bresnahan, now out of baseball, was honored with a "night" and his number 59 retired and painted on the fence at Bowman Field. The grand nephew of Hall of Fame catcher Roger Bresnahan, the erstwhile catcher was mighty proud of his fame. He noted, "Gehrig had to hit .340 and play in more than 2,000 consecutive games to get his number retired. All I had to do is hit less than .150 and throw a potato."

Impostor

It was announced that Lou Proctor of the St. Louis Browns would be dropped from the seventh edition of the *Baseball Encyclopedia*. He had been carried in previous editions as a player for the 1912 Browns. Seventy-five years later, investigators finally figured out Proctor was really a press-box telegraph operator who decided to enter his name in the box score. With only a one-game "career" in the majors, he made it on numerous trivia lists over the decades.

BASKETBALL

Look Ma, No Baskets

What is the lowest number of field goals made in a quarter by a National Basketball Association team? Would you believe . . . zero? It happened to the Sacramento Kings in what was easily the worst performance ever made in professional basketball. The Kings were facing the first-place Los Angeles Lakers in the L.A. Forum, and shot after shot they took went awry. In just a little over two minutes into the game, the Lakers had pulled into the lead 10–0. At the five-minute mark, the score was 20–0. And with just 2:54 left in the quarter, the score had widened to 29–0. Then Sacramento got its big break. Derek Smith of the Kings was fouled and went to the free-throw line and— almost unbelievably—made his first shot. The Los Angeles fans were on their feet cheering. The Kings went on to make three more free throws in the period while the Lakers managed to score a total of 40 points. In the quarter, Sacramento missed 18 shots from the floor. They could not make a jam or even a tip-in after a miss. Just plain nothing.

The Kings went on to miss their first three attempts in the second quarter before Eddie Johnson got inside and made a three-footer. Ironically, after that first atrocious quarter the two teams played exactly even, 88–88, bringing the final count to 128–92. But of course there were two games going on over the last three quarters. The Kings were going all out while the Lakers were involved in very extended garbage time.

FOOTBALL

Wait Till Next Year!

Upset after his Kansas State team went 0–10, Coach Stan Parrish declared: "I will not let it happen again. That wasn't me." In 1988 Kansas State went 0–11.

Prediction

In a quandary before his team faced Oklahoma, Iowa State Coach Jim Walden announced: "I know it's the American way to say you always have a chance, but it's also the American way not to lie." (Oklahoma beat Iowa State 56–3.)

1988

BASEBALL

Bobbler on the Mound

In a quarter century of pitching, Tommy John established himself as one of the game's better-fielding hurlers. But he still managed to do what no other pitcher in the 20th century accomplished—commit three errors on a single play. John was pitching for the New York Yankees in a game against Milwaukee when the Brewers' Jeff Leonard hit a slow roller to the right side of the mound with teammate Jim Gantner on first. John bobbled the ball and then threw to first much too late to get the batter. In addition, the throw soared past first baseman Don Mattingly and out toward right field. Gantner never stopped running and rounded third and headed for home. Right fielder Dave Winfield uncorked a throw to the plate that seemed certain to get him, but John cut it off and then pegged to catcher Joel Skinner. It was his second wild throw and third error of the play, which enabled not only Gantner but Leonard to come home as well. But proving the old axiom that good pitchers don't finish last when they have a good hitting team on their side, John was not hurt badly by his record-setting bobbles. The Yankees still won the game 16–3.

BASKETBALL

24 Free-Throw Penalty

In a game between the University of California–San Diego Tritons and the Menlo College Oaks, a fight broke out between centers Nick Campuano of the Tritons and Ken Welsh of the Oaks. As punches flew, the entire Oaks team joined in the melee, but UCSD kept all but one player from the bench out of it. When order was finally restored, the referees started toting up the technicals to be assessed against the two teams. The two fighting centers were tossed out of the game and Menlo was awarded two free throws for the Tritons' center's infraction and two for the player who came off the bench. Menlo converted three of the four shots. They had been leading in the game, 27–16, and this upped the lead to 30–16. Then the fouls were assessed against Menlo. Their banned center was hit with a two-shot penalty, and nine of the players and two coaches who had joined in the battle were hit with bench technicals, each two-shot affairs.

All 24 free throws were assigned to the Tritons' best foul shooter, Rob Rittgers. The sharp-eyed junior point guard started shooting and hit and hit and hit. He canned all 24 shots, with the crowd's applause growing with each successful hoop. Single-handedly Rittgers put UCSD ahead 40–30, in the process setting a record for making 24 straight points while the clock was stopped. Rittgers continued his hot foul shooting by hitting six more free throws in a row over the rest of the game, the 30 consecutive hits setting a new NCAA Division III mark.

As it turned out, his team needed those 30 points since the Tritons' margin of victory was 25 points, 110–85.

FOOTBALL

And the Band Played On . . .

The purpose of the college football band is to fire up both the players and the fans, but the Southern Methodist University Mustangs band may well have cost its team the game against Texas A&M. The band raised the volume of the music whenever the opponent Aggies were calling their signals. At halftime the officials warned the SMU coaches and the band that the noise level had to be cut, but the musicians played on. Despite this, the Aggies were ahead 39–35 with possession of the ball and less than a minute left in the game. Desperate to have their team get another shot at the football, the SMU band struck up extra loud to disrupt the Aggies' play calling on third down. The referee had enough and threw a flag for a 15-yard penalty, which permitted the Aggies to retain possession of the ball and run out the clock.

TRACK AND FIELD

Backward Fans

In a special New York City 5-kilometer race run *backward* through the city's streets, Yves Pol of France set a world record of 22 minutes, 33 seconds. He would have certainly made even better time if so many well-meaning people hadn't kept approaching him to inform him he was going in the wrong direction.

1990

BASEBALL

First-Base Strip

Safe at first base on a very close play in a game between Chicago and Detroit, Steve Lyons of the White Sox was more concerned about the grit in his uniform than about the argument going on around him. He calmly pulled down his pants to his knees and starting brushing the dirt from his legs, leaving himself covered only by shorts and an athletic supporter. When the crowd of 15,000 roared in laughter, the startled Lyons reversed his stripping act and hastily pulled up his pants. "I just forgot where I was," he later explained.

No-Hitter Loss

In a most unusual no-hit game, New York Yankee hurler Andy Hawkins held the Chicago White Sox hitless and still ended up losing the game 4–0. In the bottom of the eighth, errors by third baseman Mike Blowers and left fielder Jim Leyritz opened the floodgates and four runners crossed the plant in a no-hit inning. Hawkins' official pitching line read: 81 P, 0 H, 4 R, 0 ER, 3 SO. Hawkins commented: "Usually when someone pitches a no-hitter, he walks off the mound happy."

A Donation—Not a Fine

After being called out on strikes in a game, Andre Dawson of the Chicago Cubs was still fuming when he got back to the dugout and promptly heaved a bunch of bats on the field. For this he was suspended for one game and hit with a fine of $1,000. Determined to have the last word on the subject, Dawson wrote on his check, "Donation for the Blind."

"Now Playing Off the Field ..."

It got so the fans at the Seattle Mariners–Toronto Blue Jays game were more interested in the action off the field than on. They were treated to a rare view of a nude man and a towel-clad woman engaged in an intimate interlude at Toronto's Sky-Dome Hotel. While the lights were out in the $100-a-day room with a clear view of the diamond—and vice versa—the lights from the ballpark bathed the hotel scene in vivid detail. Said Blue Jays President Paul Beeston, "I never suspected in my wildest dreams that someone would be doing it right in front of the window."

By the following season, steps were taken to make sure such an X-rated show would not be repeated. Upon checking into any of the 70 rooms overlooking the playing field, hotel guests were required to sign a pledge of conduct not to engage in any activities that would be considered inappropriate in public, and that they would not be seen in a state of partial or complete undress. Any violators would be subject to eviction from the rooms—presumably in the best interest of baseball.

BASKETBALL

Double Choke

With just 1 minute, 17 seconds left in their game against Butte Community College, the Shasta College Knights just couldn't lose. Not with an 18-point lead. Yet, incredibly, they gave up that entire lead, thanks to some turnovers and the opposition's never-say-die drives to the hoop and fancy three-point shooting. With 36 seconds left, the Shasta advantage was down to six, and Butte kept up its full-court press. Just at the buzzer, Butte hit a three-pointer to tie the score and send the game into overtime.

If Shasta was in a daze, they seemed to snap out of it in overtime and with 1 minute, 54 seconds left they had built up a 103–92 lead. The crisis was over; only a second devastating collapse could stop the Knights now. But that was exactly what happened. In what has to stand as the weirdest double-choke performance in basketball history, Shasta gave up that seemingly overwhelming lead and the contest was knotted at 103-all. In the second overtime, Shasta never got a big lead to blow and ended up losing by one point, 116–115.

FOOTBALL

Good Question

Andy Van Slyke of the Pittsburgh Pirates is celebrated for his wit on the baseball field, but he demonstrated that he could spot a humorous situation on the gridiron as well. Visiting the Pittsburgh Steelers as they were working out after going four weeks without scoring a touchdown, Van Slyke turned in wonderment to Steeler offensive tackle Tunch Ilkin and asked, "Why do you guys practice kicking off?"

HORSE RACING

Last Hot One

Father Ed Droxler, a Catholic priest, thought he had seen everything at wakes, but presiding over that of Carl Schneider, a 70-year-old machinist, at Hardesty's Funeral Home in Gambrilla, MD, he got a fresh vision. The good father had seen rosaries, cards, flowers, but it was the first time he saw a copy of the *Daily Racing Form* placed snugly in Schneider's breast pocket. The departed had spent much of his free time at nearby Laurel and Bowie racetracks, and the *Form* had been a last remembrance from his widow, Ida.

The sight of the paper caused Father Droxler to recall that the wake had appeared to be peopled by horseplayers; the priest had heard two of the parishioners praising a horse named Millersville that was running that afternoon in the fourth race at Laurel. The priest told the mourners about Millersville and said, "I don't know how the horses are running up in heaven. That's not my thing to say. And I don't know Carl, but I understand by seeing the *Racing Form* that he was a fan. Wouldn't it be funny if we put a little bet on that horse and it came in?"

The suggestion made an impression on the gathering, and after the eulogy Schneider's grandson Melvin and another man collected $60 from the mourners and headed for Laurel, wagering the money on Millersville. The horse led from wire to wire. Included in those divvying up the $426 in winnings was the widow. She was asked if she thought her late husband might have been offended. "Not at all," *Sports Illustrated* quoted her as saying. "He would have liked to have been in on it."

Ringer

To investigate possible race-fixing at New York's Finger Lakes Race Track, the FBI bought a horse as a cover of its operations. No evidence of wrongdoing was found, but at least the FBI held its own. The horse won one race and placed in about half of its outings. Earning $1,000 a month in purse money, the nag covered its upkeep. Upon conclusion of its investigation, the FBI sold the horse to a private owner and it continued racing. "We wish him well," an FBI spokesman said. "He served as a real good representative of the bureau." As in the case of special informers, the horse was not named.

Heading Them Off at the Pass

After a 23-to-1 shot, Landing Officer won a mile race by 24 lengths at Delta Downs in Louisiana, the horse was disqualified, and jockey Sylvester Carmouche was banned from racing in the state for 10 years. Much of the track had been enveloped in fog, and the jockey simply hid his horse the first time around in the mist and waited until the horses came around the second time, when Landing Officer easily outran the tuckered-out nags. However, the track veterinarian noted that the horse was not breathing heavily and its leg wrappings were clean. "In my opinion, Landing Officer did not appear to have participated in a mile race," he said.

SOCCER

Good-Luck Charm

After they urinated on the field at the start of a game as part of a witchcraft rite to stem the team's eight-game losing streak, four Zimbabwe soccer players were banned for life by authorities. Soccer official Nelson Chirwa declared, "I would like to advise all football teams that next time they should go to a better witch doctor rather than indulge in such disgusting acts."

1991

FOOTBALL

No Gambling, Please

There are probably few offices in the country that don't have gambling pools on college or NFL football games, and in most places employers tend to turn a blind eye. Not one New York City company, however. It issued a memo warning employees that, "Gambling of any kind while working is a violation of company rules." The memo added, "Sports betting reflects poor judgment on the part of the participants." The name of the employer: the New York City Offtrack Betting Corporation.

1992

BASKETBALL

Home-and-Away Jinx

With the Orlando Magic's record standing at a dismal 7–27, General Manager Pat Williams declared: "We can't win at home. We can't win on the road. As a general manager, I just can't figure out where else to play."

BOXING

Ring Help Wanted

It was as bizarre a help-wanted ad as any ever to appear in the *New York Times*, offering employment to two men who "must have 4 yrs prof'l or amateur experience; must be capable of engaging in boxing matches of up to ten (10) rounds; must have excel amateur & prof'l winning record." Being looked for were a light heavyweight and junior welterweight.

Advertising for pugs was unique fare for the *Times*. It turned out the ad had been placed by Main Events, which at the time was staging fight cards in New Jersey and Virginia. The ads were an effort to comply with federal labor regulations that foreign job-seekers could be granted work permits only if qualified Americans were not handy. Dan Duva, the head of Main Events, had lined up two Canadian boxers, Egerton Marcus and Nick Rupa, for a fight card in Virginia Beach. How had Duva settled on the *Times* as the vehicle for his search for American pugilists? The advice came from John Fullmer, an official of the New Jersey Labor Department. No boxers responded, and Marcus and Rupa got their permits. Later the labor official was asked if an ad in *The Ring* might have been more productive. "*Ring* magazine?" the puzzled Fullmer replied. "I never knew it existed."

FOOTBALL

Win One for the Bull

Coach Jackie Sherrill of the Mississippi State football team provoked a storm of protest for allowing a bull to be castrated in front of his players before their game against the Texas Longhorns. Later Sherrill apologized, saying, "If this incident was in any way not perceived as proper by those who love Mississippi State, then I apologize." Sherrill insisted he had permitted the procedure because it was "educational and motivational." While others would have said "Bull!" to that, it should be noted that Mississippi State shredded the Texas Longhorns 28–10.

GOLF

Playing Around

When a 65-year-old man dropped dead of a heart attack while playing golf in Winter Haven, FL, officials of the course had him covered with a sheet and tried to contact a relative. The body remained on the 16th hole for two hours while other golfers played around the hole. "We told them they had to skip from the 15 to 17," Bob Sheffield, director of leisure services, said. "It was kind of obvious why. If they didn't understand it by the 16th tee, they understood it by the time they got to the green."

HORSE RACING

Distaste

Horse trainer Bob Klesaris claimed he hadn't been aware of the name's meaning, but one of his charges was a black thoroughbred called Hannibal Lecter. That was the name of the sociopath serial killer in *The Silence of the Lambs* who ate the flesh of his victims. A *Daily Racing Form* clocker at Belmont was more in tune with the situation than trainer Klesaris. The clocker noted in his description of the horse's last performance: "Hannibal Lecter was eating up the ground."

HUNTING

Final Hunt

It's the last hurrah for the deceased hunter, who can never again get prize game in his gunsight. Happily, reported the *Houston Chronicle*, there could still be one final adventure in the field. Canuck's Sportsman's Memorials advertised a special offer for the expired sportsman who has been cremated: They would, for a fee, load his ashes into a shotgun shell and arrange for the shell to be taken on a hunting trip by sympathetic sportsmen so that it could be shot at a duck or any other game animal of the deceased's choice.

1993

BASEBALL

The Losingest Pitcher

It was that kind of season for the hapless New York Mets. They were mired in last place, and, incredibly, one of their best gate attractions proved to be possession of the losingest pitcher in the game. He was 27-year-old Anthony Young, and when he went to the mound on June 27 against the St. Louis Cardinals in New York, he had lost 23 straight games, tying the Major League record set by Cliff Curtis in 1910–1911. Young had started his terrible streak in 1992 and extended it into 1993. In many of his losses Young pitched well enough to have won but suffered massive non-support from his team's batters. Young earned a tide of sympathy for his plight. On its editorial page the *New York Times* praised the luckless pitcher as "A Noble Loser," declaring, "Mr. Young endures all this with remarkable dignity, acknowledging the pain of his predicament but never giving in to it by whining.''

Matters were no different for decision number 24, as Young lost to St. Louis 5–3, to take the losingest pitcher title. His career stats were awesome, seldom approached by any other hurler. He now sported a record of 4–29, leaving him with a better lifetime batting average (.146) than winning pitching percentage (.121).

Young's ordeal was not over. By the All-Star break he lost two more games, and when play resumed there was another loss and then, finally, mercifully, a victory. But that win did not represent a turning point. After that Young's next decision was another loss. There was something heart-rending then about a fan's melancholy sign: ''Oh, noo! Here we go again.''

HOCKEY

Head Case

When rookie center Shaun Van Alten of the Edmonton Oilers suffered a concussion during a game, it was discovered the skater could not say who he was. ''Good,'' said Oiler Coach Ted Green. ''Tell him he's Wayne Gretzky.''

Saving Stuffing

During a World Hockey Championship game in Dortmund, Germany, a bench-clearing brawl broke out between France and Germany. In the middle of the fray was Sven Kuelmann, the tournament's penguin-attired mascot, who tried to restore order. For his efforts, Herr Penguin took a smash over the head from someone's stick, but escaped serious injury because of his padded head gear. ''I'm glad,'' he said, ''it wasn't my own head.''

TENNIS

Frantic Fan

It was between games in a match in Hamburg, Germany, between Monica Seles, the world's top-ranked female tennis player, and Magdalena Maleeva. While the 19-year-old Yugoslav star, clearly in command of the match, was resting, a burly fan lunged out of the stands

Monica Seles remained conscious after a rabid German fan lunged onto the court and stabbed the No. 1 woman tennis player between the shoulder blades, barely missing her spinal cord.

and stabbed Seles between her shoulder blades with a 4.5-inch boning knife. The weapon put a half-inch-deep cut in the muscles and barely missed the spinal cord. Seles was rushed to a hospital, where doctors closed the wound, but early indications that Seles would be back in action in a month proved too optimistic.

Under Germany's privacy laws, Seles' assailant was merely identified as Guenter P., a 38-year-old German lathe operator. Police said he gave "an insane impression" and that "he did not want to kill Monica Seles. He only wanted to injure her so Steffi Graf could become No. 1 again."

Graff visited Seles in the hospital the day after the attack and was clearly shocked by the events. Twenty-four hours later she lost the finals of the Citizen Cup to Spain's Arantxa Sanchez Vicario, 6–3, 6–3.

INDEX